How to Move to Canada

How to Move to Canada

A PRIMER FOR AMERICANS

Terese Loeb Kreuzer

with **Carol Bennett**

THOMAS DUNNE BOOKS / ST. MARTIN'S GRIFFIN
NEW YORK

To J, D, and H—TLK
To Ralph, Rafe, and Kate—CB
And to the late Robert Bridges—actor, director, playwright,
artist, and friend to both of us

Important Note to Readers:

The material in this book is intended to provide general guidelines and is for informational purposes only. Although this book is designed to offer current, accurate, and clear information, immigration is a complex process and immigration law and other laws and regulations often change. Readers should not regard this publication as a substitute for legal or other professional advice and should seek the services of a competent professional advisor for professional advice or other expert assistance. Also, reference in this book to products and to Web sites and other potential sources of additional information does not mean that the publisher or authors endorse such products or the information or recommendations in such sources. The publisher and authors have no control over, and are not responsible for, any such product or the content or policies of any such Web site or other source.

A General Note on the Text:

All dollar amounts are in Canadian dollars unless stated otherwise.

THOMAS DUNNE BOOKS.
An imprint of St. Martin's Press.

www.thomasdunnebooks.com

www.stmartins.com

Library of Congress Cataloging-in-Publication Data

Kreuzer, Terese Loeb.
　　How to move to Canada : a primer for Americans / Terese Loeb Kreuzer and Carol Bennet.—1st U.S. ed.
　　　　p. cm.
　　　ISBN-13: 978-0-312-34986-8
　　　ISBN-10: 0-312-34986-6
1. Americans—Canada—Life skills guides. 2. Relocation (Housing)—Canada—Handbooks, manuals, etc. 3. Moving, Household—Canada—Handbooks, manuals, etc. 4. Canada—Guidebooks. 5. Canada—Emigration and immigration—Handbooks, manuals, etc. I. Title.

F1035.A5　K74　2006
648'.900971—dc22

2006040203

First Edition: August 2006

10　9　8　7　6　5　4　3　2　1

CONTENTS

ACKNOWLEDGMENTS

This book could not have been written without the generous help of several dozen people. Many thanks, first, to the people we interviewed, who sometimes spent hours answering our questions about what it was like to emigrate to Canada, or what it has been like for them to live there. We thank the people who read what we had written and corrected our errors:

Bonnie Brooks and Marilyn Johnston, Ottawa teachers.

Mike Kerr, president of The Humour at Work Institute, Canmore, Alberta, and author of *What's So Funny About Alberta?*

Gina Logue, media representative, Office of News and Public Affairs, Middle Tennessee State University, Murfreesboro, Tennessee.

Diane Kinnee, who formerly worked for the British Columbia Ministry of Women's Equality and who provided many insights into British Columbia.

Arnold Bennett, filmmaker and writer.

Alex and Brenda Richmond, archivists in Quebec and New Brunswick, respectively.

Thank you to the Canadian tourism officials who provided us with materials and answered our questions.

Thanks to Karen Hammond, a Maine-based writer, who has provided many insights into Maine's relationships with her nearest Canadian neighbors.

Two librarians went out of their way to help us:

Stephen Clarke, senior legal specialist, American-British Law Division, Law Library, Library of Congress; and

Patricia Eaton, reference librarian, Victoria BC Public Library.

Several lawyers and tax and pension experts gave unstintingly of their time to help us understand the legal and financial complexities of a move to Canada:

Michelle Carney, Carney & Marchi, O.S., Seattle, Washington.

Alan Granwell, Ivins, Phillips & Barker, chartered in Washington, D.C., U.S. International Tax Counsel 1981–1984.

Louisa Helander, community tax consultant, Toronto.

Jenny Hirsch, account manager Personal Financial Services, Royal Bank of Canada (RBC) Financial Group, Toronto.

Rudi Kischer, Embarkation Law Group, Vancouver, B.C.

Ellen Lewis, attorney who worked on NAFTA (at the U.S. Commerce Department).

Tim Susel, national financial advice consultant, Royal Bank of Canada (RBC) Financial Advisory Solutions Team.

Stephen Trow, attorney, of Trow & Rahal, PC, Washington, D.C.

Most especially we thank two Canadian immigration attorneys:

David Cohen, of Campbell, Cohen in Montreal (www.Canadavisa.com); and

Linda Mark of Mark & Company Law Corporation, Surrey, B.C. (www.lindamark.com).

Each of them spent many hours in person, on the telephone, and by e-mail explaining the intricacies of Canadian immigration. The Immigration Process section of this book reflects their years of practical experience, going far beyond what could be gleaned from the numerous forms and instructions that the Canadian government provides.

Finally, thanks to our agent, Barret Neville, who thought that a book about how to move to Canada would be a good idea and who made it work, and to John Parsley, our editor, whose ideas and guiding hand are everywhere in these pages.

PREFACE

Whatever your reasons for thinking of moving to Canada, if you're an American citizen, this book is for you.

U.S. citizens have some advantages over citizens of many other countries who contemplate this move. For one thing, most of Canada is English-speaking (though if you also know French, you will find an even warmer welcome north of the U.S. border). For another, the border between the United States and Canada has historically been very open, with people going back and forth either temporarily or permanently.

Talk to a Canadian and you will often hear of U.S. ancestry. Many Americans also have Canadians in their background. Carol Bennett, coauthor of this book, is one of them. Her father, born in Manitoba, grew up and went to college in Vancouver, but immigrated to the United States, where he married an American and settled in New Orleans. Carol, born and raised in New Orleans, got her B.A. at her father's alma mater, the University of British Columbia in Vancouver, and her B.L.S. from McGill University in Montreal. Although she married an American and lives in Maryland, she has numerous friends and relatives in Canada.

For me, as for many Americans, Canada, despite its proximity, was more of a mystery. More than forty years ago I went to Quebec City and the Gaspé peninsula on my honeymoon. After that, I returned once for a brief visit to Montreal. I didn't realize, until I started working on this book, how close Canada is to much of the United States—how easy it is to get to, and how interesting it is. It is enough like what I know to be comfortably familiar, and enough different to be an adventure.

But if you're contemplating a move, you don't necessarily want adventure. You want to know what this place is really like, whether you'll be welcome and fit into a new community, whether you'll be able to make a living or to live adequately on what you already have, and, if you decide that Canada is for you, how you go about applying to be a permanent resident and possibly, at some time thereafter, a citizen.

This book will get you started on answering those questions. It will also direct you to further information. Very little about Canada gets reported in the U.S. media.

Nevertheless, you probably do know a thing or two about Canada. It's cold, there, right. Or is it? We saw flowers blooming in Victoria on Vancouver Island in February, and in Edmonton, Alberta, admittedly in the throes of an uncharacteristic warm spell, people were wearing shorts in early March.

But if you think Canada can be very cold, you're mostly correct, which is why 70 percent of the population lives within one hundred miles of the U.S. border, where it's maybe a tad warmer than it is in the tundra-covered north. If contemplating a move, climate is certainly one thing to consider.

You probably also have the impression that Canada is generally more liberal than the United States in its social policies. While it has its flaws, Canada's universal health care system is one of the things its population holds most dear. In other areas of social policy, Canadian law permits and acknowledges same-sex marriage, treats abortion as a medical procedure, prohibits the death penalty, and has stricter gun control laws than the United States.

If these values and concerns are yours, you may well feel that Canada is a place you could happily call home. We can't tell you everything you would need to know to get there and put down roots, but we've tried to give you a good start.

Terese Loeb Kreuzer

In researching this book, Terese and I visited Canada, read widely, and interviewed a random sample of U.S.-born Canadian immigrants about their experiences. We also talked to immigration lawyers, tax accountants, and other experts. We researched the larger cities in Canada, where most immigrants settle and where most of the jobs are. We have not written, though, about some of my favorite places in Canada: the Gulf Islands, Chilliwack and Cultus Lake, the Okanagan Valley, and Kaslo on Kootenay Lake, all in British Columbia.

Souris, Manitoba, is Canada's Lake Wobegon for me, with its swinging bridge, warm community spirit, and "children who are all above average." And there's Belmont, Manitoba, where my grandfather farmed, with its blue and yellow flowers in a patchwork quilt on the fields that stretch as far as the eye can see, a quilt covered with sheets of snow in winter.

Peterborough and the Rice Lake area of Ontario and Cobourg, with its historic beach on Lake Ontario, (across from Rochester, New York), are both very special to me, not just for their beauty, but for the people I've found there. For anyone who wants to get away from big city life, these and many other places are waiting to be discovered. If that sounds like a travel invitation, it is. Visiting Canada is something I hope to do for the rest of my life. Moving to another country, though, even if one can have dual citizenship, is a serious business.

Canada has a reputation as a peaceful and well-run country. Commenting on the differences between Canada and the United States, Arnold Bennett, an enthusiastic U.S. immigrant to Newfoundland, said, "It's the difference between a system that is rooted in a belief in Peace, Order and Good Government (called the POGs in Canadian parliamentary debate) instead of 'Life, Liberty and the Pursuit of Happiness' as in the U.S."

Today's Canada is truly a multicultural, sophisticated nation, a haven for refugees from less ordered places in the world. But Canada has its problems, too. The price of gasoline and the long stretches of road to be driven are not a good match. Postal strikes have threatened communication in recent years and the Canadian Broadcasting Corporation was mired in a labor-management dispute in 2005. Taxi drivers were on strike in Ottawa when we were there, and farmers were demonstrating in downtown Toronto as we left. We saw homeless people in the streets of Vancouver, Victoria, and Montreal in winter. Bureaucracy can impede rather than serve the public.

But there seems to be a conscious commitment on the part of most people to make things work. Canada's citizenship book, *A Look at Canada,* to be studied by immigrants, stresses the responsibilities as well as the rights of citizens in defining Canadian values. It says these include "Freedom, respect for cultural differences and a commitment to social justice. We are proud of the fact that we are a peaceful nation."

The border between the United States and Canada has been likened to a one-way mirror, with Canadians keeping a wary eye on the United States—"sleeping next to an elephant," as former Prime Minister Pierre Trudeau put it. We have attempted to look back through the looking glass.

Carol Bennett

IMMIGRATION TIME LINE

1. Research: To move or not to move.

Time Required: Indefinite. As long as necessary or available.

"Moving to Canada is something that most people think about very carefully for a long time before they even file a single paper," says Vancouver immigration attorney Linda Mark.

The research phase can involve visiting different parts of Canada, reading about it in books and on the Internet and talking to native and naturalized Canadians about their experiences.

If someone contemplating immigration works in a profession that requires credentials (law, medicine, accounting, engineering, architecture, for instance) and hopes to work in this profession after emigration, Mark advises that the provincial and territorial requirements be part of the initial research. She notes that credentialing requirements are under the control of provincial and territorial regulatory bodies, and therefore will vary depending on where the applicant plans to settle.

"Every profession is different in what might be required," says Mark. "For some, you may have to redo your whole training, while for others, you just have to have your previous education and experience validated."

She also says that "some licenses are easy to transfer from province to province while others are not."

While credential requirements may be an important part of the decision of whether to emigrate and if so, where to settle, they do not affect the likelihood of an immigration application being accepted or rejected. (For more information on credentialing, see pages 29–34.)

Part of the initial research phase may include talking to one or more Canadian immigration attorneys to get a general idea of their assessment of your situation and your likelihood of success, what it will cost to emigrate, and how long it might take. Many attorneys will offer a brief telephone consultation at no charge.

If a potential applicant is hoping to emigrate in the skilled worker category (see page 21 for a definition of this class of applicant), in most cases, he or she will have to accrue a minimum number of points on the immigration application and should go through the questions to get an approximate idea of whether or not the application will succeed. (See pages 25–29 for this application and an explanation of the points awarded.) "However," says Mark, "even here there are some variables. Quebec Province has a different point system than the rest of Canada, and some people who may not qualify for admission as federal skilled workers may qualify as provincial nominees if their job skills happen to be in demand in that particular province."

2. Decide: Do it yourself or hire an attorney or consultant to represent you?
Time Required: Not applicable.
Do It Yourself:
Advantages: You may save money.
Disadvantages: You may make mistakes and your application can be delayed or rejected.
Hire a Consultant:
Advantages: Consultants may be less expensive than immigration attorneys. Consultants may speak your language and be familiar with your culture.
Disadvantages: Consultants don't have the same training in regulations, immigration law, and case law as attorneys. If a case is at all complex, using a lawyer may be a wiser choice in the long run.
Hire an Attorney Who Specializes in Immigration Law:
Advantages: Familiarity with how things generally play out in practice as well as with immigration law can help avoid unnecessary delays and potentially costly mistakes.
Disadvantages: Fees add to the upfront expense.

3. Consult with your attorney or consultant, if you have hired one.
Time Required: Not applicable.

4. Assemble your supporting documents.
Time Required: Three to four months.

Obtain police background checks, transcripts, and birth certificates. (The documents required will differ depending on your immigration category.)

Be sure to determine and supply the number of copies of each form you need. Certified photocopies of all documents are acceptable, except for police certificates, which must be originals. If your documents are not in English or French, send a notarized (certified) translation with a copy of the originals.

Anything that you may need to obtain from others, such as police background checks, transcripts, or references, could take time. Determine what you will need and put that process in motion before you go on to the parts of the application you can prepare yourself.

5. Complete the forms.
Time Required: Two weeks to two months.
If any of your family members are included in your application, you will need more than one copy of some forms.

Note on Schedule 1: Background/Declaration and Additional Family Information (IMM 5406): You, your spouse or common-law partner, and each dependent child aged 18 or over (whether accompanying you or not) must complete these forms.

Use a black pen or typewriter. Answer all questions. Leave nothing blank. If something doesn't apply to you, write N/A (not applicable).

If your application is accepted and the information you provide on the forms changes before you arrive in Canada, you must inform the visa office to which you applied in writing. You must do this even if your visa has already been issued.

Make sure your application is complete. If your application is incomplete for any reason, it could seriously delay the process. Additional information may be requested at any time during the application process.

6. Submit your application.
If you are using an attorney, he or she will probably do this for you. If you do it, put all your documents and application forms in a sealed envelope and mail them to the Canadian Consulate General, Immigration Regional Program Centre, 3000 HSBC Center, Buffalo, NY 14203-2884.

7. Wait for a letter from Citizenship and Immigration Canada acknowledging receipt of the documents.
Time Required: Four to six weeks.
If Immigration says that they've done an initial review and that everything is more or less in order without need for an interview, *then* you would

arrange for medical exams for the primary applicant and all family members (see pages 49–50 for further explanation of the medical requirements) *and* pay your right of landing fees. (See pages 48–49 for discussion of fees.) Pay by certified check, bank draft, or money order. Do not send cash.

8. Wait for finalization of documents.
Time Required: Two to five months.
Sometimes Immigration does additional background checks before authorizing a permanent resident visa.

Wait for a letter from Immigration asking for your U.S. passport.

Do *not* sell your house, take your children out of school, or make any other permanent, long-lasting arrangements *until* you actually have your permanent resident visa. There could be additional delays or unexpected complications.

9. Receive permanent resident visa.
Time Required: Three weeks.
It usually takes three weeks to issue a visa that's placed inside your U.S. passport. You will also receive a Confirmation of Permanent Residence form that you and your accompanying family members must bring to your port of entry along with your visa. It contains your identification information, your photo, and your signature.

10. Land in Canada as a permanent resident.
Time Required: See below.
After your visa is issued, you have to come to Canada with it before your medical exam expires. This could give you a window of anywhere from one week to ten months. You must actually land in Canada within this window. No exceptions are made—even if this means that you land and then immediately return to the United States to complete preparations for your move.

11. Interview: Additional possible step after Step 7.
Time Required: Up to a year and a half.
"No matter how well you've prepared your case, you shouldn't be surprised if you have to go for an interview," says Linda Mark.

Though the interview itself may only take an hour to an hour and a half, it can take twelve to eighteen months to schedule. Applicants are given about eight weeks' notice to report for their interviews.

"At the interview they will often tell you if you've passed and ask you to send in your right of landing fee, but if they feel they need additional documentation, then at the interview they'll tell you what they need and ask you to submit it," says Mark.

Most people don't go for their medical exams until around the time of the interview. Even if they have passed, it can still take another two to five months to get a visa. (See pages 51–52 for more information on interviews.)

12. Arrive with possessions.
Time Required: Not applicable.
See pages 61–64 for a description of what can be brought, the required documentation, and the requirements for bringing a vehicle into Canada.

13. Make living arrangements immediately after arrival.
Time Required: Not applicable.
"Many people will rent accommodations and put their possessions in storage until they find a permanent place to live," says Mark.

Though basic health care in Canada is available to all residents, a waiting period of up to three months before enrollment is often required. Those moving from the United States to a province with a waiting period should continue their health insurance for that time.

Driver's license: A U.S. license will be good for a limited period of time after moving—in some provinces and territories, for up to six months, giving ample time to renew.

14. Find a Job?
Time Required: Indefinite.
"Most people will be arriving in Canada without a job, and if they plan to work in Canada, they will start looking for employment once they get here," says Mark. "A lot of employers won't even look at you until you're legally able to work in Canada, and you may not be able to work until you get your permanent resident visa." Expecting that many people will be coming to Canada without guaranteed employment, the federal government requires evidence of enough funds unencumbered by debt to support a family for at least six months. (See page 21 for more details on the financial requirements. See pages 66–67 for more information on finding a job.)

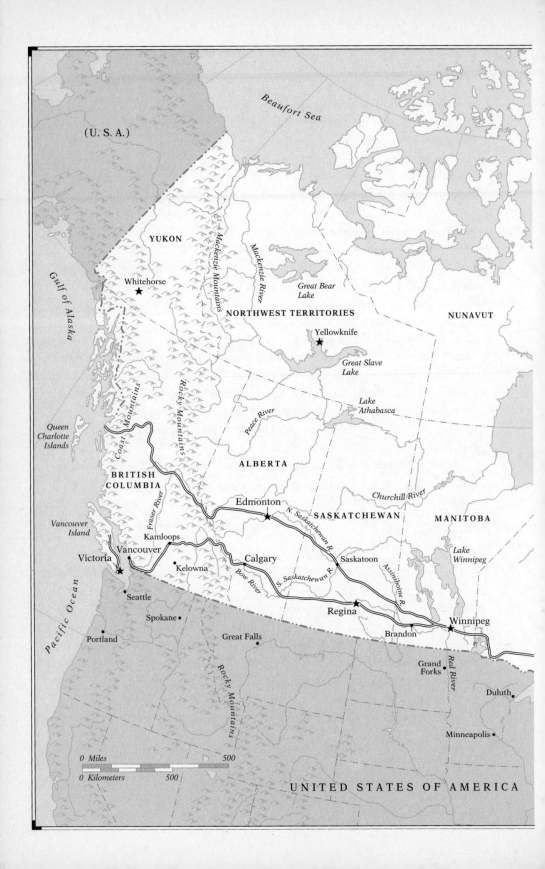

GREENLAND

ICELAND

Baffin Bay

Iqaluit ★

Ungava Bay

Labrador Sea

Hudson Bay

NEWFOUNDLAND AND LABRADOR

La Grande Rivière

James Bay

ONTARIO

St. John's ★

QUEBEC PROVINCE

Ile d'Anticosti (Anticosti Island)

Gulf of St. Lawrence

Îles de la Madeleine (Magdalena Islands)

PRINCE EDWARD ISLAND

Charlottetown ★

Cape Breton Island

NEW BRUNSWICK

Quebec ★

Fredericton ★

Moncton •

Bras d'Or Lake

Thunder Bay •

Laurentian Mountains

St. Stephen •

St. John •

NOVA SCOTIA

Superior

Ottawa River

Montreal •

Calais •

Halifax ★

Ottawa ✪

St. Lawrence River

Portland •

Bay of Fundy

Michigan

Huron

Toronto ★ *Ontario*

Boston •

Atlantic Ocean

Milwaukee •

London •

• Buffalo

Detroit •

Erie

Chicago •

Cleveland •

New York •

© 2005 Jeffrey L. Ward

How to Move to Canada

ONE

INTRODUCTION:
What Is Canada?

IT TAKES A NIGHT AND HALF A DAY TO GET FROM VANCOUVER, British Columbia, to Jasper, Alberta, by train. But this trip through some of the world's tallest and newest mountains is the dot on an "i" in Canada's great expanse. The second largest country in the world spans six time zones. It is largely uninhabited. The population of just over 32 million is roughly the same as the population of California. Most Canadians live within a hundred miles of the U.S. border.

Human beings are thought to have first entered what is now Canada around 24,000 years ago, crossing the Bering Strait from Mongolia to present-day Alaska and then moving south. Native peoples are known to have lived in some parts of Canada for at least 10,000 years. Around A.D. 1000 Vikings settled on the coast of Newfoundland for around a decade but then left.

The Frenchman Jacques Cartier was the next European of record to return. He sailed from St. Malo on April 20, 1534, with two ships and sixty-one men, looking for gold and a passage to Asia. He found instead a land "composed of stones and horrible rugged rocks," claiming it for France. Forty-nine years later, Sir Humphrey Gilbert claimed Newfoundland for England. This was the beginning of a conflict between the English and French for control of this territory that finally ended with the French defeat on Quebec City's Plains of Abraham in 1759.

However, the defeat was only partial. Canada has two official languages—English and French—and the Quebecois ("Quebecers" in English) have a culture distinct from the rest of Canada and a lingering sense of being second-class citizens in an English-speaking hegemony. Although many of Canada's premiers have been from Quebec, the province's alliance with the rest of Canada has often been uneasy.

The beaver is Canada's national animal, and rightly so. From the seventeenth to the mid-nineteenth century, the European hunger for beaver skin hats was insatiable. Starting around 1600, explorers, trappers, and traders pushed farther and farther west, seeking beaver pelts. The Hudson's Bay Company, founded in 1670, and the North West Company, founded in 1783, were built on trading fur with natives and with the European trappers who learned from them. Seeking furs, in 1793, a Scot named Alexander Mackenzie first crossed the Rocky Mountains and made his way to the Pacific Ocean.

The Hudson's Bay Company once controlled most of the land in modern Canada, from the Atlantic Ocean to the Pacific, from the Arctic Ocean to the Great Lakes. But the taste for beaver hats waned in favor of silk hats and less pricey furs. In 1870, the Hudson's Bay Company ceded most of its domain to the Dominion of Canada and became a department store supplying the needs of the farmers who flooded the prairies in response to Canada's offer of cheap land to anyone who would cultivate it.

Because of its size, terrain, and climate, and because of its political history, Canada has not been an easy country to govern—certainly not at a distance. By the 1860s, with the value of Canadian furs diminished and the United States unstable and bloody from civil war, the British Crown was quite willing to let its colony take care of many of its own problems, including defense from its neighbor to the south.

The British North America Act of 1867 established the Dominion of Canada as a confederation of provinces governed by a premier and a parliament in Ottawa. The first four provinces in the confederation were Ontario, Quebec, New Brunswick, and Nova Scotia. The Statute of Westminster, signed in 1931, further loosened the ties with Britain, giving Canada control over its external affairs. Finally, the Constitution Act of 1982 (which Quebec refused to sign) allowed Canada to change its constitution without asking permission of the British government. The Canadian Charter of Rights and Freedoms, guaranteeing Canadians freedom of religion, thought, belief, opinion, and expression, was part of that document.

When Canadians talk about what it means to be Canadian, it's often to this charter that they return as an expression of fundamental principles and beliefs. They also define themselves as a peacekeeping nation and as a nation with respect for law. "Peace, order, and good government" is how they put it—the "POGs." They will also tell you that they take care of one another. "It's not just a matter of public policy but of personal behavior," said Mary-Anne Hurley-Corbyn, who lives in New Brunswick. "I live in rural Canada," she said. "New Brunswick only has 750,000 people—but it's very community-oriented."

Canada's universal health care system is sometimes mentioned in this connection. In the fall of 2004, CBC Television initiated a contest to designate "the Greatest Canadian." The winner, with 1.1 million people voting, was Tommy Douglas, the Saskatchewan premier who spearheaded Canada's universal health care system. TV host George Stroumboulopoulos, who argued for Douglas's "candidacy," said that if Douglas were removed from the national equation, "you remove the caring, sharing legacy of everything that we value. . . . This is our most treasured national characteristic."

The name "Canada" first appeared on a map circa 1547, bestowed by Jacques Cartier after he heard the word on his second voyage of exploration. Two young Indian men on his ship used it to refer to a village; Cartier thought they meant the whole country. As it turns out, though, Canada's influx of immigrants has made it one of the most multicultural nations in the world. Cartier may have been right. Canada has many characteristics of a village, whose inhabitants are mutually dependent and who believe that the well-being of one impacts the well-being of all.

SNAPSHOT: Canada

LOCATION The northernmost country of the North American continent, bordered by the Arctic, Atlantic, and Pacific Oceans and by the United States of America. The land border with the United States is 3,145 miles long. The water border is 2,380 miles. Canada touches the states of Maine, New Hampshire, Vermont, New York, Pennsylvania, Ohio, Michigan, Minnesota, North Dakota, Montana, Idaho, Washington, and Alaska. Most of the border with the United States runs along the forty-ninth parallel.

Canada extends from latitude 41 degrees 58 minutes N at Pelee Island in Lake Erie (the same latitude as Rome, Italy) to 83 degrees 7 minutes N at Cape Columbia on Ellesmere Island, well above the Arctic Circle and within five hundred miles of the North Pole.

Canada's easternmost point is Cape Spear in Newfoundland (longitude 52 degrees 37 minutes W). The westernmost point is on the Yukon/Alaska border at 141 degrees W. It stretches 3,400 miles from coast to coast. From north to south, Canada covers 2,900 miles.

GEOGRAPHY Canada is 3.8 million square miles in area, mostly plains, with mountains in the west and lowlands in the southeast. It has seven major geological regions centered on the Canadian Shield, an area of 500-million-year-old Precambrian rocks surrounding Hudson Bay like a crescent and extending over almost half of Canada. The Canadian Shield is rugged, covered with forests, and dotted with lakes and is rich in minerals. Much of it is inaccessible. Very little of it can be cultivated.

CLIMATE Temperate to Arctic. Proximity to water (the Pacific and Atlantic Oceans, Hudson Bay, and the Great Lakes) moderates the climate in many places. The prairies are among the coldest places in Canada and get more snow than the Arctic regions. Mountain ranges in the west also have an effect. The tall Coast Mountains shield the Yukon and parts of British Columbia from moist and temperate Pacific Ocean air, leaving them very cold in winter and hot in summer.

POPULATION 32,378,122 (est., October 2005)

CAPITAL Ottawa

PROVINCES
British Columbia; Alberta; Saskatchewan; Manitoba; Ontario; Quebec; New Brunswick; Nova Scotia; Newfoundland and Labrador; Prince Edward Island.

TERRITORIES
Yukon; Northwest Territories; Nunavut.

POPULATION OF MAJOR CITIES
Toronto	4.5 million
Montreal	3.4 million
Vancouver	2 million
Ottawa	1 million

ETHNIC DIVERSITY
English, Scottish, Irish	28 percent
French	23 percent
Other European	15 percent
Asian/Arab/African	6 percent
Indigenous Amerindian	2 percent
Mixed Background	26 percent

RELIGIOUS AFFILIATIONS

Catholic	44.4 percent
Protestant	29 percent
Other Christian	4.2 percent
Muslim	2 percent
Other	4 percent

LANGUAGES English, French (official languages. Many others are widely used, particularly in areas with large immigrant populations). The Official Languages Act of 1969 made bilingual communication mandatory at the federal level. New Brunswick is the only officially bilingual province.

EDUCATION Literacy—99 percent of population aged 15 and over has at least a ninth-grade education.

HEALTH

Average Life Expectancy:
Males, 77.1 years
Females, 82.2 years
Infant Mortality Rate: 4.75 per 1,000 live births (est. 2005)

ECONOMY

Workforce: (December 2005) 17.4 million
Goods-producing sector: 25 percent
Comprises manufacturing; construction; agriculture; natural resources; utilities
Service-producing sector: 75 percent
Comprises trade; health care and social assistance; educational services; accommodation and food services; professional, scientific, and technical services; finance; public administration; transportation and warehousing; information, culture, and recreation; management, administrative, and other support
Nominal GDP (2003): $869.2 billion
Real GDP growth rate (2004): 2.4 percent
GDP per capita (2004): $40,483
Natural resources: Petroleum and natural gas, hydroelectric power, metals and minerals, fish, forests, wildlife, abundant fresh water
Agriculture: Products—wheat, livestock and meat, feed grains, oil seeds, dairy products, tobacco, fruits, vegetables

Industry: Types—motor vehicles and parts, machinery and equipment, aircraft and components, other diversified manufacturing, fish and forest products, processed and unprocessed minerals

TRADE Merchandise exports (2004): U.S. $331.74 billion: motor vehicles and spare parts, lumber, wood pulp and newsprint, crude and fabricated metals, natural gas, crude petroleum, wheat. In 2004, 84.6 percent of Canadian exports went to the United States.

Merchandise imports (2003): U.S. $289.7 billion: motor vehicles and parts, industrial machinery, crude petroleum, chemicals, agricultural machinery. In 2003, 70 percent of Canadian imports came from the United States.

GOVERNMENT Confederation with parliamentary democracy
   Confederation: July 1, 1867

CONSTITUTION The amended British North America Act of 1867 patriated to Canada on April 17, 1982, Charter of Rights and Freedoms, and unwritten custom

BRANCHES
   Executive—Queen Elizabeth II (head of state represented by a governor-general), prime minister (head of government), cabinet
   Legislative—bicameral parliament (House of Commons, 308 members; 105-seat Senate)
   Judicial—Supreme Court
   Federal-level political parties: Liberal Party, Bloc Québécois, New Democratic Party, Conservative Party of Canada

SYSTEM OF MEASUREMENT Canada uses the metric system to measure such things as distance, temperature, volume, and weight.

HEALTH CARE: How It Works

Arnold Bennett and his wife, Nancy, moved from the Washington, D.C., area to Newfoundland in 1996. They've been Canadian citizens since early 2004. Arnold Bennett, who edited a book called *Looking North for Health: What We Can Learn from Canada's Health Care System* (San Francisco: Jossey-Bass, 1993), says there are two realities about Canada's health care: "(1) Almost all Canadians believe deeply that our health care system is the best in the world and (2) that almost all Canadians complain about it all the time."

Bennett notes that Canada began the 1990s with a massive national budget deficit and managed to eliminate the deficit in a few years, running surpluses for the last several years. "That was done in large part by cutting spending throughout the nineties. One result was that the health care system was tightened up enough to cause some discomfort. Some shortages developed, and wait times for some elective services increased."

Bennett says that most of these problems have been fixed or are in the process of being fixed. The federal government, he says, has funded agreements with the provinces to increase accountability for delivery of services, create twenty-four-hour primary care centers, and improve home care services and drug insurance programs. "I live in Canada's poorest, most rural, province," he says, "and I'd take our health care system over what I saw in the richest, least rural, U.S. states any day."

Basic health care in Canada is publicly funded and available to all residents, though a waiting period of up to three months before enrollment is often required. Those moving from the United States to a province with a waiting period will want to continue their health insurance for that time. Those moving from one province to another are generally covered by their previous province for the first few months.

Anyone moving from the United States to Canada who is 65 or over should know that, while Social Security goes with them, U.S. Medicare does not. They should get short-term insurance to cover the first three months, if necessary, until they are registered in Canada's system.

Canada's national health care system is called Medicare, but unlike Medicare in the United States, it is not just for senior citizens. Canada's Medicare evolved in the 1960s from what was termed "socialized medicine" in Saskatchewan, and by 1967, Canada's centennial year, universal health care was a national commitment.

As Arnold Bennett noted, budget cuts in the 1990s have strained the system, but many of the problems were already being addressed when, in June 2005, the Canadian Supreme Court handed down a ruling that led some to fear that Medicare would be seriously and permanently undermined by the creation of a parallel private insurance system for basic care.

Ruling in a case brought by a Montreal doctor and a patient who had to wait a year for hip replacement surgery, the court said, "The evidence in this case shows that delays in the public health care system are widespread, and that, in some serious cases, patients die as a result of waiting lists for public health care."

Specifically, the court struck down Quebec's ban on private medical insurance for core medical services, saying, "The prohibition on obtaining private health insurance is not constitutional where the public system fails to deliver reasonable services."

Then Prime Minister Paul Martin's response was to say that Canada would not have a two-tiered health care system that could siphon off doctors from the public system. He said his government was making progress in strengthening the public health care system, allocating additional funds toward reducing wait times.

In fact, the Supreme Court ruling thus far applies only to the province of Quebec, and the net effect there and in other parts of Canada may simply be to make fixing the health system a legislative and financial priority. In August 2005, the Supreme Court issued a second ruling saying that the implementation of the first one would be delayed by twelve months to give Quebec and the federal government time to address the waiting period problems.

HOW GOOD IS CANADIAN HEALTH CARE? Canada spends less per capita on health care than the United States (U.S. $2,931 per person in Canada vs. U.S. $5,267 in the United States, both figures, 2002) but Canadians live longer on average. In 2005, the estimated Canadian life expectancy at birth was 80.1 years, compared with 77.7 years in the United States.

Americans who have been in Canada since the early 1970s recall a golden age of medical care. Many feel it is unraveling a bit today, but are grateful for the national commitment. Judith Wouk has been a Canadian citizen since 1975: "I find it is very good for acute care, but a little slow on follow-up care. Compared to the experiences of my friends and family in the United States, I am very happy with Canadian health care."

"There are definite problems and there are very definite advantages from what we've seen," says University of Winnipeg history professor Dan Stone, who moved to Manitoba from New York City in 1969. "There's a shortage of high-tech diagnostic equipment, and this can sometimes be a serious issue. There are some operations where they're not as quick as they should be. In Manitoba, it seems to be particularly hip and knee replacement. Other provinces, for some reason, that's better, and other things are worse. In emergencies, they all function extremely well."

Canada's health minister in May 2005 announced a five-year, $75 million initiative aimed at helping more than two thousand "internationally educated" health care professionals join Canada's health care system. "This initiative will strengthen our health system by helping to increase the supply of health care professionals, which will improve access to quality health care and reduce wait times," said Health Minister Ujjal Dosanjh. He noted that the initiative is part of a wider Internationally Trained Workers Initiative, involving fourteen federal departments and agencies. There is an on-line Canadian Information Centre for International Medical Graduates with more information at www.IMG-Canada.ca.

Canada's health system is funded largely by the federal government, though "premiums" are charged in some provinces, such as Alberta and British Columbia, while Ontario and Quebec have placed income-related surcharges on their provincial income taxes to help pay for health care. The care itself is administered and delivered at the provincial level, in keeping with the provisions of the Canada Health Act, which guarantees residents universal access to medically necessary hospital and medical services.

WHAT'S COVERED Universal health coverage applies to many aspects of medical care, but not all. In some cases, employers will offer coverage for many uncovered services. In others, people pay out of pocket or take out private insurance.

Medically necessary hospital services are covered whether provided on an inpatient or outpatient basis and include a bed in a standard ward, meals, X-rays, most laboratory tests, and nursing care.

Physician services that are covered by Medicare include diagnosis and treatment of illness and injury, surgery, obstetrical care (including pre- and postnatal care), eye exams and treatment or operations by an ophthalmologist.

Not covered are hospital charges above the standard ward rate for private or semiprivate rooms and services not medically required, such as cosmetic surgery, experimental services, ambulance services, or dental services, other than procedures related to jaw injury or disease.

Physician services not covered by Medicare include annual physical exams, cosmetic surgery, experimental services, prescription drugs, and physical exams done at the request of a third party for such things as preschool or pre-employment requirements or for medical insurance. Optometry and dental services (other than those related to injury or disease) are also not covered.

The services of chiropractors, naturopaths, podiatrists, and osteopaths as well as acupuncture treatments are generally not covered. Physiotherapy, speech therapy, and psychological services received in a facility that is not an insured outpatient facility are also not covered.

Also not covered by Medicare are services to which a resident is entitled under other legislation such as the Workers Compensation Act, Public Health Act, or other territorial or federal legislation. Veterans, for example, are entitled to treatment as a result of their service in the armed forces.

Additional services, such as prescription drugs, eyeglasses, and dental care, can be covered by an employee's benefit package, or private insurance can be purchased to supplement the federal Medicare. Canada does have private clinics offering specialized services.

A Seniors' Benefit program covering the costs of some prescription drugs and some of the things listed above is available in most of the provinces and territories, but coverage and costs are variable and often linked to income. Nursing home and home care are generally not covered under Medicare, but physician and hospital care is.

Full-time students from the United States enrolled at Saskatchewan colleges and universities are covered by Saskatchewan Health if they have valid study permits. British Columbia and Alberta offer some coverage for a fee, but students generally buy private insurance or pay for insurance with their registration fees at school.

Travel insurance is available through private insurers for residents of Canada who travel outside the country. Rates depend on the traveler's age, preexisting health conditions, and the length of the trip.

HOW TO APPLY Application forms to enroll in Canada's Medicare are available from the provincial and territorial health ministries (see Appendix, page 211, for contact information). They can also be found at doctors' offices, hospitals, and in pharmacies. Enrollees receive a health care card with a personal, lifetime health number. Once a resident is enrolled in a province, care is portable from province to province. There's usually a three-month waiting period for eligibility in the new province, but, with proper notification, it is covered by the previous province.

Each member of a family, even newborn babies, must have his or her own card. The applicant will need a birth certificate or confirmation of permanent residence and passport to obtain a card.

OBTAINING PRIVATE HEALTH INSURANCE

The Consumer Assistance Centre for Life and Health Insurance of the Canadian Life and Health Insurance Association in Toronto has a list of private carriers offering temporary coverage for visitors, newly arriving permanent residents, and others going to Canada. Within Canada, the Centre can be reached by calling 800-268-8099. This toll-free number does not work from the United States. The association can be reached from the United States by calling 416-777-2344 and has information on insurance providers throughout Canada. They have a Web site at www.CLHIA.ca.

SIDE BY SIDE: CANADIAN VERSUS U.S. HEALTH CARE

In 2001, the United States spent approximately 13.9 percent of the GDP on health care compared to 9.7 percent in Canada. What did this money buy?

Coverage   45.8 million Americans do not have any health insurance, the lowest level of comprehensive health care coverage of any G-7 nation (France, the United States, Great Britain, Germany, Japan, Italy, and Canada) or OECD (Organization for Economic Co-operation and Development) nation (those listed above plus Australia, Austria, Belgium, the Czech Republic, Denmark, Finland, Greece, Hungary, Iceland, Ireland, Korea, Luxembourg, Mexico, the Netherlands, New Zealand, Norway, Poland, Portugal, the Slovak Republic, Spain, Sweden, Switzerland, Turkey). A further 24.5 million have only basic coverage through Medicaid.

Canadians have universal health care coverage.

Life Expectancy   Canadian life expectancy is more than two years higher than U.S. life expectancy, which ranks lowest in the G-7 countries.

Infant Mortality Rate   The rate in the United States is 37 percent higher than the rate in Canada (6.5 deaths per 1,000 live births in the United States compared with 4.75 deaths per 1,000 live births in Canada, both figures est. 2005).

HOT BUTTON ISSUES

Is Canada really more liberal than the U.S.?

Canada wrestles with many of the same issues that divide people in the United States.

Abortion

Although the U.S. Supreme Court legalized abortion in 1973, a ban on late-term abortions was enacted by Congress in 2003, and many states restrict the availability of abortion in one way or another.

In 1988 Canada's Supreme Court found Canada's abortion law violated section 7 of the Charter of Rights and Freedoms. Chief Justice Brian Dickson wrote: "Forcing a woman, by threat of criminal sanction to carry a foetus to term unless she meets certain criteria unrelated to her own priorities and aspirations, is a profound interference with a woman's body and thus a violation of her security of the person." Attempts to enact a new law have failed, and Canada treats abortion as a medical procedure.

However, the provinces vary widely in the availability of abortion services. As of 2003, 34.8 percent of the hospitals in Quebec provided abortions which, if performed in hospital, were fully paid. In Ontario 23.4 percent of hospitals performed abortions, and in British Columbia it was 22 percent. Access is more difficult in the Atlantic provinces. Since 1983 there have been no abortion facilities in Prince Edward Island. In Nunavut and the other territories, abortions performed in hospitals are paid for, but facilities are limited. In 2003, women in Nunavut seeking abortions flew to Ottawa or Montreal. In the Northwest Territories two hospitals performed abortions, in the Yukon, just one.

Death Penalty

The United States has a federal death penalty and many states do as well, but it was abolished in Canada in 1976. In doing away with the death penalty, Canada's Parliament substituted imprisonment for life as a mandatory sentence for both first- and second-degree murder, with no eligibility for parole for twenty-five and ten years, respectively.

Same-Sex Marriage

Whether same-sex marriages are recognized in the United States is up to the individual states. In Canada, it's a federal matter. Canada's Supreme Court in December 2004 unanimously ruled that same-sex marriages are constitutional, and in February the prime minister introduced same-sex marriage legislation in the House. It was voted into law in June 2005.

In recent years, Canada has afforded both same-sex and opposite-sex couples as well as common-law partners equal treatment for immigration purposes. Same-sex couples in the United States can apply for permanent resident status in Canada as a couple, assuming they meet the eligibility criteria. Canadian citizens and permanent residents are also allowed to sponsor their same-sex partners.

Guns

Canada's Parliament passed a strict gun control bill in 1991 nearly two years after a young antifeminist gunman shot and killed fourteen women students and wounded fourteen more at Montreal's École Polytechnique before killing himself.

Canada's laws ban the import into Canada of military-style assault weapons and require the registration of all guns. Gun purchases are restricted to persons 18 and over. Minors aged 12 to 17 can get a minor's license allowing them to possess a nonrestricted rifle or shotgun, but a licensed adult must be responsible for the firearm.

Canada has a gun registry and requires gun owners to take the Canadian Firearms Safety Course (CFSC) and pass a test to get a license.

The United States has more firearm homicides than Canada not just in absolute numbers, but also proportionate to population. For 1987–1996, the average firearm homicide rate was 5.7 per 100,000 people in the United States, compared with 0.7 per 100,000 for Canada.

Robberies involving firearms are also far more numerous both in absolute numbers and proportionate to population in the United States than in Canada. Between 1987 and 1996, firearms were used in 38 percent of robberies in the United States, compared with 25 percent in Canada. The average firearm robbery rate in those years was 91 per 100,000 in population in the United States, compared with 26 per 100,000 in population in Canada.

Nonresidents of Canada who wish to bring a firearm to Canada and who are at least 18 years old can meet Canada's license and registration requirements by filling out a Non-Resident Firearms Declaration and having it confirmed by a customs officer. (The form is available on the Internet at www.cfc-ccaf.gc.ca/online-en_ligne/form-assistance/indiv_forms/909_e.asp.) They can also get a Possession and Acquisition License (PAL) and register their firearms in Canada. (Extensive information about firearms possession plus required forms are on the Internet at the Canada Firearms Centre site, www.cfc-ccaf.gc.ca/default_e.asp or by contacting the Canada Firearms Centre, 50 O'Connor St., Ottawa, ON K1A 1M6. Phone: 800-731-4000.)

TAXES

"There's a substantial apparent difference between taxes in the United States and Canada, but I don't think there really is that much difference," says Daniel Stone, a history professor at the University of Winnipeg who was born in New York City and emigrated to Canada. "Canadians get medical benefits and pensions," he points out.

Taxes fund many of Canada's social programs—not only health care and pensions for those over 65 but also unemployment and workman's compensation insurance.

Canada appears to have one of the highest tax rates in the world, but before comparing tax burdens in the United States with those of Canada, it makes sense to factor in what it costs a U.S. family to pay for health care insurance. According to a study by Mercer Human Resources Consultants quoted in the *Washington Times* (May 3, 2005), in the United States, medical insurance cost an individual US $6,679 on average in 2004.

In addition to premiums, there are likely to be co-payments, which can add thousands of dollars a year to health care costs, even for those with insurance. More than 45 million people in the United States have no health care insurance, often because they can't afford it.

The income tax system in Canada is administered by the federal government and the money is collected by the federal government. Annual income up to $35,595 is taxed at 15 percent. From $35,595 to $71,190 the tax rate is 22 percent. From $71,190 to $115,739 it's 26 percent. Over that, it's 29 percent. Provincial taxes are on top of that and depend on one's income level, except in Alberta, where everyone earning above a minimum income pays 10 percent.

Ontario has a health care tax based on income with a maximum tax of $900 a year. Those earning $20,000 or less pay nothing.

There are a variety of other taxes, such as the federal goods and services tax (GST) of 7 percent across the board, and provincial sales taxes. In Ontario, Nova Scotia, New Brunswick, and Newfoundland the sales tax is 8 percent. In Quebec the sales tax is 7.5 percent. It's 7 percent in British Columbia, Saskatchewan, and Manitoba. In Prince Edward Island, the sales tax is 10 percent, except for clothing, which isn't taxed. In Alberta there is no provincial sales tax, only the GST.

Those earning $30,000 or less are entitled to a GST tax credit.

Anyone living in Canada must report all of their worldwide income on their Canadian income tax return. The same applies to U.S. citizens wherever they live. The two countries have a treaty aimed at preventing double taxation, but U.S. citizens living in Canada as permanent residents or dual citizens must file federal income tax returns in both countries. The returns are due April 15 in the United States and April 30 in Canada.

Each individual's tax situation is likely to vary, but the basic rule, according to international tax attorney Alan Granwell, of Ivins, Phillips & Barker (chartered in Washington, D.C.), is: "If you retain your U.S. citizenship, you continue to be a U.S. taxpayer for income, estate, gift, and generation-skipping transfer tax purposes."

Granwell, who was U.S. international tax counsel from 1981 to 1984, advises those moving to another country to seek the advice of tax specialists competent on cross-border movement in both countries. He also suggests getting recommendations from immigration lawyers, bankers, or others. "The trouble is, the way the legal fees are structured, people who don't have that much money, but who want to move, might get sticker shock in trying to seek competent advice. It's just an exceedingly complicated area because you're dealing with a multijurisdictional analysis."

Granwell says, "There are two basic rules. If you have your passport, you're a taxpayer. And get good advice."

In Canada, husbands and wives file individually. There are no joint returns, meaning each partner is taxed based on his or her own income. There is no tax due on the first $8,000 earned.

If one of the couple has no income and the other does, the one with taxable income can deduct the other. If there are child care expenses, they can be deducted by the person with the lower income.

Dependent children are not deductible unless they are children of a single parent, who can deduct one child, no matter how many children he or she has.

There are no mortgage interest deductions allowed on a house in Canada, but neither are there capital gains taxes for the sale of a primary residence. There are city and municipal property taxes on a residence, as in the United States. Some investment expenses can be deducted, as can some medical expenses.

Residents of Canada need a Social Insurance Number (SIN) to work and to file income taxes, just as residents of the United States need a Social Security Number (SSN). The nine-digit SIN is also used to connect the Canadian taxpayer with such programs as Employment Insurance (EI) and Canada's Pension Plan (CPP).

Louisa Helander, a community tax consultant in Toronto, says it's important for people with low or no income to file an income tax return every year anyway in order to be eligible for government benefits such as the Canada Child Tax Benefit, known previously as the Baby Bonus. The amount of that credit is determined by the number and age of children and the combined family income.

CITY TO CITY TAX COMPARISONS

In March 2004, *Saskatchewan Finance* published statistics comparing taxes and household charges for a family with $50,000 in total income in ten cities throughout Canada.

Factoring in provincial income tax, tax credits and rebates, health premiums, retail sales tax, and gasoline tax, total provincial taxes for each city were as follows:

St. John's, Nfld.	$5,206
Saint John, N.B.	$4,726
Halifax, N.S.	$4,606
Charlottetown, P.E.I.	$4,417
Vancouver, B.C.	$4,188
Saskatoon, Sask.	$3,644
Winnipeg, Man.	$3,316
Montreal, Que.	$2,915
Calgary, Alta.	$2,757
Toronto, Ont.	$2,598

CANADA'S GOVERNMENT

Americans who become Canadian citizens will find they have a Queen at the top of their government, even though the Queen's influence is largely symbolic. The Queen is represented in Canada by a governor-general, whom she appoints on the recommendation of Canada's prime minister.

The Canadian government is modeled on the British Cabinet system with a Parliament and a prime minister exercising the main power. The prime minister is not directly elected by the people but traditionally is the leader of the party that wins the most seats in the House of Commons in a federal election.

The House of Commons has 308 members, called members of parliament or MPs. They are elected from districts, called ridings, based on the population of those districts, as are members of the U.S. House of Representatives. Sixty percent of House of Commons members currently come from Ontario and Quebec, where the majority of Canadians live.

Occasionally a member of parliament will be an independent, but most belong to a political party such as the Liberal Party, the Progressive-Conservative Party, the Canadian Alliance Party, the Bloc Québécois, or the left-of-center New Democratic Party. Party leaders are chosen at conventions held at least every five years.

After a national election, the party with the most seats in the House of Commons becomes the governing party and its leader is the prime minister. The prime minister then appoints a cabinet of twenty to thirty ministers to head departments of the government, such as Agriculture or Immigration and Citizenship. These departments are responsible to the House of Commons.

The runner-up party in a national election becomes the official opposition party and its leader chooses a shadow cabinet. There is an hour-long question period every day the House meets during which the opposition parties can ask questions of the prime minister and the cabinet ministers on almost any topic they wish.

There is a Senate in Canada with 105 members, but they are not elected. The Canadian Senate resembles the British House of Lords. Senators are appointed by the governor-general on the recommendation of the prime minister and hold office until they are seventy-five years old. Vacancies normally occur on the death or retirement of a sitting senator.

As in the U.S. Congress, the House initiates all funding bills. They and other bills must also pass in the Senate, but the Senate's chief role has been to make policy recommendations and to conduct long-term investigations.

Canada's Parliament makes the laws. The judiciary, appointed by the governor-general on the recommendation of the cabinet, interprets and enforces them.

The Canadian judiciary resembles the U.S. judiciary in that decisions by lower courts are appealed to higher provincial courts and ultimately to the Supreme Court of Canada.

Criminal law in Canada is based largely on British law and is uniform throughout Canada and under federal jurisdiction. Civil law is also based on British law except in Quebec, where the root is Napoleonic law. Civil and criminal cases generally begin in lower courts (small claims, provincial or district) and can be appealed to the Court of Appeals of the province and ultimately to the Supreme Court of Canada.

The Supreme Court of Canada also hears appeals involving the government and its departments from the Federal Court (which hears suits against the government) and decides all constitutional questions relating to the powers of the federal and provincial governments. Since 1982, the High Court also makes decisions about the rights and freedoms guaranteed in the Canadian Charter.

Canada's Constitution Act was signed by Queen Elizabeth in 1982. The act, now Canada's governing document, effectively succeeded the British North America Act of 1867 that united what became the four provinces of Ontario, Quebec, Nova Scotia, and New Brunswick into a confederation called the Dominion of Canada.

Succeeding Acts added British Columbia, Manitoba, Prince Edward Island, Alberta, Saskatchewan, and Newfoundland to the Dominion. In 1931 the Statute of Westminster gave Canada control over its foreign and domestic policy. All of these acts were passed in the British Parliament.

Even though the Westminster statute gave Canada its independence, amendments to it continued to need Britain's approval. Finally, in 1982, as a result of Canadian proposals, the Constitution Act effectively brought Canada's Constitution home. It also added to the Constitution the Canadian Charter of Rights and Freedoms, which is not unlike the U.S. Constitution's Bill of Rights.

Included in the Charter are the fundamental freedoms of conscience and religion; freedom of thought, belief, opinion, and expression; freedom of the press; freedom of peaceful assembly; and freedom of association. Among legal rights afforded to Canadians are the right to life, liberty, and security of the person, and the right not to be deprived thereof except in accordance with the principles of fundamental justice. The Equality Rights section of the Charter states that every individual is equal before and under the law and has the right to the equal protection and equal benefit of the law without discrimination and, in particular, without discrimination based on race, national or ethnic origin, color, religion, sex, age, or mental or physical disability.

TWO

THE IMMIGRATION PROCESS:
Immigration Categories

CANADA NEEDS IMMIGRANTS AND SEEKS THEM. IN 2004, ALmost 236,000 people became permanent residents of Canada. In addition, there were around 90,000 people who came to the country to work temporarily and another 130,000 who came to study, not including those who came to Canada specifically to learn French or English as a second language.

While there is some information on temporary residency in this section of the book, it is primarily directed to U.S. citizens thinking of moving to Canada permanently.

Any U.S. citizen may visit Canada for six months or less without needing a visa or a permit. (For more information on temporary residency, see page 45.) But applications for permanent residency have sometimes complex requirements.

PERMANENT RESIDENCY

U.S. citizens who wish to emigrate to Canada on a permanent basis have a number of options. In 2004, 57 percent of Canada's permanent immigrants came into the country as skilled workers or as business class applicants. Most of the remainder were sponsored by a family member or were refugees.

Would-be immigrants should note that applications are processed according to the rules and regulations in effect at the time the application is filed. The most up-to-date information is available on the federal government's immigration Web site: www.cic.gc.ca.

In some cases, several years can elapse between the time of filing and the issuance of a permanent residency visa. If an applicant meets the required criteria at the time of filing, he or she must still meet them when the visa is finally granted. (The one exception has to do with the evaluation of age. Skilled worker applicants are qualified under a point system in which age is a criterion. The applicant's age at the time of filing is the age that is used in evaluating the application.)

CANADA'S IMMIGRATION LAWS AND HOW THEY'VE CHANGED

In 2002, Canada enacted a new Immigration and Refugee Protection Act (IRPA), which differed from previous laws in several important ways. The old law, according to David Cohen, an immigration lawyer in the Montreal firm of Campbell, Cohen, "was somewhat subjective," awarding points for what the government referred to as "Personal Suitability." This was determined by a visa officer based on documents submitted at an interview. The officer was also empowered to evaluate English language ability based on that interview.

"These subjective factors were changed in the new law," says Cohen. The Personal Suitability requirement was eliminated and evaluation of language fluency was based on standardized tests. "The new legislation, IRPA, is more objective than the previous legislation," Cohen says.

There were some other changes under the new law having to do with education and work experience. Now educational criteria are simply evaluated on the number of years of study and the degrees awarded.

Most of this was a step forward. Problems, however, arose because there were a huge number of applications in process when the new law went into effect. The government attempted to apply the new selection criteria retroactively, which caused some applicants to take the matter to court. They said that they were being treated unfairly because they would have qualified under the old Immigration Act, but no longer qualified under the new one.

The lawsuits created a processing backlog that is only now being resolved.

Economic Applicants: Skilled Worker Class

Who is a Skilled Worker? How are they evaluated for immigration?

SKILLED WORKER These are people whose education and job experience may qualify them for permanent residence. Skilled workers are assessed according to a system that awards points for education, job experience, English and French language proficiency, age, previously arranged employment, and adaptability. This last category includes an assessment of a spouse's or common-law partner's level of education, previous study in Canada, previous work in Canada, arranged employment, and having relatives in Canada.

At the present time, an applicant's points must total 67 or more out of 100, though this could change. (For the current pass mark, consult the government's Web site at www.cic.gc.ca/skilled.)

When a couple—either married or in a common-law conjugal partnership that has lasted at least a year—wants to immigrate in the skilled worker category, both should take the self-assessment test to see which scores higher. The other person should then apply for admittance as a family member. This applies for same sex or opposite sex couples. (If the couple has dependent children, they can be included on the application.)

If a skilled worker has sufficient points, he or she must still pass a background check and get health clearance. Unless the worker has a prearranged job, the would-be immigrant in this category must also have sufficient funds unencumbered by debts or other obligations. The sum required varies according to family size, from $9,897 for one person to $25,210 for a family of seven or more.

Only certain occupations qualify for immigration as a skilled worker. These are listed and explained on the Web at www.cic.gc.ca/skilled.

QUALIFYING OCCUPATIONS

Examples of the occupations listed in Skill Type 0, Skill Level A or B of the National Occupation Classification List. (Many other occupations qualify.)

Aerospace Engineers
Architects
Archivists
Athletes
Audio and Video Recording Technicians
Authors and Writers
Automotive Service Technicians, Truck Mechanics, and Mechanical Repairers

Bakers
Banking, Credit, and Other Investment Managers
Biologists and Related Scientists
Boilermakers
Bookkeepers
Bricklayers

Cabinetmakers
Cardiology Technologists
Chefs
Chiropractors
Computer and Information Systems Managers
Conservation and Fishery Officers
Crane Operators

Dancers
Database Analysts and Data Administrators
Dentists
Dry Cleaning and Laundry Supervisors

Economists and Economic Policy Researchers and Analysts
Editors
Employment Counselors

Continued on next page

Farmers and Farm Managers
Firefighters
Funeral Directors and Embalmers

Government Managers—Economic Analysis, Policy Development
Grain Elevator Operators
Graphic Designers and Illustrators

Hairstylists and Barbers
Head Nurses and Supervisors
Heavy-Duty Equipment Mechanics

Insurance Adjusters and Claims Examiners
Interior Designers
Ironworkers

Jewelers, Watch Repairers, and Related Occupations
Journalists
Judges

Land Surveyors
Lawyers and Quebec Notaries
Librarians
Loan Officers
Logging Machinery Operators

Machinists and Machining and Tooling Inspectors
Managers in Social, Community, and Correctional Services
Mathematicians, Statisticians, and Actuaries
Meteorologists
Midwives and Practitioners of Natural Healing
Ministers of Religion
Musicians and Singers

Nursery and Greenhouse Operators and Managers

Occupational Therapists
Oil and Gas Well Drillers, Servicers, Testers, and Related Workers
Opticians

Continued on next page

QUALIFYING OCCUPATIONS

Painters and Decorators
Petroleum Engineers
Pharmacists
Physicians—General Practitioners and Family Physicians
Plumbers
Professors—University

Real Estate Agents and Salespersons
Registered Nurses
Restaurant and Food Service Managers

Sales, Marketing, and Advertising Managers
Secretaries
Social Workers
Supervisors, Fabric, Fur, and Leather Products Manufacturing

Tailors, Dressmakers, Furriers, and Milliners
Teachers—Elementary School and Kindergarten
Telecommunications Line and Cable Workers
Translators, Terminologists, and Interpreters
Transportation Managers

Underground Production and Development Miners
Upholsterers

Veterinarians

Water Well Drillers
Web Designers and Developers
Welders and Related Machine Operators

Skilled workers must have had the equivalent of at least one year of full-time employment (37.5 hours per week or more) in one or more of the occupations listed in Skill Type O (management occupations) or Skill Level A (primarily professional occupations) or B (technical or skilled trades and para-professional occupations) of the National Occupational Classification (NOC). The work experience must have occurred in the previous ten years.

Level C, which includes occupations mainly of intermediate level, clerical, or supportive functions, and D, which includes elemental sales or service and primary laborer occupations, don't meet the criteria for admission to Canada as a skilled worker.

SKILLED WORKER SELF-ASSESSMENT TEST

Could you qualify to enter Canada as a skilled worker? Take the self-assessment test.

1. Education:
   - Master's Degree or Ph.D. and at least 17 years of full-time or full-time equivalent study: 25 points.
   - Two or more university degrees at the Bachelor's level and at least 15 years of full-time equivalent study: 22 points.
   - A three-year diploma, trade certificate, or apprenticeship and at least 15 years of full-time equivalent study: 22 points.
   - A university degree of two years or more at the Bachelor's level and at least 14 years of full-time or full-time equivalent study: 20 points.
   - A one-year university degree at the Bachelor's level and at least 13 years of full-time or full-time equivalent study: 15 points.
   - A one-year diploma, trade certificate, or apprenticeship and at least 13 years of full-time or full-time equivalent study: 15 points.
   - A one-year diploma, trade certificate, or apprenticeship and at least 12 years of full-time or full-time equivalent study: 12 points.
   - Completion of high school: 5 points.

YOUR POINTS FOR EDUCATION:_____

2. English and/or French Language Proficiency: Applicants receive a maximum total of 24 points for fluency in both official languages of Canada. Listening, speaking, reading, and writing are evaluated. Americans should have little problem with English fluency in all four areas, which would be worth 16 points. Points for the second language are ranked at two for each of the four areas (listening, speaking, reading, and writing), for a maximum of eight points.

YOUR POINTS FOR LANGUAGE PROFICIENCY:_____

SKILLED WORKER SELF-ASSESSMENT TEST

A list of approved organizations to assess language skills is available at www.cic.gc.ca/skilled. Assessment results should be submitted with immigration applications. The testing must have occurred within the previous twelve months.

Americans do not have to submit proof of language ability in the form of a standardized English test. "A statement of language ability signed and dated saying that I was born and raised in the U.S. and I went to school here and I worked in the U.S. will get you the 16 points," says David Cohen.

The Paris Chamber of Commerce and Industry administers the Test d'Evaluation de Français (TEF). TEF is offered worldwide including in many cities in the United States (Los Angeles; San Francisco; Chicago; Philadelphia; New York; New Orleans; Washington, D.C.; Houston; San Jose, Calif.; Lynchburg, Va.; and White Plains, N.Y.). The test is a standardized assessment of reading, writing, listening, and speaking skills in the French language.

As an alternative, an applicant may establish French proficiency levels through a written explanation and supporting documentation. "It's somewhat on the honor system," says Cohen. "If the visa officer for any reason doubts that, then they could ask you to take the TEF."

Interestingly, he adds, "Quebec does not have the same requirements of standardized testing in French. Quebec relies on an interview either by telephone or in person, and they test only oral and listening ability."

3. Work Experience: Maximum 21 points for four years or more of full-time work within the previous ten years. Three years earns 19 points, two years 17 points, and one year 15 points.
YOUR POINTS FOR EXPERIENCE:_____

4. Age: Maximum 10 points if you are between age 21 and 49 at the time of application. Subtract two points for each year over 49 or under 21.
YOUR POINTS FOR AGE:_____

5. Arranged Employment in Canada: In all cases, the applicant must have a job offer in one or more of the occupations listed in Skill Type O (management occupations) or Skill Level A (primarily professional

occupations), or B (technical or skilled trades and paraprofessional occupations) of the National Occupational Classification (NOC). The applicant must be able to perform the job and be likely to accept it.

Maximum 10 Points If You Are:

- working in Canada on a temporary work permit that was issued after receipt of a confirmation of your job offer from Human Resources and Skills Development Canada (HRSDC). (Conditions: Your work permit was valid at the time you applied for a permanent resident visa and at the time the visa, if any, is issued; your employer has offered you a permanent job once the permanent resident visa is issued; you are currently working in that job.)
- working in Canada on a temporary work permit that was exempted from the requirement of a confirmed job offer from HRSDC on the basis of an international agreement such as the North American Free Trade Agreement (NAFTA) or the General Agreement on Trade in Services (GATS), a significant benefit to Canada (e.g., intracompany transfer) or public policy on Canada's academic or economic competitiveness (e.g., postgraduate work). (Conditions: Your work permit was valid at the time you applied for a permanent resident visa and at the time the visa, if any, is issued; your employer has offered you a permanent job once the permanent resident visa is issued; you are currently working in that job.)
- working in Canada on a temporary work permit that does not fall under either of the two situations above. (Conditions: Your employer has offered you a permanent job once the permanent resident visa is issued; your employer has had the permanent job offer confirmed by HRSDC; it is a genuine, full-time job offer and not part-time or seasonal; and it pays wages consistent with Canadian standards.)
- not working in Canada, do not currently hold a work permit, and do not intend to work in Canada before being issued a permanent resident visa. (Conditions: The employer has offered you a permanent job once the permanent resident visa is issued; the employer has had the permanent job offer confirmed by HRSDC; you meet the Canadian licensing or regulatory requirements necessary for the job; it is a genuine, full-time job offer and not part-time or seasonal, and it pays wages consistent with Canadian standards.)

SKILLED WORKER SELF-ASSESSMENT TEST

The would-be immigrant cannot arrange for HRSDC confirmation. This must be done by the employer. If you have a temporary work permit, it must be valid at the time of your application and also if and when a permanent residency visa is issued. In addition, your employer must have made an offer to give you a permanent job if your application is successful.

YOUR POINTS FOR ARRANGED EMPLOYMENT:_____

6. Adaptability: Maximum 10 points from a variety of sources. Although the possible points in this category add up to more than 10, only 10 will be awarded, even if the applicant or his or her spouse could qualify for more. Arranged employment appears in this category, as it does in the one above, constituting, in effect, a 5-point bonus for arranged employment.

Points Are Awarded For:

- spouse's (or common-law or conjugal partner's) education: 3-5 points;
- at least one year of full-time authorized work in Canada on a valid work permit (by applicant or spouse): 5 points;
- at least two years of authorized postsecondary study in Canada (by applicant or spouse) after the age of 17 and with a valid study permit: 5 points;
- the applicant or spouse/partner's having a relative (parent, grandparent, child, grandchild, sibling, aunt/uncle or grandchild of a parent, niece, or nephew) who lives in Canada and is a Canadian citizen or permanent resident: 5 points;
- the applicant's having arranged employment in Canada (see page 26–28 for specific qualifications): 5 points

YOUR POINTS FOR ADAPTABILITY:_____

YOUR TOTAL POINTS:_____ (YOU NEED A MINIMUM OF 67 OUT OF 100.)

ARRANGED EMPLOYMENT

"This is a tricky part of the immigration regulations," says immigration attorney Linda Mark of the Vancouver firm of Mark & Co. It's tricky, she explains, "partly because you have human resources officers approving parts of it and visa officers approving other parts. A person may think they have approval and will be successful, but their application could be rejected several years down the road by the visa officer." For this reason, she says, she first tries to assess whether someone can qualify without arranged employment. "If not, that would be a second alternative. It's a technical part of the regulations that can easily be misinterpreted."

The current regulations were instituted in 2002. "It's only now that we're beginning to see how the laws are actually getting interpreted by the visa officers," Mark says. She advises anyone trying to come into Canada under arranged employment to get legal help.

If not enough points are accrued, the applicant may submit a formal application with a detailed letter and supporting documentation explaining why he thinks he could become economically established in Canada. Or the applicant may seek to qualify under the Provincial Nominee Program. (See page 38.) Another alternative might be to apply as a skilled worker in the province of Quebec, which has a different point and weighting system than the rest of Canada.

CREDENTIAL ASSESSMENT Twenty percent of people working in Canada work in regulated or licensed occupations such as nursing, teaching, or engineering. Provincial or territorial regulatory bodies are responsible for establishing entry requirements for such occupations, for recognizing prior credentials, training, and experience, and for issuing licenses required to practice. This assessment can take time and can generally only be completed once the applicant is in Canada. (There are credential-assessment services outside of Canada, but some employers and some regulatory bodies may ask for additional assessments once the applicant is in Canada.)

Having your credentials assessed does not guarantee that they will be recognized by a regulatory body, Canadian educational institution, or employer or that you will be issued a license to practice by a regulatory body.

In most cases, there are fees for credential assessment. A basic assessment, which, for instance, might evaluate an immigrant's diploma for authenticity, the standing of the educational institution from which it came, the country's educational profiles, and the individual's educational standing, will cost around $100 to $125, but more elaborate assessments could cost many times that amount.

Most assessments take eight weeks to complete, but they can take longer if extensive research or correspondence is required. One credential assessor, World Education Services, a not-for-profit organization funded in part by the government of Ontario, promises a seven-day turnaround for a basic assessment, but that is unusual.

For more information, contact:

Canadian Information for International Credentials
95 St. Clair Avenue West, Suite 1106
Toronto, ON M4V 1N6
Canada
    Phone: 416-962-9725
    Fax: 416-962-2800

CREDENTIAL ASSESSMENT SERVICES, BY PROVINCE

People who work in licensed professions (doctors, nurses, engineers, architects, for example) will need to have their credentials assessed and approved in order to practice these professions in Canada. Students transferring to Canadian universities may need their previous academic record evaluated for admission and placement.

Alberta and Saskatchewan
International Qualifications Assessment Service (IQAS)

www.learning.gov.ab.ca/iqas

International Qualifications Assessment Service (IQAS)
9th Floor, 108 Street Building
9942 108 Street
Edmonton, AB T5K 2J5
    Phone: 780-427-2655
    Fax: 780-422-9734

Continued on next page

British Columbia
International Credential Evaluation Service (ICES)

International Credential Evaluation Service
3700 Willingdon Ave.
Burnaby, BC V5G 3H2
   Phone: 604-432-8800 (available between 8:30 A.M.-12:00 P.M.
   PST)
   Fax: 604-435-7033
   E-mail: icesinfo@bcit.ca
   Toll-free within North America: 866-434-9197

Manitoba
Academic Credentials Assessment Service-Manitoba (ACAS)

For an appointment, call 204-945-6300.

www.gov.mb.ca/labour/immigrate/newcomerservices/7a.html

Manitoba Labour and Immigration
Settlement and Labour Market Services Branch
5th Floor, 213 Notre Dame Ave.
Winnipeg, MB R3B 1N3
   Phone: 204-945-6300
   Fax: 204-948-2148
www.immigratemanitoba.com

Quebec
*Evaluation comparative des Etudes effectuées hors du Québec
(Comparative Evaluation for Studies Done Outside Quebec)*

For more information, applicants living outside Quebec can contact:

Ministére de l'Immigration et des Communautés culturelles
Service des Evaluations comparatives d'Etudes (Demandes inter-
nationales)
255, boulevard Crémazie Est, 8e Etage
Montréal, QC H2M 1M2
   Phone: 514-864-9191
   E-mail: Renseignements@micc.gouv.qc.ca

Continued on next page

CREDENTIAL ASSESSMENT SERVICES, BY PROVINCE

Ontario
World Education Services

WES is a not-for-profit organization recognized, and funded in part, by the government of Ontario.

Canadian Office
World Education Services
45 Charles St. East, Suite 700
Toronto, ON M4Y 1S2
  Phone: 416-972-0070 or 866-343-0070
  Fax: 416-972-9004
  canada@wes.org

New York
  Phone: 212-966-6311
  Fax: 212-739-6100
  info@wes.org

Southeast
  Phone: 305-358-6688
  Fax: 305-358-4411
  south@wes.org

Midwest
  Phone: 312-222-0882
  Fax: 312-222-1217
  midwest@wes.org

West Coast
  Phone: 415-677-9378
  Fax: 415-677-9333
  sf@wes.org

Continued on next page

Washington, D.C.
> Phone: 202-331-2925
> Fax: 202-331-2927
> dc@wes.org 1S2

New Brunswick, Newfoundland, Nova Scotia or Prince Edward Island, Yukon

You may contact any of the credential assessment services listed above.

Other assessment services

International Credential Assessment Service of Canada

(Phone: 519-763-7282; www.icascanada.ca) Service centers in Ontario. Basic fees, $80–$160.

Comparative Education Service, a Service of the University of Toronto.

(Phone: 416-978-2190; www.adm.utoronto.ca/ces) Basic fee, $100.

CREDENTIALS FOR PROFESSIONALS

Many highly educated professionals have come to Canada in recent years only to find themselves seriously and woefully underemployed because of problems in getting their credentials and experience recognized.

In April 2005, then Immigration Minister Joe Volpe announced a $269 million plan to help foreign-born professionals such as engineers, doctors, and nurses get their Canadian credentials more quickly than they have in the past.

Canada has a shortage of trained medical personnel. At the same time, many immigrants with medical training in other countries find themselves unable to work in their fields. If approved by Parliament, some of the money requested by Volpe would be spent to set up a national agency to evaluate the credentials of all international medical graduates.

Several Web sites would be funded under the proposal. One would help prepare medical personnel to be licensed in Canada.

Continued on next page

CREDENTIALS FOR PROFESSIONALS

Another would improve an existing site called Going to Canada that helps prospective immigrants understand the Canadian labor market and how to prepare for it. Language training would also be funded, with an emphasis on vocabulary needed by professionals.

Immigrant engineers would be aided by the creation of a database of foreign institutions offering engineering degrees.

Economic Applicants: Business Class

People with capital to invest in Canada or with experience owning and running a business may qualify in this category.

INVESTORS Must demonstrate business experience and have a minimum net worth of $800,000, which may include a house, property, and a spouse's property. Must be able and willing to make an investment of $400,000, which the investor loans to the Canadian government for five years, after which it is returned without interest. Investor applicants only need 35 points from the six categories by which skilled workers are assessed and are not required to start a business, but must show they have certain types of business experience in two of the past five years. This is an option for people who are older, have the money, and don't want to worry about starting or running a business, but do want to go to Canada to retire.

ENTREPRENEURS Must have experience owning and managing a business that will contribute to the Canadian economy and create jobs. Must demonstrate business experience and have a minimum net worth of $300,000. Entrepreneurs are only required to have 35 points from the six categories used to rate skilled workers, but must show two years of having run their own business in the past five years.

SELF-EMPLOYED Must have the intention and the demonstrated ability over two of the past five years to create their own employment. This could be in cultural or athletic fields or in farming. At the federal level, there are no specific financial requirements in this category but applicants must demonstrate that they have enough money to support their proposed work in Canada. In Quebec Province, self-employed applicants must have minimum net assets of $100,000, which can have been accumulated through the work of both the principal applicant and an accompanying spouse.

Family Class Immigration

If one member of a family is already a Canadian citizen or a permanent resident and is 18 years old or older, he or she may sponsor other family members including

- a spouse, a common-law or conjugal partner 16 years old or older of the same or opposite sex
- parents and grandparents
- dependent children, including adopted children
- children under 18 for whom there are adoption plans
- brothers, sisters, nephews, nieces, or grandchildren who are orphans, less than 18 years old, and not married or in a common-law relationship

The law also permits the sponsorship of one relative of any age if the sponsor has no aunt, uncle, or family member from the list above.

Children are considered dependent if

- they're under the age of 22 and don't have a spouse or common-law partner
- they're full-time students and have primarily relied on a parent for financial support since before the age of 22
- they've married or become a common-law partner before age 22 but still depend financially on a parent
- they've been financially dependent on a parent since before the age of 22 because of a disability

With sponsorships there is no point system to meet, just the relationship criteria. The sponsee should not have a criminal record. Health problems are not usually an issue, especially for spouses and dependent children, though anyone with a contagious disease might be barred from Canada to protect the overall population. "If there are any significant health issues," says Linda Mark, "you may want to get legal advice."

Sponsors must be willing and able to support the relative or family member and their accompanying families for three to ten years to help them settle in Canada. The government requires the sponsor to sign a document entitled an Undertaking with the Minister of Citizenship and Immigration spelling out the commitment. In Quebec, this formal document is signed with the province of Quebec. Family members must also sign a Sponsorship Agreement with one another. This is a legal document detailing their mutual commitments.

FAMILY CLASS

Up till now, bringing a parent or grandparent into Canada could take five to ten years, but in April 2005, Citizenship and Immigration Minister Joe Volpe announced a $72-million plan to speed up the process. Over a two-year period, half of that money ($36 million) will be used to cover the costs of processing and integrating parents and grandparents. In the meantime, CIC will make it easier and faster for parents and grandparents to obtain multiple-entry visas so that they can visit their families while their sponsorship applications are pending.

Though there's a backlog of a hundred thousand people now waiting for their immigration applications to be considered and, hopefully, approved, marriage to a Canadian or a permanent resident who then acts as a sponsor can move things along relatively quickly, taking six to twelve months instead of one to two years.

Linda Mark, who practices immigration law in Vancouver, notes that immigration officials will look carefully at conjugal situations to make sure that they're bona fide relationships. "They look at how long people have known each other, whether they've traveled together, if they have photos of themselves as a couple, and so on." Interestingly, she says, immigration officers look for signs that U.S.-Canadian relationships are love matches. "But if an Indian spouse were trying to immigrate, the officials would be more inclined to look on the application favorably if it was an arranged marriage."

Sometimes, says Mark, legitimate relationships get rejected as do the applications of some adoptees and would-be adoptees. "If it appears to immigration officials that an adoption was done mainly to get someone into Canada, the application could be rejected." Mark advises getting legal assistance for adoption sponsorship applications.

Refugees

To be accepted as a refugee in Canada you generally have to show that you are afraid of your own government or that authorities are not protecting you. This is not an easy thing for Americans to prove according to Linda Mark. She says if a U.S. citizen came to her and wanted to know what his options were, that would be the last option she would select. If a person does go through the refugee application process and is deemed a refugee, he or she then can apply for permanent resident status and ultimately citizenship.

MILITARY REFUGEES

In the late 1960s and early 1970s when the United States had a military draft, many U.S. citizens fled to Canada to avoid serving in the war in Vietnam or because they were unsympathetic with that war. Now, some soldiers who believe that the U.S. invasion of Iraq is wrong are attempting to find asylum in Canada, thus far with little success.

In March 2005, U.S. Army Specialist Jeremy Hinzman was denied refugee status in Canada where he had sought asylum because he believed that the invasion of Iraq was criminal. The Immigration and Refugee Board ruled that Hinzman had not made a convincing argument that he would face persecution if he returned to the United States. Hinzman's lawyer is attempting to appeal that decision before the Federal Court of Canada.

If Hinzman is forced to return to the United States, he would face a court-martial as a deserter and a possible five-year jail sentence if convicted.

In April 2005, Celeste Zappala, whose son, Sherwood Baker, joined the Pennsylvania National Guard and was sent to Iraq where he was killed, appealed to Parliament in Ottawa to permit deserters to find sanctuary in Canada. Zappala claimed that her son didn't know what he was getting into when he joined the National Guard, which he thought would be called up to handle natural disasters.

Provincial Nomination

The Provincial Nominee Program can help applicants who may not have the 67 points needed to enter Canada under the Skilled Worker Program, but who have skills needed in eight of the ten Canadian provinces and one territory that have agreements with the federal government under the Immigration and Refugee Protection Act of 2002.

A growing number of applicants are utilizing the Provincial Nominee Program according to recent statistics from the Ministry of Citizenship and Immigration. The goal for 2005 was to admit 8,000 to 10,000 immigrants as provincial nominees.

Alberta, British Columbia, Manitoba, New Brunswick, Newfoundland, Nova Scotia, Prince Edward Island, Saskatchewan, and the Yukon Territory all have provincial nominee agreements, allowing them to recruit a certain number of foreign individuals to fill permanent, full-time, skilled positions for which no Canadians are available, so long as the recruitment efforts don't conflict with existing collective bargaining agreements.

A Provincial Nominee Program application can be useful, but it isn't for everyone. "You have to have the right set of circumstances," says Linda Mark. "The criteria can be subjective. In most instances, there's no point system, which can make it difficult to assess the end result at the beginning of the process."

Generally the nominee must meet the requirements of a preapproved provincial (or territorial) employer and have a valid job offer. Sufficient language skills to begin working soon after arrival enhance the possibility of being accepted as a provincial nominee.

Acceptance by the Provincial Nominee Program can speed up the application process, but the applicant must still meet all federal requirements for health, criminal, and security checks before an immigration visa is issued.

In addition to accepting skilled worker applicants for this program, some provinces also accept business class applicants. Manitoba, for instance, recruits qualified business people from around the world who have a net worth of at least $250,000 and are able to make an equity investment in Manitoba of at least $150,000. They must also have demonstrated experience running their own businesses or as senior managers of a successful company and have visited, or planned to visit, Manitoba to explore business opportunities. They are required to make a cash deposit of $75,000 with the government of Manitoba, which is usually refunded when the intended business is opened.

Potential economic nominees in Nova Scotia, another province that seeks business class applicants, must have a minimum net worth of $300,000 acquired by their own work (documentation of this is required). They must also be willing and able to make a one-time, nonrefundable economic contribution of $128,000 to the province. This is held in trust and returned without deduction or interest if the applicant is refused a Canadian residence visa.

An unusual feature of Nova Scotia's program is that it enables the nominee to live and work in the province for six months before making a long-term commitment. During this time, the nominee can hold a salaried middle-management job with a Nova Scotia employer while he or she assesses other options either for self-employment or for working in a management position with an existing company.

To use any of the Provincial Nominee programs, the applicant contacts the province before applying for federal immigration. The province will consider the applicant based on the needs of the province and the applicant's genuine interest in settling in that province. Once nominated by the province, the applicant then makes a separate application to the federal Citizenship and Immigration Canada for permanent residency.

FOR MORE INFORMATION ON
PROVINCIAL NOMINEE PROGRAMS

Alberta
Provincial Nominee Program
Economic Immigration
Alberta Economic Development
4th Floor, Commerce Place
10155 102 St.
Edmonton, AB, T5J 4L6
   Phone: 780-415-1319
   www.alberta-canada.com/pnp

British Columbia
Provincial Nominee Program
Ministry of Community,
Aboriginal & Women's Service
P.O. Box 9915 Stn Prov Gov
Victoria, BC V8W 9V1
   Phone: 250-387-2190
   Fax: 250-387-3725
   www.mcaws.gov.bc.ca/amip/pnp/

Manitoba
Provincial Nominee Program
Immigration Promotion & Recruitment Branch
Labour and Immigration Manitoba
9th Floor, 213 Notre Dame Ave.
Winnipeg, MB R3B 1N3
   Phone: 204-945-2806
   Fax: 204-948-2256
   E-mail: immigratemanitoba@gov.mb.ca
   www.gov.mb.ca/labour/immigrate/english/immigration/
   1.html

Continued on next page

New Brunswick

Provincial Nominee Program

Training and Employment Development

P.O. Box 6000

Fredericton, NB E3B 5H1

   Phone: 506-453-3981

   Fax: 506-444-4277

   E-mail: immigration@gnb.ca

   www.gnb.ca/immigration/english/index.htm

Newfoundland and Labrador

Provincial Nominee Program

Industry, Trade and Technology

Confederation Building

West Block, 4th Floor

P.O. Box 8700

St. John's, NL A1B 4J6

   Phone: 709-729-2781

   Fax: 709-729-3208

   www.gov.nf.ca/itrd/prov_nominee.htm

Nova Scotia

Provincial Nominee Program

The Office of Economic Development

World Trade and Convention Centre

1800 Argyle St.

P.O. Box 519

Halifax, NS B3J 2R7

   Phone: 902-424-8322

   www.gov.ns.ca

Continued on next page

FOR MORE INFORMATION ON
PROVINCIAL NOMINEE PROGRAMS

Prince Edward Island

Immigration & Investment Division

PEI Department of Development & Technology and Island
Investment Development Inc.

P.O. Box 1176, 94 Euston St., 2nd Floor

Charlottetown, PE C1A 7M8

Phone: 902-894-0351

Fax: 902-368-5886

E-mail: peinominee@gov.pe.ca

www.gov.pe.ca/immigration

Saskatchewan

Saskatchewan Immigrant Nominee Program

2nd Floor, 1919 Saskatchewan Dr.

Regina, SK S4P 3V7

Phone: 306-798-SINP (7467)

Fax: 306-798-0713

E-mail: immigration@graa.gov.sk.ca

www.immigrationsask.gov.sk.ca

Yukon Territory

Business Development and Immigration

Department of Economic Development

P.O. Box 2703

Whitehorse, YT Y1A 2C6

Phone: 867-667-3014

E-mail: bob.snyder@gov.yk.ca

www.economicdevelopment.gov.yk.ca

Immigration to Quebec Province

Quebec is responsible for selecting immigrants who wish to settle in Quebec. The Canada-Quebec Accord of 1991 gives Quebec selection powers and control over its own settlement services. The federal government, however, retains exclusive jurisdiction in the areas of visa issuing and medical and criminal checks.

The province of Quebec has somewhat different selection criteria than the rest of Canada, giving more weight to French language ability (up to sixteen points for French fluency but only a maximum of six points for English fluency) and to certain occupations as well as to families emigrating with children. However, even without fluent French, a well-educated individual could qualify to live in Quebec as a skilled worker, according to David Cohen.

"Quebec awards bonus points for certain kinds of education and training, whereas the rest of Canada treats a bachelor's degree as a bachelor's degree, no matter what area it's obtained in," says Cohen. "Someone might be able to qualify to come into Quebec Province even if they couldn't qualify to come into another province."

Highly qualified workers in the information technologies and telecommunications, biotechnology, and aeronautics industries get extra points on their skilled worker applications.

Quebec has a free, on-line form that will give a preliminary evaluation of whether an applicant is likely to qualify for emigration to the province. It asks questions about education level, work experience, French and English fluency, number and ages of children, whether the applicant will be accompanied by a conjugal partner, whether the applicant has family members or friends in Quebec, and whether the would-be immigrant has ever studied in Quebec or visited for any length of time.

APPLYING AS A SKILLED WORKER The first step is to fill out a Certificat de Sélection du Québec (CSQ), which can be obtained from the Quebec government (contact information for the U.S.-Quebec immigration office, below). The form is also available on the Internet at www.immigration-quebec.gouv.qc.ca/anglais/forms/dcs-general.html. (Note that there are two different Certificat de Sélection forms, one for skilled workers and business class applicants and the other for family class applicants.) If Quebec approves, the applicant must then apply to Citizenship and Immigration Canada for permanent residence. The six selection criteria applied to federal skilled worker applicants differ for skilled workers applying to immigrate to Quebec Province.

To qualify as a skilled worker in Quebec, the applicant must either have assured employment (a valid job offer from a Quebec employer who has demonstrated that no current Quebec resident could fill the position), have skills in an occupation that is in demand in Quebec Province, or meet the requirements of the Employability and Occupational Mobility category. The latter entails scoring at least 30 points (35 points if married or in a common-law relationship) plus at least 60 points (68 points if married or in a common-law relationship) under the Quebec skilled worker grid.

Most applicants in the Quebec skilled worker category are expected to appear for an interview with a provincial immigration officer who will ascertain that the information in the application is accurate, verify documentation, and provide some initial counseling on the resettlement process.

BUSINESS CLASS Within the business category of immigration, the Quebec definition of a business person differs from the federal definition. Quebec accepts three years of business management experience and does not require business ownership in order to qualify as an entrepreneur. (People applying as entrepreneurs through the federal Provincial Nominee Program would find that Prince Edward Island, Nova Scotia, and Manitoba accepted their business management experience, but with those exceptions, the federal immigration program requires business ownership for an applicant who wants to be considered as an entrepreneur.)

Investor applicants are also measured somewhat differently in Quebec Province than they are under the federal program. Quebec will accept people with management experience in a government office or a nongovernmental organization (NGO), whereas in the federal program, the management experience must have been for a profit-making business.

Applications to immigrate to Quebec are usually processed faster than federal applications. "How much faster? That depends on which visa office is involved and which Quebec government office is involved," says Cohen. "If one were applying from Hong Kong, it would be significantly faster. If you were a business applicant from the United States, currently—and this is always subject to change because service standards change within visa offices—it is taking in excess of two years to qualify under the business program to come to Canada under the federal side, but you can get a visa coming through Quebec in a year—plus or minus. Quebec is more efficient in selecting, and once Quebec has made the selection, the federal side only handles health and security, and they can handle that quite quickly."

QUEBEC IMMIGRATION OFFICE IN THE UNITED STATES

Direction de la sélection des travailleurs New York
Délégation générale du Québec
One Rockefeller Plaza, 26th Floor
New York, NY 10020
   Phone: 212-843-0960
   Fax: 212-376-8984
   E-mail: siq.newyork@mri.gouv.qc.ca
   (If using e-mail, also include your postal address.)
Skilled worker and family class applications should be submitted to
the New York office, above. Business class applications (investor, en-
trepreneur, and self-employed) should be submitted to:

Centre de Services aux Gens d'Affaires (CSGA)
Ministère de l'Immigration et des Communautés Culturelles
19e Étage, Bureau 1915
360, Rue Saint-Jacques
Montreal, QC H2Y 1P5
   E-mail: CSGA-selection@micc.gouv.qc.ca

TEMPORARY RESIDENCY

U.S. citizens don't need a visa to visit Canada. At the present time, they need only present a photo ID such as a driver's license or passport at the border and then they can enter the country and stay for up to six months. (As of Dec. 31, 2006, a passport will be required to enter and leave Canada by air or sea. Passports will be required for land crossings by Dec. 31, 2007.)

Sometimes a visitor can arrive at the border with a dual purpose. He or she may, for instance, have an application for permanent residency pending, but be coming to Canada to visit. "As long as the border officer is satisfied that you intend to leave at the end of that visit, you will be admitted," says David Cohen. "But," he adds, "you're here at the permission of the host country. Where there is some doubt about the person's real intentions, the immigration officer at the border can exercise his or her judgment and let the person in or not. The border immigration officer's decision is pretty much final."

STUDY PERMITS Study permits are granted to people who have been accepted by a Canadian university, college, or private institution and have satisfied a Canadian immigration official that they're bona fide students. They must have enough money to support themselves and demonstrate that they're likely to return to the United States at the end of their study. They can be accompanied by their spouse or common-law or same-sex partner. Their dependent children will be permitted to attend Canadian schools for free. The partner is eligible for a work permit so long as the applicant is attending a publicly funded institution. Courses of less than six months don't require study permits, but in that case a partner would be ineligible for a work permit.

WORK PERMITS U.S. citizens who are offered a job in Canada can enter the country on a work permit. These are quick to arrange, sometimes taking only a few hours. When one member of a spousal or common-law partnership has a bona fide job in an approved HRSDC category (see pages 22–24) and a work permit valid for more than six months, the other can also get a work permit. It will be good for the same amount of time as the main applicant's. A work permit is generally valid only for a specified job, employer, and time period. If you are issued a work permit and your employer changes, you will probably have to reapply. Talk to an attorney to clarify the situation.

Work permits are usually required to work in Canada unless you are a permanent resident or a citizen. There are certain occupations and certain circumstances where they are not required. Business visitors who enter Canada for international business activities without entering the Canadian labor market are exempt. A journalist, for instance, coming to Canada to write for a publication based outside the country would not need a work permit.

NAFTA Some temporary residents of Canada enter under the 1994 North American Free Trade Act, which was designed to facilitate the free movement of goods and services across the U.S.-Canadian and U.S.-Mexican borders. The free movement of workers could be subsumed under NAFTA as well. "NAFTA is not specifically about immigration," says Cohen. "It's about the temporary relocation of individuals, either as intracompany transfers or as professionals under the NAFTA agreement. There are sixty-three occupations whereby, if you're an American citizen or Canadian or Mexican, you could cross the border to work."

In addition, NAFTA offers options through intracompany transfers. "Let's just take a hypothetical situation," says Cohen. "You are a business owner in Los Angeles and you've gone to visit Vancouver and you love it. You can open a branch of your Los Angeles–based business in Vancouver and transfer yourself there the next day. And you would get a work permit under NAFTA to do that. That would not be one of the sixty-three open occupations but what we call an intracompany transfer. Or you could acquire a Canadian business and transfer yourself over that way, as a NAFTA investor."

TEMPORARY RESIDENCY

In April 2005, the Canadian government sweetened the rules that apply to foreign-born students in Canada. Now they can work either on campus or off and can work in the country for up to two years after graduation instead of the previous one year if they're willing to work in places other than Montreal, Toronto, and Vancouver. The new rules were designed to make a Canadian education more affordable and more attractive to foreigners.

RETIRING TO CANADA

"It used to be easier than it is now to retire to Canada," says Linda Mark. "Formerly you could just apply for a special category of permanent residence. You had to show that you were independent financially, that you had no criminal record, and that your health was good. That was it. Now you have to enter the country under one of the categories that apply to everyone else."

Under the present skilled worker category, an applicant over the age of 54 would get no points for age, which might lower his or her total score below the accepted threshhold.

An alternative would be to come into the country as an investor, but that takes a substantial amount of money.

Mark has several suggestions for people who think they might like to retire to Canada. One of them is to apply while still young enough to qualify for age points as a skilled workers. If a couple is trying to emigrate, the younger of the two might be the stronger applicant for that reason.

Another possibility would be to enter the country with arranged employment, which would give an applicant up to 15 extra points. This could overcome the loss of points based on age, Mark observes.

U.S. citizens born in 1947 or earlier and who have a Canadian parent are a special category. They may legally qualify for Canadian citizenship as opposed to just permanent residence without having to pass the point test. These people could immigrate to Canada as retirees or during their working years. They would bring with them any U.S. Social Security benefits that they might have accrued. If you think you might be in this category of immigrants, consult an immigration attorney.

THREE

THE IMMIGRATION PROCESS:
Immigration Mechanics

FEES

FEDERAL GOVERNMENT FEES VARY DEPENDING ON THE KIND of visa or permit being applied for. Fees are subject to change without notice and must usually be submitted at the time of application.

For permanent resident visas as a skilled worker, there is a nonrefundable processing fee of $550 for the principal applicant, $550 for his or her spouse or partner, and $550 for each dependent child 22 years of age and over. The fee for dependent children under 22 is $150.

The Right of Permanent Residence fee is $975 for the principal applicant and another $975 for that person's spouse or common-law partner, if any, plus $975 for each dependent child, 22 years old or older. (A child 22 or older is considered a dependent if they are financially dependent and continue to go to school full-time.) That fee is refundable if a permanent resident visa isn't issued or used or if the application is withdrawn. It can be paid at any time during the application process but must be paid before a permanent resident visa can be issued.

These fees can be paid in Canadian dollars or an equivalent amount in another currency.

There are additional fees assessed by a nominating province or territory (for provincial nominees). These fees vary widely. There are also fees for medical examinations, police certificates, and language assessments.

Permanent resident visas for family class applicants include a $75 fee per sponsorship application, a $475 fee for the principal applicant who is 22 years old or older, $550 for a family member of the principal applicant who is 22 years old or older or who is younger than 22 and is the spouse or common-law partner of the principal applicant, and $150 for a family member of the principal applicant who is less than 22 years old and is not a spouse or common-law partner. (Note: Principal applicants who are less than 22 years old and not a spouse or common-law partner of the sponsor pay $75 instead of $475 to apply. They may be a dependent child, a child to be adopted, or an orphaned brother, sister, niece, nephew, or grandchild.)

In the investor, entrepreneur, or self-employed persons class, the fee is $1,050 for the principal applicant. An accompanying family member who is 22 years old or older, is a spouse or common-law partner of the principal applicant pays a fee of $550, while a family member of the principal applicant who is less than 22 years old and is not a spouse or common-law partner pays $150.

The fee for a work permit is $150. The fee for a study permit is $125.

In Quebec Province, applicants for permanent skilled worker admission pay a nonrefundable fee of $390 plus $150 for each dependent. In addition, the government of Quebec charges $175 to review an assured job offer for a foreign worker.

Investor applicants in Quebec Province pay a nonrefundable fee of $3,850 to have their application for Selection Certification reviewed. Entrepreneurs and self-employed applicants pay $950. In all cases, the fee for a spouse and each dependent child is $150.

Fees for Dependent Children

Anyone with children around the age of 20 faces the possibility that the permanent residency application won't be approved until the child is 22 or older. Although fees for such a child would not increase, the child may no longer meet the definition of "dependent child" after 22 if he or she is no longer attending school and depending financially on parental support.

MEDICAL EXAMS

All immigrants and some visitors need to undergo a medical exam before receiving a visa. The Canadian government wants to be sure no one coming into the country has a condition, such as active tuberculosis, that would be a danger to public health or that would cause excessive demand on health or social services in Canada. Examples of excessive demand include ongoing hospitalization or institutional care for a physical or mental illness. The exam also screens for conditions that would keep the prospective immigrant from being employed or productive.

The medical exam includes blood and urine tests and X-rays as well as a standard physical. Prior medical records of physical and mental condition may be required.

Family members of the immigration applicant must undergo a medical examination even if they will not be immigrating to Canada. If one member of a family is unable to pass the medical exam, all members of the family will be denied permission to immigrate.

The exams are good for twelve months and in some cases, longer. If a final visa hearing comes up shortly after the twelve months have expired, the visa officer may, at his or her discretion, accept the results of the medical exam without requiring further testing.

Applicants pay for these exams and must go to a designated practitioner to have them done. (After receiving your application and approving it to the next stage, the Canadian government will send a list of designated doctors in the United States; or you can go to www.cic.gc.ca/english/contacts/dmp/usa.html to see who they are and where they are located.)

SECURITY REQUIREMENTS

Police certificates and clearances are required from each country in which an applicant for permanent residency plus his or her spouse or common-law partner and dependent children 18 and over have lived for six months or more since reaching the age of 18. Certificates attesting that the applicant and accompanying family members have "no criminal record or conviction" must be originals and issued within the three months prior to application.

A full set of fingerprints is required of each applicant and family member and may be obtained from a local police department or from a private organization in the fingerprinting business. For U.S. background checks, fingerprints are sent to the FBI and can take three to six weeks to process.

Those who have been convicted of a criminal offense in Canada or have committed a criminal act with or without a conviction outside of Canada have to either apply for a pardon in the first case or be found rehabilitated to be considered for immigration. Pardons came from the National Parole Board and rehabilitations are determined by Canada Immigration. Before filing an immigration application, those who need them should first apply for a pardon to the:

Clemency and Pardons Division
National Parole Board
410 Laurier Ave. West, Ottawa, ON K1A 0R1,
   Fax: 613-941-4981
   www.npb.cnlc.ge.ca (Pardon application forms can be downloaded from this Web site.) Rehabilitation applications can be downloaded from www.cic.gc.ca or call Canada Immigration at 888-242-2100.

Montreal immigration attorney David Cohen advises anyone with potential problems or concerns in this area to consult an immigration attorney. He notes that discussions with an attorney are confidential and that Canada's courts recognize consultation with a lawyer as a guarded privilege.

NOTE: Immigrants to Canada carrying more than $10,000 Canadian (which can be in the form of cash, securities, etc., negotiable instruments such as bankers' drafts, checks, or money orders) must tell Canadian officials this at the border. Failure to do this may result in fines and imprisonment.

INTERVIEW REQUIRED?

Much of the application process for permanent residency is in the form of documents that get submitted and reviewed, but sometimes an immigration official may ask that an applicant come in for an interview. To some extent, applicants can pick their venue, but immigration can change venues without the applicant's permission if the one selected is too backlogged.

For U.S. citizens, the interview locations are in Seattle, Detroit, Los Angeles, and New York City. The cost of travel to an interview location is obviously another expense that must be considered.

Vancouver immigration attorney Linda Mark says that she spends a lot of time preparing her clients for an interview, but rarely goes with them because of the expense. Still, she says, "even for people where it's straightforward and it looks good, there's a lot of stress. It's a life-changing situation, and of course, there's a lot of anxiety."

THE INTERVIEW: ONE PERSON'S EXPERIENCE

In the interview, they [an official representing Citizenship and Immigration Canada] ask about why you want to come to Canada. They inspect your money status, and try to persuade you to settle outside of the cities, but not in remote areas. They also educate you—they advised me to not try to work in the Yukon thinking I would make a lot of money, as it was too much of a change from New York City. They made a few comments about receiving my papers and how easily some people have forged them, then waited to see what I would say to that. I remarked the people must be very clever, and the guy smiled broadly telling me when my documents would arrive in the mail. They also discuss the application and add up your points there so you know how you did in your application. You are advised to keep the documents safe and that they need to be stamped when you land in Canada. I landed in the Quebec airport, ran in, and got the paper stamped. Someone shook my hand and said, "Welcome to Canada."

—Sharon Andersen, a nurse, now living in British Columbia

TAKING A CHANCE

Linda Mark, Vancouver immigration attorney, sees quite a few people in her practice who live in the United States but were not born there and who want to immigrate to Canada.

"Some of them don't have status in the United States," she says, "meaning that their visas have expired or they entered the country illegally.

"They need to be aware," she continues, "that if they want to immigrate to Canada, they may have to go back to their home country for an immigration interview and that they may not be permitted back in the United States afterward. They have to be able to make arrangements to stay in their home country for a short period, or permanently, if necessary."

In order to take that chance, she says, they have to be pretty sure that their application to move to Canada will be successful. Also, she adds, "they have to be able to get passports from their own country."

HOW LONG DOES IT TAKE TO BECOME A PERMANENT RESIDENT?

To become a permanent resident can take as little as a year but usually takes one to two years, or more. The immigration system itself is backlogged, but the process can also be delayed because of errors or omissions by the applicant or complications that arise. These might include incomplete or unsigned application forms, missing documents, insufficient postage, missing fees, unclear photocopies, documents not accompanied by a certified English or French translation (where that is required), a medical condition that requires additional tests, involvement in criminal activity, family situations such as divorce, custody, or maintenance issues, or failure to notify of a change of address.

"Don't sell your house or your business or take your kids out of school until you actually have your visa," advises Mark. "You don't know that you're going to have a visa until it's been issued."

A permanent residency visa, once granted, must be exercised by actually landing in Canada before the expiration date on the visa. There is no way to extend that date. Mark says that she tells clients who have business to wrap up in their original countries to fly to Canada, even if they immediately turn around and go back where they came from. The fact of having landed in Canada will satisfy the visa requirement.

Once permanent residency status has been granted, a person must accumulate two years of residency days in each five-year period to retain it. The two years are cumulative and need not be consecutive. Since some people are employed by Canadian companies but actually work outside of Canada on their behalf, this is taken into consideration in assessing whether the residency requirement has been fulfilled. Mark also notes that a permanent resident with a Canadian-born spouse is considered to be resident in the country, even if they are actually living outside of Canada. "Anyone in this position should probably get legal advice early in the process to make sure they meet all the criteria to retain their permanent residency status," she says.

If a permanent resident commits a serious crime, he or she can be deported, which is not true of citizens.

BECOMING A CANADIAN CITIZEN

Eventually, many permanent residents of Canada wish to become citizens so that they will be eligible to vote in Canadian elections. There was a time when American law made it impossible for U.S.-born citizens to become citizens of other countries without losing their U.S. citizenship. That is no longer true. People who are citizens of the United States can become citizens of Canada without losing their U.S. citizenship. They will still be able to travel with a U.S. passport if and when they wish to, and to vote in federal elections in the United States, using their last place of U.S. residence as their voting address.

Steve Trow, an immigration attorney in Washington, D.C., says that "the U.S. government has adopted a policy that presumes an American citizen intends to remain American. That's the default outcome. If you don't say anything one way or the other, you're still American. If you want to stop being American, you have to raise your hand and say, 'I quit.' You do that by filling out a questionnaire from the U.S. consulate and checking a box to indicate that you intended to give up U.S. citizenship when you got Canadian citizenship."

Usually it takes three years from the time a person becomes a permanent resident of Canada to become eligible to apply for citizenship. Up to one year of that time may be counted if the applicant was working in Canada on a temporary permit or was in Canada for any other reason.

The applicant for citizenship receives a booklet on Canada, its history and government, and must pass a test on the information. To pass the test, applicants must correctly answer questions about the right to vote in Canadian elections, the right to run for elective office in Canada, how to register to vote, and what the voting procedures are. Other questions concern Canada's main historical and geographical features, the rights and responsibilities of citizens, and the structure of Canadian government and Confederation. In addition, there are questions about the geography, economy, and history of the province or territory in which the applicant lives.

The rights of Canadian citizens are stated in the Canadian Charter of Rights and Freedoms. They include the right to be a candidate in federal, provincial, and territorial elections; be educated in either official language; apply for a Canadian passport; vote in federal and provincial or territorial elections; and enter and leave Canada freely.

BECOMING A CITIZEN

Daniel Stone, a professor of history at the University of Winnipeg and his wife, Kay, a storyteller and folklorist, immigrated to Canada in 1969 when he was offered a teaching job at the university. In 1990, they became Canadian citizens.

As Dan recalls, "We could have applied [for Canadian citizenship] after a few years, but we did not apply until American regulations changed, making it possible to acquire Canadian citizenship without losing U.S. citizenship. There were a whole series of cases that came to the U.S. Supreme Court starting in the 1960s. We decided that it was safe enough—though not absolutely safe—in 1990. We filled out a card. There was a date set for an interview and we took our multiple choice test and had an interview with the judge."

Did they study for this test? "Oh, yeah," Kay says emphatically.

After they were approved, says Dan, "The date came up. We came to the citizenship swearing-in and there were fifty or sixty people, I suppose. Most of them were Third World immigrants or Eastern European immigrants. It was quite moving. It was difficult for me to swear allegiance to the Queen. I think the Queen's fine, but the idea of swearing allegiance to the Queen was rather odd, but I succeeded—and that was that."

For Kay, swearing allegiance to the Queen wasn't a problem. "I thought it was quite wonderful," she says.

Now the Stones carry two passports. Their two children, born in Canada, consider themselves Canadian though they could claim U.S. citizenship, too, if they wished.

DUAL CITIZENS

Approximately 2 percent of Canadian citizens are also citizens of other countries. Canada has accepted dual citizenship since 1977—one of the first countries to do so. Canada's Citizenship Act allows Canadians "to have two or more citizenships and allegiances at the same time." Canada's governor-general, Michaëlle Jean, is an example. Born in Haiti, she was a citizen of both Canada and France for many years.

IS A LAWYER NECESSARY?

The Canadian government spells out the steps applicants must take to apply for immigration at its Web site (www.cic.gc.ca) so applicants can do this themselves. The government does caution them to fill in all the forms carefully and completely in order to avoid having their entire application returned, significantly delaying the process.

Those who find the numerous documents too complex may prefer to have a representative tackle the job for them. Paid representatives must be lawyers or immigration consultants whom the applicant hires to assist in the process. Only one immigration representative can be designated at a time.

As of April 2004, paid immigration representatives must be authorized by the Canadian Society of Immigration Consultants, a Canadian law society (or students-at-law under a lawyer's supervision), or the Chambre des Notaires du Québec (or students-at-law under a notary's supervision.) If an applicant appoints a paid representative who is not in one of the above categories, the application will be returned.

An unpaid representative requires no formal accreditation but has to be formally designated by the applicant as his or her representative.

The Canadian Society of Immigration Consultants was formed in 2003 to provide supervision and standards for nonlawyers who act as immigration consultants. Members must pass the society's knowledge and ethics test and demonstrate good character. For more information on the Canadian Society of Immigration Consultants, go to www.csic-scci.ca. (The address of the Society is Canada Trust Tower, 161 Bay St., 27th Floor, Toronto, Ontario M5J 2S1; phone: 416-572-2800; fax: 416-572-4114).

The Canadian government emphasizes in its materials that people who hire immigration consultants or lawyers do not receive preferential treatment in the immigration process. Nevertheless, they have the advantage of knowing the ropes and being able to anticipate potential problems.

"If you give me enough time, I could probably build my own house and file my own taxes," says immigration attorney Rudi Kischer of the Embarkation Law Group in Vancouver when asked if a lawyer is necessary. But, he continues, "I wouldn't advise anyone to do it themselves. It's the biggest move in their life. Do you want to be unsure what time things are going to happen and whether you're going to qualify or not?"

Applicants who deal with Citizenship and Immigration Canada through a representative, be the representative a lawyer or another paid immigration representative, must fill out a Use of Representative form to authorize the individual to act on their behalf.

The Canadian government does not get involved in disputes between applicants and their representatives. Before hiring a representative, applicants should ask for references and proof that the person is currently a member in good standing of the Canadian Society of Immigration Consultants or a Canadian law society.

Fees for immigration legal services should be discussed in advance. Fees can vary widely, according to David Cohen. He says that the average for a skilled worker application would be between $2,000 and $5,000 in attorney's fees plus whatever filing costs and other costs might be entailed.

Including legal fees, filing fees, medical exam fees, possible travel for an interview, and credentialing fees, if that is required, Linda Mark estimates that a couple with two children applying under the Skilled Worker Program could expect to pay $8,000 to $10,000. Many lawyers, she says, will offer a short initial consultation without charge to help determine whether the applicant has a case.

For U.S. citizens wishing to apply for immigration on their own, the main office to contact is in Buffalo, New York (Canadian Consulate General, Immigration Regional Program Centre, 3000 HSBC Center, Buffalo, NY 14203-2884; phone: 716-858-9501).

Mark suggests that even if you opt to do it yourself, it would be a good idea to consult an attorney at the beginning of the process so that you understand exactly what you need to do and after you've filled out the forms to make sure that you've done them correctly. If you do the work yourself but simply consult an attorney for advice, your legal costs should be around one quarter of what they might be otherwise.

LAW SOCIETY ADDRESSES

Federation of Law Societies of Canada
445-480 Saint-Laurent Blvd.
Montreal, QC H2Y 2Y7
   Phone: 514-875-6350
   Fax: 514-875-6115
   www.flsc.ca

Continued on next page

LAW SOCIETY ADDRESSES

Law Society of Alberta

Calgary Office (Main)
500, 919 11th Ave. S.W.
Calgary, AB T2R 1P3
  Switchboard: 403-229-4700
  Toll-free: 800-661-9003 (Toll-free numbers valid only in: Alberta,
  Saskatchewan, Lower Mainland British Columbia, Yukon, N.W.T.,
  and Nunavut)
  Fax: 403-228-1728

Edmonton Office
201 10060 Jasper Ave.
Scotia Place Tower II
Edmonton, AB T5J 3R8
  Switchboard: 780-429-3343
  Toll-free: 800-272-8839 (Toll-free numbers valid only in Alberta,
  Saskatchewan, Lower Mainland British Columbia, Yukon, N.W.T.,
  and Nunavut)
  Fax: 780-424-1620
  www.lawsocietyalberta.com

Law Society of British Columbia

845 Cambie St.
Vancouver, BC V6B 4Z9
  Phone: 604-669-2533
  Toll-free in BC: 800-903-5300
  Fax: 604-669-5232
  www.lawsociety.bc.ca

Law Society of Manitoba

219 Kennedy St.
Winnipeg, MB R3C 1S8
  Phone: 204-942-5571
  Fax: 204-956-0624
  www.lawsociety.mb.ca

Continued on next page

Law Society of New Brunswick

206 1133 Regent St.
Fredericton, NB E3B 2Z2
  Phone: 506-458-8537
  Fax: 506-451-1421

Law Society of Newfoundland and Labrador

Mailing Address
P.O. Box 1028
St. John's, NL A1C 5M3

Courier Address
196-198 Water St.
St. John's, NL A1C 1A9
  Phone: 709-722-4740
  Fax: 709-722-8902
  www.lawsociety.nf.ca

Nova Scotia Barristers' Society

Centennial Building
1101-1645 Granville St.
Halifax, NS B3J 1X3
  Phone: 902-422-1491
  Fax: 902-429-4869
  www.nsbs.ns.ca

Law Society of Upper Canada

Osgoode Hall
130 Queen St. W.
Toronto, ON M5H 2N6
  Phone: 416-947-3300
  Toll-free: 800-668-7380
  Fax: 416-947-5263
  E-mail: lawsociety@lsuc.on.ca
  www.lsuc.on.ca

Continued on next page

LAW SOCIETY ADDRESSES

Law Society of Prince Edward Island
P.O. Box 128, 49 Water St.
Charlottetown, PE C1A 7K2
   Phone: 902-566-1666
   Fax: 902-368-7557
   E-mail: lawsociety@lspei.pe.ca
   www.lspei.pe.ca

Barreau du Québec
Maison du Barreau
445, Boulevard Saint-Laurent
Montreal, QC H2Y 3T8
   Phone: 514-954-3400
   Toll-free: 800-361-8495

Chambre des Notaries du Québec
Tour de la Bourse
800, Place-Victoria, Bureau 700
C.P. 162, Montréal, (QC) H4Z IL8
   Phone: 514-879-1793
   Toll-free: 800-263-1793
   Fax: 514-879-1923

Law Society of Saskatchewan
1100-2500 Victoria Ave.
Regina, SK S4P 3X2
Phone: 306-569-8242
Lawyer Referral Service: 800-667-9886
   Fax: 306-352-2989
   E-mail: reception@lawsociety.sk.ca
   www.lawsociety.sk.ca

Continued on next page

Law Society of the Northwest Territories
Lower Level, Laurentian Building
4918 50th Street
P.O. Box 1298
Yellowknife, NT X1A 2N9
  Phone: 867-873-3828
  Fax: 867-873-6344

Law Society of Nunavut
Mailing Address
P.O. Box 149
Iqaluit, NU X0A 0H0

Courier Address
8-Storey Building #105
Iqaluit, NU X0A 0H0
  Phone: 867-979-2330
  Fax: 867-979-2333
  General inquiries: lawsoc@nunanet.com
  www.lawsociety.nu.ca

The Law Society of Yukon
202-302 Steele St.
Whitehorse, YT Y1A 2C5
  Phone: 867-668-4231
  Lawyer Referral Service: 867-668-4231
  Fax: 867-667-7556
  E-mail: lsy@yknet.yk.ca
  www.lawsocietyyukon.com

ARRIVING IN CANADA

For people who have never lived in Canada before and are arriving as permanent residents or as temporary residents for more than three years, there are special provisions as to what can be brought into the country.

Goods that have been owned, possessed, and used can be brought in duty- and tax-free. Sales receipts and registration documents can help to establish that these requirements have been met. If something has been owned and possessed but never used, it would be subject to duties. Likewise, leased goods would be subject to duties because they don't meet the ownership requirement.

WEDDING GIFTS Wedding gifts are a special case. They can be imported free of duty if the marriage has taken place three months or less before coming to Canada or will take place within three months after arrival. (Bring documentation.) The ownership and possession requirements apply, but not the use requirement. Household goods that are part of a bride's trousseau are likewise exempt from duties.

PERSONAL AND HOUSEHOLD EFFECTS Items that can be imported duty- and tax-free include such personal and household effects as: antiques; appliances; boats and the trailers to carry them (trailers are subject to Transport Canada requirements); books; family heirlooms; furnishings; furniture; hobby tools and other hobby items; jewelry; linen; musical instruments; private aircraft; private collections of coins, stamps, or art; silverware; and vacation trailers.

Any goods that will be used commercially are not part of personal or household effects and are subject to regular customs duties. Mobile homes would also be taxed.

VEHICLES Personal effects can include vehicles so long as they are used for noncommercial purposes. However, Transport Canada has many restrictions on vehicles. They must meet Canadian safety and emission standards, which are not necessarily the same as U.S. standards. No vehicle can be imported that cannot be modified to meet Canadian standards. For more information, call Transport Canada at 800-333-0371.

The Registrar of Imported Vehicles (RIV) administers a national program to make sure that imported vehicles comply with Canadian standards. Call the RIV to verify that a vehicle is eligible for importation into Canada. The phone number is 888-848-8240.

If a vehicle doesn't meet Canadian standards but can be modified to meet them, it can be brought into Canada, with a forty-five-day window in which to bring the vehicle into compliance. It can't be licensed in Canada until it's successfully modified and passes federal inspection under the RIV program. The fee to enter a vehicle into this program is payable at customs at the time of entry into Canada. It is $182, except in Quebec, where the fee is $197.

In addition to federal requirements, each province may have its own safety requirements as well as provincial and territorial sales taxes. Those considering importing a vehicle into Canada should check with the province to which they intend to move.

ALCOHOL AND TOBACCO To import the contents of a bar or wine cellar intended for personal use, provincial or territorial fees and assessments must be paid in advance of shipment. Receipts for these payments must be presented before the shipment will be released. In addition, there may be federal assessments. Wine not exceeding 1.5 liters or any alcoholic beverages not exceeding 1.14 liters can be imported as personal effects, without paying duty. Up to 50 cigars, 200 cigarettes, 200 tobacco sticks, and 200 grams of manufactured tobacco can be brought into Canada without duty.

FIREARMS There are numerous regulations surrounding the importation of firearms. For more information on what is allowed and under what circumstances and also on licensing requirements, see page 13 and contact the Canada Firearms Centre, 50 O'Connor St., Ottawa, ON K1A 1M6; phone: 800-731-4000. Web site: www.cfc.gc.ca.

CURRENCY AND MONETARY INSTRUMENTS Currency and monetary instruments that are physically imported into Canada or exported from Canada and have a value equal to or greater than $10,000 must be reported to Canada customs. The penalties for failure to report could be fines and imprisonment. The funds could be in the form of cash, securities such as stocks, bonds, debentures, or treasury bills, or negotiable instruments such as bankers' drafts, checks, traveler's checks, or money orders.

HOUSEPLANTS Houseplants for indoor use can be imported from continental United States as part of baggage or household effects without requiring any special certificates or import permits. However, houseplants coming into Canada from Hawaii are only admissible if they are bare-root and free of soil and all other growing media and if the container bears a stamped certificate from the Department of Agriculture of the State of Hawaii.

PETS Dogs or cats younger than three months can be imported from the United States without requiring any documentation. Seeing-eye dogs can be imported regardless of age without documentation if they accompany the owner.

Dogs or cats coming from the United States that are three months old or older must have a certificate signed and dated by a veterinarian for each pet. It must identify the animal by breed, age, sex, coloring, and any distinguishing marks and certify that the animal has been vaccinated against rabies within the last three years.

Pet birds can be brought into Canada with certain restrictions. They must be species commonly known as "caged" birds and must have been personally owned and cared for by the owner for at least ninety days prior to coming to Canada. They must accompany the owner to Canada and must be found to be healthy when inspected at the port of entry. The owner must sign a declaration stating that they are personal pets, not for resale, and that they have not been in contact with other birds for ninety days preceding importation.

Neither the owner nor any member of his or her family can have imported birds into Canada for the preceding ninety-day period.

If these conditions can't be met, an import permit is required from the Canadian Food Inspection Agency regional office in the province to which the owner will be moving.

For more information, contact the Canada Border Services Agency (www.cbsa-asfc.gc.ca). From within Canada, call: 800-461-9999. From outside Canada, call: 204-983-3500 or 506-636-5064.

MAKING A LIST On arrival in Canada, two copies of a list, preferably typewritten, of everything being brought into Canada as settler's effects must be presented to the customs officer. The list should show the value, make, model, and serial number (where applicable) of all possessions. It must be divided into two sections: goods accompanying the owner and goods to follow.

Even if no goods are being brought in at the time of entry, the list must be presented to customs.

Jewelry should be described using wording from an insurance policy or appraisal document and, if possible, be photographed.

At the border, the customs officer prepares Form B4, "Personal Effects Accounting Document," based on the list of goods provided.

MAKING A LIST

A recent émigré to Canada describes what it was like to bring his possessions across the border:

You have to get permission to bring in your furniture and your clothes and everything. So we called the Canadian government and they told us to list what we have. So my wife made up a list—we have clothes and we have a TV set and we have a computer—and she listed everything. And they said, "No. We want to know how many men's socks you have and what you paid for them, how many women's socks and what you had to pay for them, how many shirts were men's and how much they cost, and how many women's shirts and what they cost, how many handkerchiefs and what they cost." They went to every single item and you have to have exact details. If we didn't exactly know, they said, "Do as close as you can." My wife spent weeks going through the whole house and doing everything. It was so time-consuming. When we got to Canada, they looked at the list and said to my wife, "You did such a beautiful job. We're not going to inspect the inventory. We're just going to let you go." It was a breeze to go through but she worked very hard.

FOUR

LIVING IN CANADA FOR NEWCOMERS

SETTLEMENT SERVICES AND REQUIREMENTS VARY BETWEEN REGIONS AND provinces. The Citizenship and Immigration Web site provides some information. Go to www.cic.gc.ca/english/newcomer.

FINDING A JOB

Throughout this book you will find information relevant to a job search. The local economy is profiled in each province and city listing (Chapter 5, "Where to Move in Canada," starting on page 71), an indicator of possible job openings.

Once you are a permanent resident or citizen of Canada, a work permit is no longer required, as it is for temporary residents. However, you will need a Social Insurance Number.

SOCIAL INSURANCE NUMBER To work in Canada, you must have a Social Insurance Number (sometimes called an SIN). You can get an application through the nearest Human Resources Skills and Development Canada Centre or from the post office. Downloadable forms are available on the Internet at www.hrdc-drhc.gc.ca/sin-nas. There is a small processing fee.

LABOR MARKET INFORMATION Information about the Canadian labor market including job requirements, local, regional, and national market conditions, current and future job or career prospects, and educational and skill-building opportunities are available on the following Web sites:

Labor Market Information: www.labourmarketinformation.ca
Work Destinations: www.workdestinations.org
Job Futures 2000: www.jobfutures.ca

JOB OPPORTUNITIES BY PROVINCE AND TERRITORY

Alberta: www.alis.gov.ab.ca
British Columbia: http://workinfonet.bc.ca
Manitoba: www.mb.workinfonet.ca
Newfoundland and Labrador: www.gov.nf.ca/nlwin/
Nova Scotia: http://workinfonet.ednet.ns.ca/
Northwest Territories: http://northwin.ca/
Ontario: www.onwin.ca
Prince Edward Island: www.gov.pe.ca/infopei/Employment/index.php3
Saskatchewan: www.sasknetwork.gov.sk.ca/
Yukon: http://yuwin.ca/

GENERAL INTERNET SITES There are many Internet sites that list job opportunities in Canada. Here are some of them:

Listings for more than 35,000 jobs:
  Workopolis: www.workopolis.com/
A network of industry-centered job leads and information:
  SkillNet: www.skillnet.ca/pub/index.html?iin.lang=en
A Canadian government Web site where between 300,000 and
  500,000 jobs are posted each year:
  Job Bank: http://jb-ge.hrdc-drhc.gc.ca/Intro_en.asp
A Canadian government Web site with information about jobs,
  training, and careers:
  JobsEtc.ca: www.jobsetc.ca/
Comprehensive information on available jobs, economic trends, and
  training and education:
  The Workplace: www.theworkplace.ca
Internships for recent college graduates, graduates with disabilities,
  and internationally qualified professionals:
  Career Edge: www.careeredge.org/

ENROLLING CHILDREN IN SCHOOL

Most children start school by the age of 5. By law, they must attend school until they are 15 or 16, depending on where they live. (In New Brunswick, the age is 18 or the completion of high school, whichever comes first.)

To enroll a child in public school, go to the local school or school board office, bringing the child's Permanent Resident Card, Record of Landing, or Confirmation of Permanent Residence. Also bring the child's birth certificate, vaccination certificate, and previous school records. Some schools will test language and mathematics skills before assigning a child to a class.

OPENING A CANADIAN BANK ACCOUNT

To open a Canadian bank account, you will need a Social Insurance Number and some other identification such as a passport or your Permanent Resident Card. You may also need something that proves where you live, such as a telephone bill or a driver's license.

The major banks in Canada include the Royal Bank of Canada, the Canadian Imperial Bank of Commerce (CIBC), the Bank of Montreal, Scotiabank, and the Toronto-Dominion Bank. All have offices in the United States as well as in Canada, which should facilitate banking for U.S.-born citizens seeking to move to Canada.

All of these banks (or their holding companies) trade on the Toronto and New York Stock Exchanges.

ROYAL BANK OF CANADA Canada's largest bank as measured by assets and market capitalization. www.royalbank.com.

CANADIAN IMPERIAL BANK OF COMMERCE (CIBC) Branches and offices across Canada, the United States, and worldwide. www.cibc.com.

THE BANK OF MONTREAL The BMO Financial Group includes the BMO Bank of Montreal, which was founded in 1817 and was Canada's first bank. Offices throughout Canada, in the United States, and worldwide. www4.bmo.com.

TORONTO-DOMINION BANK The Toronto-Dominion Bank and its subsidiaries are collectively known as the TD Bank Financial Group (TDBFG). Headquartered in Toronto with offices around the world. www.tdcanada-trust.com.

SCOTIABANK Offices in fifty countries worldwide. Headquartered in Toronto. www.Scotiabank.com.

PENSIONS

Those who qualify for Social Security retirement in the United States will receive payments in Canada, though U.S. Medicare will not cover health care for individuals living in Canada. Given Canada's universal health care system covering residents (sometimes immediately and generally after three months) as well as citizens, this may not matter much.

CANADA PENSION PLAN A national pension plan called the Canada Pension Plan (CPP) is available to anyone who worked in Canada (except Quebec, which runs its own similar provincial program with the same benefit payment). It is a mandatory contribution program designed to provide a minimum amount of retirement income. Pension amounts received are based on the employee's earnings and contributions to the plan and the age of the employee when receiving them.

Contributions by employees and employers are required during the working years. Reduced monthly payments are available at age 60; full payments are available at age 65 and premium payments can be started any time before age 70. Survivors' benefits go to the spouse and children of a pensioner who dies. The maximum current benefit is $828.75 a month.

A pensioner may be eligible for disability benefits if he or she is between the ages of 18 and 65, has enough contributions in the plan at the time of becoming disabled, and meets the plan's definitions of the severity of the disability and its likely duration. Applications for the CPP are made through the Canada Pension Plan branch of Social Development Canada (SDC). QPP applications are available from Revenue Quebec. This plan is most similar to the U.S. Social Security program.

EMPLOYER PENSIONS These can be set up under federal or provincial legislation. They are similar to the U.S. IRA plans. As a general rule, federal legislation governs large national organizations and federal government employees. Provincial legislation governs companies that chiefly do business in one province.

There are two general types: defined benefit, which is usually employer funded, and defined contribution, which is generally funded by employer and employee. This is most similar to a U.S. 401(k) plan.

REGISTERED RETIREMENT SAVINGS PLAN (RRSP) This retirement savings account is similar to a cash account, but the contributions to the plan are deductible from income, and contributions or withdrawals to and from the account (more commonly referred to as a plan) are reported to the government. Many Canadians contribute both to RRSPs and to pensions to supplement finances in retirement years.

There are limits as to how much can be contributed in a year. It is a percentage of the previous year's income (18 percent to a maximum of $16,500 for 2005). This is most similar to a U.S. IRA.

There are also pension plans that are most beneficial for the self-employed and highly paid executives called Retirement Compensation Agreements (RCAs) and for individuals (IPPs.) Many major brokerage firms offer these plans.

Other Income Benefits

OAS Canada has an Old Age Security Benefit Program (OAS) for all Canadian citizens and permanent residents over the age of 65. Full benefits go to those who have lived in Canada for forty years after the age of 18 with reduced amounts for fewer than forty years of residence. The 61- to 64-year-old spouse of an OAS recipient who has died may qualify for a survivor's benefit. Applications are made through Social Development Canada (SDC).

GIS Those over 65 with little or no income may also be eligible for the Guaranteed Income Supplement (GIS). The GIS is available to low-income seniors receiving the OAS. The maximum payment to a single person is $388.90 a month. For full rate information see: http://www.sdc.gc.ca/asp/gateway.asp?hr=/en/isp/oas/oasrates.shtml&hs=fyf.

Given the number of years required for eligibility, few immigrants from the United States are likely to be enrollable in these programs, which are not pensions, but income-tested benefits. In 2005, the maximum amount of $471.76 was available to everyone who earned less than $60,806. Above that amount, payments were reduced by $0.15 for every dollar earned. If someone earned over $98,547 (for 2005), they were no longer eligible for the OAS.

FIVE

WHERE TO MOVE IN CANADA

SNAPSHOTS: An Introduction

IF YOU'RE SERIOUS ABOUT MOVING TO CANADA AND TRYING TO
decide where to live, this section of the book will get you started.

Winters are long and cold in most of Canada, but in some places the
snow that doesn't melt for months is accompanied by crisp blue skies.
Southern British Columbia, which is much warmer than elsewhere in
Canada, is also much rainier. Information on climate in these pages will al-
low you to consider the places that best meet your needs and preferences.

If you prefer big cities to small towns—or vice versa—population statistics will help narrow your search. Though we profile the largest cities of
each province, you can be sure that if the largest city is still relatively small,
there will be plenty of towns even smaller. (Compare Charlottetown, capital
of Prince Edward Island, for instance, population 32,245, with Toronto, the
capital of Ontario, where the population exceeds 4 million.)

If you enjoy and seek a multiracial, multiethnic environment, the listings
of the ethnic background of the population will tell you where to look.
Some parts of Canada are a mosaic of people from many parts of the world.
Others are predominantly English, Scottish, and Irish. Quebec Province is
predominantly French. Ethnic origins affect the cultural life of a region or
city, including its music and food, and are likely to affect the religious affiliations of its population.

If your plan is to go to Canada and work, information on the economy of each province and city will indicate the kinds of jobs that might be available. The unemployment statistics will give you an inkling of your likelihood of finding a job. Statistics on average earnings will suggest what you might hope to make—and you can weigh that against typical housing costs, which we also list.

Car ownership is usually a necessity, and can be a big expense; however, some places have practical public transportation systems. Some small cities are so walkable that many residents don't need cars much of the time. So that you can factor the car into your living equations, we tell you something about auto insurance and driving regulations. We also profile transportation access to other parts of the world via airports, trains, ferries, and highways.

The information on schools will certainly be of interest if you have children, but even if you don't, the proximity of a college campus often means a range of interesting cultural opportunities, bookstores, and libraries.

If you do have children and they are not yet of college age, the information on tuition costs may help sway your choice of a community. In most cases, in-province students pay far less tuition than those from other parts of Canada—and a third to a half of what international students would pay. Some Canadian colleges and universities are ranked among the best in North America.

The festival listings will give you an idea of what the people of that province honor and think is important. The culture sections will suggest the depth, range, and type of cultural offerings, and again, may be a reflection of a region's or a city's values and ethnicity.

Recreational sports opportunities are related to geography. We describe both in the following "snapshots." Most Canadians, you will find, can romp in the outdoors within a stone's throw of home, even if "home" is a large city. Hiking, bicycling, swimming, ice skating, and cross-country skiing are present everywhere in Canada. Other than these, we mention special or unique recreational opportunities in each locale.

All Canadian citizens receive free basic health care; however, accessibility and, to some extent, quality vary within the provinces and territories. Life expectancy and infant mortality rates are among the indicators of how well the health care system is working. You will find both indicators in these snapshots.

In terms of violent crime, Canada is pretty safe, but some places are safer than others. Public safety information will give you an idea of what to expect.

Finally, there are political issues. Though Canada recently elected a Conservative government, it is in general a relatively liberal country. Some places, however, are more liberal than others in their social values, as is reflected in their politics and laws. There are several litmus tests: the political parties represented in the provincial or territorial legislatures, the party in power, provincial attitudes toward gays, tax structures, and laws. Depending on where you fall on the conservative-liberal spectrum, you may want to consider these sections carefully as you think about where you might like to live.

SNAPSHOT: BRITISH COLUMBIA

International travelers at Vancouver's busy airport learn something about British Columbia before they even leave the arrivals terminal. A huge, wooden, sculpted circle by First Nations artist Susan Point (of the Coast Salish) stands at the top of the stairway leading to the Immigration Room. Behind it is a wall flowing with water that burbles in two streams toward two tree-sized totemic figures. This is an indication, which proves to be accurate, of British Columbia's remarkable natural beauty and of the prominent First Nations presence. ("First Nations" is the term often used in Canada to describe the people who were living there prior to the arrival of the Europeans.)

Canada's third largest province in area and population is more diverse geographically than any other region of Canada. The landscape ranges from mountains to prairie, from rain forest on the northwestern coast of Vancouver Island to desert. Mountain ranges known as the Canadian Cordillera cover much of the province. There are numerous glacial lakes. The forests are vast and thick.

Aboriginals once lived in every part of what is now Canada, but in many places their culture has been submerged. Not here. While indigenous people are only 4 percent of British Columbia's population, their artwork is enshrined in museums, sold in galleries, erected in parks. It seems to capture the spirit of the place—the majestic landscape, the bears, whales, ravens, and other animals, the misty, sometimes brooding beauty.

Asia provides another pervasive cultural influence. When Hong Kong reverted to mainland China in 1997, many residents immigrated to Canada—but even before that, there were a large number of Chinese and other Asians in British Columbia. "It's extremely multicultural and also integrated," observes Vancouver resident Linda Bates. She also mentions that when her son was in the Vancouver public school system, "he was one of the few kids who spoke English as his first language."

Native people have lived in British Columbia for at least ten thousand years, sustained by the salmon-rich rivers and the game, berries, and edible roots of the forests. Within a little more than a century after the arrival of the first Europeans in the late eighteenth century, they were forced onto reservations, and essential aspects of their culture were forbidden.

Elsewhere in Canada, the British Crown had signed treaties with native people spelling out land rights and other legal issues before a province or territory could become part of the Canadian Confederation. When British Columbia joined the Confederation of Canada on July 20, 1871, as the sixth province, only fourteen treaties with First Nations people were in place, all of them on Vancouver Island. Aboriginal claims to the rest of the province were still unresolved.

Now the weight of Canadian law states unequivocally that the First Nations people have rights to their lands and must be compensated or given jurisdiction over them. The provincial and federal governments are in the process of trying to work out treaties with fifty-three First Nations groups, the most complex treaty negotiations that Canada has ever undertaken.

LOCATION Canada's most westerly province is part of the Pacific Rim. (See map on pages xviii–xix.) British Columbia has 1,347 miles of borders with the United States, specifically with Alaska on the west, and Montana, Idaho, and Washington on the south.

GEOGRAPHY The province includes Vancouver Island, which is 323 miles long, and the Queen Charlotte Islands off the western coast as well as a number of smaller islands in the Strait of Georgia between Vancouver Island and the mainland. All are part of a partially submerged mountain range. Area: 364,764 square miles; 810 miles north to south and 780 miles east to west.

The Rocky Mountains run the length of the province, flanked by a series of other ranges. The highest peak, Mount Fairweather (15,299 feet), is in the Saint Elias Mountains, part of the Coast Mountain system. The northeastern part of British Columbia (the Peace River District) includes Rocky Mountain foothills and prairie. The Lower Fraser Valley in the southwest is flat and fertile. The province has many streams and large rivers. The Fraser, 850 miles long, is the longest river.

Canada's only microdesert, with sagebrush, cactus, and even rattlesnakes, is just north of the U.S. border near Osoyoos.

CLIMATE Because of the great variations in geography within the province, there are also large variations in temperature and precipitation from region to region. Mild on the coast, with average temperatures of 32°F in January and 60° to 70°F in July.

The eastern and northeastern parts of the province experience greater temperature extremes, with cold winters and hot summers. Average temperatures in January range from 5° to 14°F and from 60° to 74° in July.

B.C. has some of Canada's wettest and driest climates. Precipitation varies markedly, from 12 inches annually to 100 inches, depending on height above sea level and the location vis-à-vis the mountains. Precipitation on the western coast of Vancouver Island usually exceeds 100 inches annually.

PROVINCIAL CAPITAL Victoria

POPULATION 4,271,210 (est., Oct. 2005)

POPULATION DENSITY 1.63 people per square mile. (But most people live in Vancouver, where the population density is 1,636 per square mile.)

ETHNIC DIVERSITY In 2001, immigrants constituted 26.1 percent of British Columbia's population. Only Ontario had a larger percentage of immigrants (26.8 percent). Around 35,000 new immigrants settle in B.C. annually.

Visible Minorities: 836,445 people, constituting 21.6 percent of the population (2001 census). (This is the highest percentage of any province in Canada. Compare it to 19.1 percent for Ontario, and 13.4 percent for Canada as a whole.)

Among visible minorities, the percentages are: Chinese 44 percent; South Asian 25 percent; Filipino 8 percent; Japanese 4 percent; Korean 4 percent.

Religious Affiliations:

None	36 percent
Protestant	31 percent
Catholic	17 percent
Sikh	3 percent
Buddhist	2 percent

In 2001, there were 56,220 Muslims in the province, 31,495 Hindus, and 21,230 Jews.

Languages: The top ten languages spoken in British Columbia are (in order of frequency): English, Chinese, Punjabi, German, French, Tagalog, Spanish, Italian, Korean, and Dutch.

HEALTH See Appendix, page 212, for details on B.C.'s health care coverage and how to apply for it.

Average Life Expectancy (2001):
　　Males, 78.0 years
　　Females, 82.8 years
Infant Mortality Rate: 4.1 per 1,000 live births (2001)
This was the lowest in Canada in 2001. (The rate for Canada that year was 5.2 percent.)
Health Care Satisfaction: In 2003, British Columbians responded to questions about the quality of the health care they had received in the previous twelve months (Statistics Canada, Canadian Community Health Survey, 2003). They were much less satisfied with their care than Canadians as a whole.

ECONOMY B.C.'s largest and most lucrative industries are wood and pulp related. In 2003, they accounted for $15.5 billion—nearly 42 percent of all manufacturing revenue. Other major industries are tourism, fishing, and agriculture. Secondary industries are high-tech and mining.

Construction in British Columbia is booming. The province leads Canada in building permits. In 2004, they were worth $7.9 billion, up from $6.39 billion a year before—a 24 percent increase.

The United States is B.C.'s top trading partner (with $30.5 billion in 2003), followed by Japan ($10.1 billion), China, South Korea, and Taiwan.

Filmmaking, which had accounted for $1.4 billion in revenues in 2003, has taken a nosedive in B.C. because the strength of the Canadian dollar against the U.S. dollar has made film production in the province less economically attractive. However, the B.C. government is attempting to resusitate the industry through tax credits.

The 2010 Winter Olympics, which will be held in B.C. at Whistler/Blackcomb, will bring substantial tourism revenue to the province.

EARNINGS
　　Average earnings, working full year, full-time: $44,307 (2001)
　　Median family income (couples): $60,278 (2001)
　　Average earnings of the population, 15 and over, for holders of a
　　　　university certificate, diploma, or degree: $44,066 (2001)

UNEMPLOYMENT RATE 4.4 percent (Dec. 2005). The national average for that month was 6.1 percent. British Columbia led the nation in job growth in 2005 with gains in construction, trade, information, culture, and recreation and educational services.

HOUSING Housing costs are very high in British Columbia and got even higher in 2004. First-time home buyers could expect to pay 44.3 percent of their monthly pretax income for a typical starter home. This would go for mortgage payments, utilities, and property taxes.

Among renters, 43.8 percent spend 30 percent or more of their household income on shelter. (That figure rises to 50.5 percent in central Vancouver Island.) Among owners, 20.6 percent spend 30 percent or more of their household income on shelter. (All figures as of the 2001 census.)

Average value of dwelling: $230,645 (2001)

Average gross monthly payments for renters: $751 (2001)

Average monthly payments for owner-occupied dwellings: $904 (2001)

EDUCATION Schooling is free and compulsory for children ages 7 to 15. There are seventy-five public school districts with locally elected school boards. Also, private and religious schools. The provincial Ministry of Education is responsible for overall funding of the public school system and for setting educational policy.

Children in the British Columbia public school system tend to do well on standardized tests that measure academic achievement. Their scores on the Student Achievement Indicators Test and the Program for International Student Achievement have been among the highest in Canada.

Between 1998 and 2003, the high school graduation rate in British Columbia climbed to 77.1 percent from 71.4 percent, the largest increase of any province.

British Columbia funds nonprofit private schools proportionately to the degree to which they are regulated by the government, with the most regulated getting the most funding. Approximately 6 percent of British Columbia K-12 students attend private schools.

Universities and Colleges: University of British Columbia in Vancouver; Simon Fraser University in Burnaby; University of Victoria in Victoria; Trinity Western University (religious) in Langley; Open Learning Institute (education by correspondence); University of Northern British Columbia in Prince George. Colleges in Kamloops, Kelowna, Nanaimo, and the Fraser Valley. Two-year colleges in most cities.

Vocational and Technical: British Columbia Institute of Technology in Burnaby; Emily Carr Institute of Art and Design in Vancouver.

Libraries: More than 550 municipal, regional, academic, and special libraries. The largest public library system is in Vancouver. The University of British Columbia has a large, important research library. Legislative library and provincial archives are in Victoria.

Proportion of the population, aged 25 to 54, with one or more postsecondary degrees: 57.7 percent (2001). (The overall proportion for Canada was 55.7 percent in 2001.)

TAXES A personal income tax credit instituted in 2005 reduces or eliminates provincial income taxes for around 730,000 British Columbia residents. Most people earning up to $16,000 a year pay no provincial income tax. Those earning up to $26,000 pay a lower tax.

GOVERNMENT *Premier:* Gordon Campbell (British Columbia Liberal Party). British Columbia has a unicameral Legislative Assembly of seventy-nine members elected by the first-past-the-post system (meaning the winner is the person or party with the most votes even if that person or party does not have a majority of all the votes cast). Representatives serve for up to five years.

British Columbia has numerous political parties. As of the May 2005 election, those represented in the Legislative Assembly are the British Columbia Liberal Party with forty-six seats and the New Democratic Party of British Columbia with thirty-three seats. Other parties on the ballot in this election included the Democratic Reform British Columbia and the Green Party.

Right to Vote: Citizens 18 years old or older can vote. In recent elections, only 25 percent of eligible voters in the 18–24 age group have voted, causing discussions in B.C. (as elsewhere in Canada) about how to bring them to the polls and whether the voting age should be lowered to 16 in the hope that younger people would feel more involved in the political system. In January 2004, a Citizens' Assembly on Electoral Reform was convened to examine the B.C. electoral system. After months of deliberations, the Assembly recommended proportional representation rather than winner-take-all. In a referendum in May 2005, the proposal received a majority of the votes (57 percent affirmative) but not the 60 percent required to turn the recommendation into law.

The province elects thirty-six members to the federal House of Commons. The federal government appoints six members to the Senate.

TRANSPORTATION Vancouver International Airport is B.C.'s major airport, serving thirty-three international destinations as well as many within the province and within other parts of Canada. Most of British Columbia is accessible by air; the province's mountains make road access difficult or impossible in many areas. There are only four passes through the Rocky Mountains.

B.C. Ferries, linking Vancouver Island and the Lower Mainland, operates the largest passenger ferry fleet on the Pacific Coast. B.C. Ferries also go to the Sechelt Peninsula and the Queen Charlotte Islands and to small coastal communities, some of which are inaccessible by other means. The service is government-owned and carries vehicles as well as passengers.

Other ferry services connect Vancouver Island to Seattle, Anacortes, and Port Angeles, all in the state of Washington.

VIA Rail provides passenger service on Vancouver Island and from Vancouver and Prince Rupert to Alberta and the rest of Canada as well as to the United States. (VIA Rail does not own the tracks on which the trains run, and sometimes passenger trains get stuck behind long freight trains, which have priority.)

Bus service is available throughout the province as well as to many U.S. cities.

CARS AND AUTO INSURANCE The Insurance Corporation of British Columbia (ICBC), a government corporation, provides basic liability insurance to all British Columbia car owners. Insurance is mandatory with car ownership. ICBC also handles vehicle registration and accident claims.

Supplementary insurance can be purchased from private insurers.

Driver's Licenses: A British Columbia license must be obtained within six months of moving to the province. Licensed drivers moving to B.C. from another province or the United States simply have to pass a vision test. Otherwise, written and road tests are required.

ATTITUDES TOWARD GAYS Same-sex marriage has been legal in British Columbia since July 2003. Vancouver Pride Week Celebration is an annual event in late July or early August. The Gay and Lesbian Business Association of Greater Vancouver is an association of business and community service organizations that are lesbian- or gay-owned or supportive.

CULTURE B.C. has produced some outstanding artists—the painter Emily Carr, born in Victoria in 1871, and the sculptor, Bill Reid, of Haida (a First Nation People), German, and Scottish ancestry, born in 1920, are among them. Some of their finest work is on display in Vancouver.

Both Victoria and Vancouver have a variety of museums and venues for concerts, dance, and theatre (see pages 85 and 89–90, respectively). Kelowna is the third largest city in British Columbia and the hub city of the Okanagan Valley. The Okanagan Cultural Corridor spanning the Okanagan and Similkameen Valleys harbors more than a hundred art studios and galleries, heritage sites, museums, and agritourism attractions. Prince George, the major city of north-central British Columbia, has a symphony orchestra.

FESTIVALS Victoria Independent Film and Video Festival (February); Whale Festival in Ucluelet and Tofino, Vancouver Island (mid-March); Greater Victoria Performing Arts Festival (April); Wine Festival in the Okanagan Valley (late April/early May and also in late September/early October); JazzFest International in Victoria (June); Whistler Mountain Biking Festival (July); Edge of the World Music Festival in Tlell, Queen Charlotte Islands (July); South Cariboo Gathering of the Dancers Competitive Powwow (July); Squamish Days Logger Sports (July/August); Gibsons Landing Fibre Arts Festival (August); Dawson Creek Annual Stampede and Fall Fair (August); Victoria Dragon Boat Festival (August); Vancouver Fringe Festival (September); Vancouver Writers and Readers Festival (October).

SPORTS Winter: Skiing and snowboarding at Whistler/Blackcomb where the 2010 Winter Olympics will be held. (This is just one of thirty-five ski resorts in the province.) Cross-country skiing (more than thirty Nordic skiing destinations), helicopter skiing, snowshoeing, dogsledding, snowmobiling, snowboarding, ice hockey. Summer: Golfing (four golf courses at Whistler plus many others elsewhere), kayaking, rafting, canoeing, windsurfing, mountain biking, scuba diving (off Vancouver Island), fishing, rock climbing, caving, horseback riding.

PARKS National Parks include Glacier National Park of Canada with dense rain forests and glaciers; Gulf Islands National Park Reserve of Canada in the southern Strait of Georgia; Gwaii Haanas National Park Reserve and Haida Heritage Site, preserving Haida culture and coastal rain forest on the Queen Charlotte Islands; Kootenay National Park of Canada, a UNESCO World Heritage Site with Radium Hot Springs; Mount Revelstoke National Park of Canada, a rain forest of thousand-year-old cedars and spectacular mountains; Pacific Rim National Park Reserve of Canada, a marine and forest environment in the Pacific Coast Mountains; Yoho National Park of Canada, a UNESCO World Heritage Site in the Rockies with rock walls, spectacular waterfalls, and soaring peaks.

More than eight hundred provincial and regional parks. Among the provincial parks: Nisga'a Memorial Lava Bed Provincial Park commemorates two Aboriginal villages buried by lava more than two hundred years ago; Desolation Sound Marine Provincial Park is the province's largest marine park; Barkerville Provincial Historical Park is a restored Gold Rush mining town and one of many historic sites in the province that preserve the history of the early settlers.

PUBLIC SAFETY For the past two decades, British Columbia has had the highest rate of drug crimes of any province—more than double the national average. In 2003, it reported a 6 percent increase in drug offenses. This included a 3 percent rise in arrests for marijuana possession.

Counterfeiting incidents nearly doubled in British Columbia in 2003; however, there were many fewer homicides than in 2002. Violent crimes were down 0.3 percent in 2003 over the rate for 2002, and down an additional 1.5 percent between 2003 and 2004. Between 2003 and 2004, property crimes decreased by 2.9 percent.

In 2003 and again in 2004, British Columbia had the third highest crime rate of any province—due in part to high crime rates in both Vancouver and Victoria. In 2004, the province reported 12,522 criminal code offenses per 100,000 population.

SNAPSHOT: Victoria

A statue of a beautiful, lithe Queen Victoria stands on a pedestal facing the inner harbor of the city that bears her name. Since 1871, when British Columbia became Canada's sixth province, western Canada's oldest city has been its capital.

Home to First Nations people for around ten thousand years, European settlement of the area began with an outpost of the Hudson's Bay Company named Fort Victoria that was completed in 1843. Whaling and sealing fleets put in at the harbor, which soon became a major port of entry to British North America.

The building of the Canadian Pacific Railway did the trick of pulling British Columbia into the Canadian Confederation and away from union with the United States, as some American businessmen in Victoria wanted. The Chinese laborers who did much of the hard, dirty work of railroad building stayed on after the job was finished in 1886. Victoria has the oldest Chinatown in Canada. It also has one of the grand, château-like hotels built by the Canadian Pacific Railroad in every major city along its route. Since Victoria is on an island, the first occupants of the Empress Hotel arrived by steamship. Now they mainly come by ferry or float plane, but they can still take afternoon tea as they've been doing since 1908 among potted palms in a regal room overlooking the city's inner harbor.

The city of Victoria loves its English traditions, but it also embraces change. Retirees may move to the city because it has the mildest climate in Canada, where plum and cherry trees bloom even in February, but young people also come (or stay, if they were born there) because they can kayak, hike, surf, sail, ski, skate, snowshoe, and snowboard on Vancouver Island.

Bicycles are a favored means of transportation. People who live in downtown Victoria don't really need a car. It's a different story in the suburban areas, where shopping malls proliferate along traffic-clogged roads, driving nature lovers ever farther up island to escape.

In the city and its immediate environs, housing prices inch upward yearly, but there's still plenty of room on 323-mile-long Vancouver Island for those who yearn for solitude.

LOCATION On the southern end of 19,356-square-mile Vancouver Island, with the Strait of Georgia to the east and the Strait of Juan de Fuca to the south. On the other side of Juan de Fuca, the snowcapped Olympic Mountains in Washington State are clearly visible. Victoria is closer to the United States than it is to mainland Canada.

The distance by car between Victoria and Port Hardy at the northern end of the island is 301 miles. It takes just under eight hours to drive from one end of the island to the other.

Latitude: 48°25' N; Longitude: 123°19' W; Elevation: 62 feet above sea level

CLIMATE Average January temperature, 39°F; average July temperature, 61°F. An average of 275 frost-free days a year.

Victoria is sheltered by the Olympic and Vancouver Island Mountains from the rains that deluge other parts of Vancouver Island and the mainland. The city's average annual precipitation is 33.3 inches. The region averages 2,207 hours of sunshine annually.

POPULATION 77,538 (2004); 330,200 in the metropolitan area (2004)

POPULATION DENSITY 1,521 per square mile

ETHNIC DIVERSITY In 2001, 43 percent of the population of the Victoria metropolitan area was of English ancestry. In descending order of numbers, residents identified themselves as Canadian, Scottish, Irish, German, French, Dutch, Ukrainian, Chinese, North American Indian, Welsh, Polish, and Italian.

There were 5,910 people who said they were of U.S. ancestry (2 percent of the population).

Visible Minorities: 8.6 percent of the population (2001)
Religious Affiliations:

Protestant   38 percent
None   38 percent
Catholic   16 percent

In 2001, there were 3,470 Sikhs in the Victoria metropolitan area, 3,315 Buddhists, 1,680 Christian Orthodox, 1,550 Jews, and 1,230 Muslims.

ECONOMY Major employers are government and other public sector organizations or companies. There are close to 50,000 public sector employees in the Victoria region. Many people also work in tourism-related businesses and in health care and education.

Most businesses in the Victoria area have five or fewer employees. Though the region has no industry or major manufacturing facilities, Victoria is affected by the rest of British Columbia's economy.

UNEMPLOYMENT RATE 7.1 percent (2002)

EARNINGS

Average annual earnings for full-time workers (2001): $42,121
Median family income (couples, 2001): $64,606

HOUSING Housing costs are high compared with many places in Canada.

Average price of a house (2004): $325,412

In 2004, the rental vacancy rate in Victoria was 0.6 percent, making the city one of the most difficult places in Canada to rent an apartment.

Average rent for a three-bedroom apartment (2003): $900
Average rent for a two-bedroom apartment (Oct. 2004): $799

EDUCATION There are three school districts in the Capital Region. School District 61 (Victoria) is the largest, serving approximately 22,300 students. The others are District 62 (Sooke) and District 63 (Saanich). Each of the districts offers some French immersion programs and has funding and programs for special-needs students.

In addition to the public school system, there are several private schools.

Universities and Colleges: University of Victoria, with around 18,000 students in bachelor's, master's, and diploma programs (tuition $4,841 for in-province undergraduate students and $13,102 for international students); Camosun College, with 7,800 students in credit and vocational programs and another 10,000 in noncredit courses; Royal Roads University, a "special purpose" university offering distance learning and on-campus residencies to midcareer professionals. There are also specialized schools in Victoria for photography, art, and design.

The Greater Victoria Public Library has public access Internet and CD-ROM terminals.

HEALTH There are three hospitals in the Victoria region and nineteen walk-in medical clinics where no appointment is necessary to see a doctor.

The Vancouver Island Health Authority, South Island provides hospital, community, home, environmental, and public health services. For more information, go to www.viha.ca.

Average Life Expectancy (2001):

Males, 79.7 years

Females, 83.2 years

The life expectancy in Victoria is one of the highest in Canada.

MEDIA Daily newspaper, the *Times-Colonist*. Also, a chain of twice-weekly newspapers, a free weekly "alternative" paper, three television stations, nine radio stations, and two free monthly magazines, one of which focuses on women and the other on parenting.

TRANSPORTATION Ferries to the B.C. mainland run every hour in the summer between 7:00 A.M. and 10:00 P.M. In winter, the sailings are usually every other hour. Pacific Coach Lines operates bus service from downtown Victoria to downtown Vancouver and also goes to the Vancouver International Airport.

Seaplane flights go from Victoria's Inner Harbor to downtown Vancouver, with several scheduled flights daily. Helicopters and small twin-engine jets fly from Ogden Point to downtown Vancouver. Two airlines offer daily seaplane flights between Seattle and Victoria.

Ferries carry passengers and vehicles between Victoria and Washington State year-round. They put in at Port Angeles and Anacortes. Passenger-only service is available between Victoria and Seattle and between Victoria and Bellingham.

VIA Rail train service connects Victoria with Courtenay, 131 miles away in the central part of Vancouver Island. Several bus services also connect Victoria with other parts of Vancouver Island.

Victoria International Airport is located thirty minutes from downtown Victoria.

URBAN TRANSIT People in Victoria walk, cycle, car-pool, and ride the bus in addition to using their own cars to get around.

Buses run daily, 6:00 A.M. to midnight. Day passes and monthly passes are sold at a discount. There are also fare discounts for seniors and young people, aged 6 to 18. Children under 6 ride free.

Most buses accommodate wheelchairs and scooters. Half of the buses in the system have bike racks.

CULTURE Victoria has one of the finest museums in Canada, the Royal British Columbia Museum, with an outstanding collection of First Nations artifacts and imaginatively displayed exhibits relating to the natural and human history of the region. Other museums include the Art Gallery of Greater Victoria, with a permanent collection of over 15,000 objects, the Maltwood Art Museum and Gallery at the University of Victoria, and the Maritime Museum of British Columbia.

Victoria has several theatres—the professional Belfry Theatre, the Victoria Theatre Guild (the oldest community theatre in Western Canada), and the Phoenix Theatre at the University of Victoria. Kaleidoscope Theatre Productions stages plays for young audiences. The Victoria Operatic Society presents musicals and operettas, while Pacific Opera presents operas from the classic repertoire.

The Victoria Symphony plays over fifty concerts annually from classical to pops. The Victoria Conservatory Music School has students at all levels, from beginners to advanced, and sponsors concerts.

SPORTS Victoria's $30-million, 7,300-seat multiplex sports arena opened in March 2005. Saanich Commonwealth Place, one of six municipal recreation centers, has an Olympic-sized swimming pool. Victoria has six eighteen-hole golf courses (two of them public, one, semiprivate) and two public nine-hole golf courses. Other recreational activities in or near Victoria: Tidal and freshwater sportfishing, kayaking, canoeing, sailing, scuba diving, horseback riding.

Mount Washington Alpine Resort, Vancouver Island's premier ski and snowboard area, is located four hours north of Victoria.

There are forty-eight regional, provincial, and federal parks in the Greater Victoria area. Some of the regional parks have beaches, some have manicured trails, while others are in wilderness settings. The thirty-seven-mile-long Galloping Goose Trail runs from Leechtown to Victoria along an old railroad right-of-way and is used by cyclists, joggers, and walkers.

Victoria and the surrounding area are known for beautiful gardens. Butchart Gardens on the Saanich Peninsula are world famous.

PUBLIC SAFETY In 2003, Victoria had one of the highest crime rates in Canada, with 10,588 criminal code offenses per 100,000 population. There were 1.5 homicides, 77 robberies, 720 break-ins, and 284 motor vehicle thefts, all per 100,000 population. The crime rate increased by 3.7 percent between 2002 and 2003.

SNAPSHOT: Vancouver

On a night when the Canucks, the hometown hockey team, won a big game, all hell broke loose on Robson Street, the main drag through Vancouver's downtown. Banners waved and horns blared as the occupants of car after car whooped it up, making this city of more than half a million seem like a small town.

Vancouver is big enough to be sophisticated but small enough to be friendly. It has a raffish charm and an idyllic setting. Kayaks and other recreational boats ply its waterways; joggers and cyclists exercise in thousand-acre Stanley Park. Skiers drive fifteen minutes out of town to snowcapped mountains. The shops in its lively downtown stay open well into the evening. Its numerous restaurants, some of world-class caliber, are stocked with delectable produce and wines from the nearby Okanagan Valley. Though rainy, it has one of the most temperate climates in Canada.

Vancouver was named for English captain George Vancouver, who stepped ashore in 1792 while looking for a route to China. Today, as Canada's principal gateway to the Pacific Rim, numerous shops and restaurants reflect the Asian presence. A city-operated phone service gives information on municipal services in five languages: English, Chinese, Punjabi, Spanish, and Vietnamese.

Polyglot Vancouver can be the ne plus ultra of trendy. In Yaletown, for instance—a former warehouse district now converted to boutiques, restaurants, and apartment buildings—a hip hotel offers meeting facilities that include matcha tea breaks, guided breathing breaks, and canisters of oxygen for "increasing energy levels and cognitive performance."

Some Americans, particularly those from the East Coast or smoggy L.A. might say that a sniff of Vancouver's fresh air would do the trick all by itself.

Newer immigrants from the United States find that they have predecessors who have come to Vancouver and thrived. Stanley Park's numerous gray squirrels descend from eight pairs of immigrant squirrels. They were a gift from New York City in 1909 when the city of Vancouver was a mere twenty-three years old but already growing hand over fist. In 1887, the Canadian Pacific Railway's first train arrived—the final stop of the first transcontinental trip. By 1920, Vancouver was bigger than Winnipeg, which had been the major city of western Canada. It's still bigger—and still growing.

LOCATION Vancouver is twenty-four miles north of the Washington State border, bounded by the Strait of Georgia (part of the Pacific Ocean) to the west, the Fraser River to the south, the Coast Mountains to the north, and the Fraser Valley to the east.

Greater Vancouver is made up of twenty-one municipalities on and around the Fraser River delta.

Latitude: 49°16' N; Longitude: 123°07' W.

CLIMATE Average January temperature, 40°F; average July temperature, 65°F. Average annual precipitation, 48 inches. Vancouver weather is highly variable because of the variety of topography within a small area. Within the space of a few miles, the city goes from sea level to mountains.

POPULATION 583,296 (2004); 2,132,824 metropolitan area (est., 2004)

POPULATION DENSITY 1,963 per square mile (city of Vancouver, 2004)

ETHNIC DIVERSITY In order of frequency, Vancouver residents cited their ancestral background as follows in the 2001 census: English, Canadian, Chinese, Scottish, Irish, German, East Indian, French, Ukrainian, Italian, Dutch, Filipino, Polish, Norwegian, North American Indian, Welsh, Russian, Swedish, Korean, Japanese, American (USA), Vietnamese, Spanish, Jewish, Iranian, Hungarian, Danish, and Austrian.

Religious Affiliations:

None	35 percent
Protestant	25 percent
Catholic	19 percent
Sikh	5 percent
Buddhist	4 percent

There were 52,590 Muslims living in the Vancouver metropolitan area in 2001, 26,520 Orthodox Christian, and 17,270 Jews.

ECONOMY Vancouver is Canada's busiest port, handling an average of twice as much cargo as its nearest competitor, St. John. In 2003, 66.7 million tons of goods were shipped through Vancouver, up 6.2 percent from 2002. Key growth sectors: business services, engineering, scientific and technical services, life sciences and bio-technology, construction, transportation, entertainment, education, health services, and retail.

UNEMPLOYMENT RATE 7.2 percent (2003)

EARNINGS
Average annual earnings for full-time workers (2001): $46,806 (metropolitan area)
Median family income (couples, 2001): $63,146 (metropolitan area)

HOUSING The average price for a house in Greater Vancouver in 2004 was $373,877 (far more than anywhere else in the country. Toronto was in second place, with an average housing price of $315,266 in 2004.)
Average rent for a three-bedroom apartment (2003): $1,116.
In 2001, 56 percent of Vancouver residents rented their homes compared with 33.7 percent in British Columbia as a whole. Vancouver had the highest percentage of people in the province paying 30 percent or more of their pre-tax income on housing costs. (Forty-four percent of tenants fell into this group, as did 25.1 percent of owners, for a total of 35.7 percent.)

EDUCATION There are ninety-one elementary and eighteen secondary public schools in the city. School trustees and board members are elected.
In 2001, 30.5 percent of Vancouver residents had university degrees, compared with 17.6 percent province-wide.
Universities and Colleges: University of British Columbia (more than 28,000 undergraduate students, 6,400 graduate students, and more than 40,000 noncredit, certificate, or distance students). Undergraduate tuition for in-province students, $4,595. Tuition for international students, $16,844 to $16,853.
Also, Ashton College, British Columbia Institute of Technology, Century College, Imperial Hotel Management College, Institute of Indigenous Government, Kingston College, Regent College, Simon Fraser University, Vancouver Film School, Vancouver Premier College, Vancouver School of Theology, Kwantlen University College, and several community colleges.
The Vancouver Public Library is the second largest public library system in Canada, with a main building and twenty branches. The collection of more

than 2.5 million items includes books, magazines, newspapers, videotapes, CDs, DVDs, and e-books in English, French, Chinese, German, Japanese, Hindi, Italian, Korean, Portuguese, Punjabi, Russian, Spanish, Tagalog, Polish, and Vietnamese.

HEALTH The Vancouver Coastal Health Authority is responsible for delivering acute, residential, and community health care. There are forty-one hospitals in the Greater Vancouver area.

Average Life Expectancy (2001):
Males, 77.8 years
Females, 83.5 years
Infant Mortality Rate: 4 per 1,000 live births (average, 1999–2003)

MEDIA Daily English-language newspapers, the *Vancouver Sun* and the *Province*. Daily Chinese-language newspapers: *Sing Tao* and *Ming Pao*. Weekly paper, *The Georgia Straight*. Also, monthly entertainment and shopping guides. Four major TV news stations and three radio news stations. Local news is presented and discussed on GVTV on the Shaw Cable Channel.

TRANSPORTATION Vancouver International Airport is the second largest in Canada. VIA Rail trains travel between Vancouver and Toronto with stops in Kamloops, Jasper, Edmonton, Saskatoon, Winnipeg, and Sudbury Junction. Amtrak trains travel daily between Seattle and Vancouver. For other transportation information, see British Columbia listing (pages 78–79).

URBAN TRANSIT Vancouver Regional Transit System operates a network comprising rapid transit, ferries, and buses. Skytrain, the city's rapid transit, connects downtown Vancouver with Burnaby, New Westminster, and Surrey. It runs daily between 5:30 A.M. and 7:00 P.M. Day passes and multiple-trip tickets offer substantial discounts. Ferries operate daily between Vancouver and the North Shore. West Coast Express is a commuter rail service between Vancouver and Mission in the Fraser Valley.

A car is not absolutely necessary for people living in downtown Vancouver where public transportation is good and many places are walkable, but it is in the suburbs. Bicycling is encouraged.

CULTURE The city owns and operates three performing arts facilities: Queen Elizabeth Theatre, Vancouver Playhouse, and the Orpheum Theatre, where the Vancouver Symphony Orchestra plays. Vancouver has twenty-seven professional theatrical groups and several major theatre festivals. There are twenty-nine dance companies, including Ballet British Columbia.

Museums: UBC Museum of Anthropology (on the campus of the University of British Columbia), Vancouver Art Gallery, Chinese Cultural Centre Museum and Archives, Vancouver Aquarium Marine Science Centre, B.C. Sports Hall of Fame and Museum, Granville Island Museums of sports fishing, model ships, and model trains, Vancouver Museum and H. R. MacMillan Space Centre, Vancouver Maritime Museum.

SPORTS B.C. Lions Football Club (Canadian Football League); Vancouver Canadians (baseball; minor league affiliate of the Oakland Athletics); Vancouver Canucks (National Hockey League); Vancouver Whitecaps (United Soccer League).

BC Place Stadium is the largest air-supported domed amphitheatre in the world. It holds up to 60,000 people.

Recreational Sports: Summer: swimming (sandy beaches and cool water), also nine indoor pools and seven outdoor pools, kayaking, sailing, fishing, golf, tennis, rafting, windsurfing, scuba diving. Winter: cross-country and downhill skiing on nearby mountains, snowboarding.

Parks: Vancouver has more than two hundred parks and many community centers with swimming pools, skating rinks, fitness centers, racquet courts, and golf and pitch and putt courses.

Stanley Park, the third largest city park in North America, is the crown jewel of the system. Douglas firs, western hemlocks, and western red cedars shelter raccoons, squirrels, coyotes, and numerous resident and migrating birds. Recreational activities include tennis, golf, swimming, cycling, rollerblading, jogging, and walking. Cricket, bowling, and rowing clubs maintain handsome clubhouses, as does the Royal Vancouver Yacht Club, to which Queen Elizabeth's husband, Prince Philip, belongs. The renowned Vancouver Aquarium Marine Science Center is in the park. In the summer, plays are presented in an outdoor amphitheatre. There are several restaurants. At the Brockton Point Visitors Centre, totem poles are a reminder of the First Nations people who once lived on this land. Queen Elizabeth Park is large and lovely, with tennis courts, a restaurant, sunken gardens, and the Bloedel Conservatory, which houses tropical and desert plants.

Vancouver's gardens include VanDusen Botanical Garden and the Sun Yat-Sen Classical Chinese Garden.

PUBLIC SAFETY In 2003, Vancouver had one of the highest crime rates in Canada, with 2.1 homicides, 153 robberies, 1,350 break-ins, and 1,261 motor vehicle thefts, for a total of 11,576 criminal code offenses per 100,000 population. This was a 4.5 percent increase over 2002 levels.

SNAPSHOT: ALBERTA

Like Texas, Alberta is huge, oil rich, and agricultural. Real, twenty-first-century cowboys ride herd over the beef cattle for which the province is famous.

Alberta is Canada's most prosperous province, due largely to its vast supplies of oil and natural gas. It has the lowest rate of unemployment in Canada, the most affordable housing as a ratio of cost to income, and the lowest taxes. The province has no deficit, but this has been achieved in part by curtailing some social programs.

In social and religious matters, Alberta is Canada's most conservative province. There is continuing talk of partially privatizing health care, for instance, and Alberta is the only province whose government officially opposed same-sex marriage (now legalized throughout Canada by federal law).

Along with Saskatchewan, Alberta joined the confederation on September 1, 1905. The province was named for Princess Louise Caroline Alberta, a daughter of Queen Victoria, who was married to the then governor-general of Canada.

Alberta has some of the grandest mountain scenery in the country in two of its five national parks, Banff and Jasper, where visitors marvel at emerald green lakes in summer and the dense turquoise blue ice of glaciers in winter.

On the Alberta-Montana border, Waterton Lakes National Park is geologically indistinguishable from Glacier National Park on the U.S. side—a fact that was recognized in 1932 with the formation of Waterton-Glacier International Peace Park.

Two hours east of Calgary, Alberta's largest city, the surrealistic pinnacles and buttes of Dinosaur Provincial Park are the remains of what was a subtropical landscape 75 million years ago. The region abounds in ancient bones and fossils. Dinosaur Provincial Park is one of Alberta's five UNESCO World Heritage sites.

The Calgary Stampede, which takes place in July, is a world-famous rodeo with chuckwagon races, midway rides, and many kinds of live entertainment.

Edmonton's Klondike Days, also in July, celebrate the 1890s when miners bound for the Yukon gold fields passed through Edmonton on their way north.

LOCATION The westernmost of Canada's prairie provinces (see map on page xix). To the south, Alberta shares a 185-mile-long border with the state of Montana.

GEOGRAPHY At 255,303 square miles, Alberta is Canada's fourth largest province. It is three times the size of Great Britain. The northern half of the province is largely uninhabited and is covered with forests and lakes. The southern half is mostly broad, fertile plains that give way to the snow-covered Rocky Mountains. Alberta has 600 lakes and 245 named rivers, most of which originate in the mountains and are fed by melting snow and glaciers.

CLIMATE Alberta claims to receive more hours of sunshine per year than any other province. Average annual precipitation, 16 inches. Average summer temperatures, June to August, 68°F; average winter temperatures, December to February, 12°F.

PROVINCIAL CAPITAL Edmonton

POPULATION 3,281,296 (est., Oct. 2005). Between 2000 and 2004, the population of Alberta grew faster than that of any other province. About 58 percent of Albertans are under the age of 40.

POPULATION DENSITY 2.89 people per square mile. Two-thirds of the population lives in or around Edmonton and Calgary.

ETHNIC DIVERSITY Most Albertans are of English, German, Scottish, and Irish descent. Among other ethnic groups, the greatest number are French, followed by Ukrainians, Dutch, American Indians, and Poles.

There are around 90,000 people of Indian ancestry in the province and about 65,000 Métis, descended from French fur trappers and Natives.

Visible Minorities: 11.2 percent of the population. Most live in Calgary, Alberta's largest city, where 16.1 percent of the population belongs to a visible minority, or in Edmonton, where the visible minority population is 14.6 percent of the total.

Religious Affiliations:

Protestant	39 percent
Catholic	27 percent
None	24 percent

Other Christian	4 percent
Christian orthodox	2 percent
Muslim	2 percent

HEALTH In 2001 and 2002, Alberta had the third highest life expectancy at birth among the provinces.

Average Life Expectancy (2001):

Males, 77.1 years

Females, 82.0 years

Infant Mortality Rate: 5.6 per 1,000 live births (2001)

Health Care Satisfaction: In 2003, Albertans responded to questions about the quality of the health care they had received in the previous twelve months (Statistics Canada, Canadian Community Health Survey, 2003). They were slightly less satisfied with their care than Canadians as a whole.

ECONOMY With millions of acres of fertile land, Alberta's economy had traditionally been based on agriculture. The province raises more than 40 percent of Canada's beef. In addition, since the 1950s, Alberta has become Canada's largest producer of oil and natural gas.

In 2003, the Alberta Energy and Utilities Board reported that the province had 176.10 billion barrels of proven oil reserves, more than any other Canadian province and far more than the United States and Mexico combined.

EARNINGS

Average earnings, working full year, full-time: $44,130 (2001)

Median household income (couples): $62,343 (2001)

Average earnings of the population, 15 and over, for holders of a university certificate, diploma, or degree (2001): $50,069 (This was the highest in the prairie provinces and higher than the Canadian national average of $48,648.)

UNEMPLOYMENT RATE 3.9 percent (Dec. 2005). The national average for that month was 6.1 percent.

HOUSING Typical homeowners in Alberta pay 25.5 percent of their pretax household income for shelter, a lower percentage than in any other province.

Average value of dwelling: $159,698 (2001)

Average gross monthly payments for renters: $674 (2001)

Average monthly payments for owner-occupied dwellings: $875 (2001)

EDUCATION In 2003, fifteen-year-olds in Alberta scored significantly higher in reading, mathematics, and science tests than students elsewhere in Canada or in the United States. Alberta has the best-educated workforce in Canada. Approximately 65 percent of Albertans aged 25 to 64 have a post-secondary education.

TAXES Alberta has a flat income tax of 10 percent. It has no general retail sales tax; however, the federal government's 7 percent goods and services tax is levied on most purchases. Property taxes are among the lowest in Canada. In Alberta, a typical two-income family with two children earning $60,000 pays around $4,000 in combined taxes and health care insurance. This is 34 percent less than the average in other provinces.

Gasoline taxes in Alberta are the lowest in Canada.

GOVERNMENT *Premier:* Ralph Klein (Progressive Conservative Party). There are currently eighty-three constituencies in Alberta, each of which sends a representative to the provincial legislature, but constituency boundary lines change every few years as determined by the Electoral Boundaries Commission.

Political Parties: The Progressive Conservative Party has been in power in Alberta for more than three decades.

There are currently nine political parties registered in Alberta, but only four of them are represented in the provincial legislature. They are the Progressive Conservative Party, the Liberal Party, the New Democratic Party, and the Alberta Alliance Party.

Alberta has twenty-six representatives in the federal House of Commons and six in the Senate.

Right to Vote: Women have been able to vote in Alberta since 1916, but First Nations people have only been able to vote since 1965.

LAWS Alberta's small claims court limit of $25,000, which took effect on November 1, 2002, is the highest in Canada. Claims can be heard in Provincial Court, Civil Division, without needing a lawyer.

PROVINCIAL HOLIDAY Heritage Day, the first Monday in August. While not an official holiday, it is a day for honoring the province's multiethnic heritage with music, dancing, games, and food. Alberta Family Day, which is uniquely Albertan, is celebrated the third Monday in February. Some employees in Alberta, in fact, don't get Heritage Day off anymore, but get this as a holiday instead.

TRANSPORTATION Two international airports, one in Edmonton and one in Calgary. VIA Rail offers regularly scheduled train service through Edmonton and Jasper. Royal Canadian Pacific and Rocky Mountaineer Vacations run touring trains through the province. Two Trans-Canada routes traverse parts of Alberta, east and west—Highway 1 in the south and the Trans-Canada Yellowhead Highway (Highway 16) in the central part of the state. Drivers going north can choose between Highway 2 and the scenic route on the Icefields Parkway.

CARS AND AUTO INSURANCE Auto insurance continues to be controversial in Alberta. In an effort to control ever-rising premiums, the government in October 2004 limited the amount that auto accident victims could collect, including a $4,000 cap for minor injuries. However, the insurance companies (all of them private) did not lower their rates, yielding record profits for the industry. In April 2005, Alberta's finance minister ordered the insurance companies to cut their rates by 6 percent. Meanwhile, the Alberta Civil Trial Lawyers Association is challenging the auto insurance reform laws in court saying that they deprive Albertans of adequate compensation for lost quality of life and pain and suffering.

For the last fifteen years, Calgary and Edmonton have had the lowest gasoline prices in Canada.

ATTITUDES TOWARD GAYS Alberta is one of three provinces that did not legalize same-sex marriage (the other two were Prince Edward Island and New Brunswick) before it became legal by federal law, and has the only provincial government that officially opposed it. Opposition has been particularly vehement from the Catholic church. (In 2001, Protestants were the most numerous religious group in the province, followed by Catholics.)

CULTURE Edmonton and Calgary have concert halls, theatres, museums, and galleries, but Alberta has many cultural sites and activities that have nothing to do with traditional art forms. Weekend rodeos are common throughout the province during the summer. First Nations powwows with drumming, dancing, and native food are also common.

FESTIVALS Edmonton is known for its festivals. (See listing on pages 100–101). Some other festivals: Cowboy Poetry Gathering in Pincher Creek (June); Calgary International Jazz Festival (June); Medicine Hat Jazz Fest (June); Athabasca River Rats Festival (July); Calgary Stampede (July); Big Valley Country Jamboree in Camrose (late July–early August); Banff Summer Arts

Festival (May–August); Calgary Dragon Boat Race and Cultural Festival (August); Calgary International Horse Show (September); Banff Mountain Film Festival (late October–early November), Calgary Winter Festival (February).

SPORTS For professional teams, see the listings under Edmonton and Calgary (pages 101 and 105, respectively).

Recreational Sports: Climbing, horseback riding, fishing, canoeing, kayaking, skiing, snowshoeing, skating, dogsledding, and snowmobiling. Alberta has 280 golf courses.

Banff, the country's oldest national park, and Jasper National Park are both in Alberta. The province's other national parks are Waterton Lakes in the Rockies, Elk Island near Edmonton, and Wood Buffalo, the largest national park in Canada, on the border between Alberta and the Northwest Territories. Kananaskis, a 1,544-square-mile network of five provincial parks near Banff, has many recreational facilities, including groomed cross-country ski trails that were built for the 1988 Olympics. In summer, they're used for mountain biking.

PUBLIC SAFETY In 2003, there were more vehicles stolen in Alberta than in any other province. Crimes of violence and property both decreased by 1.3 percent between 2003 and 2004 (figures per 100,000 of the population). Of the three Prairie provinces (Alberta, Manitoba, Saskatchewan), Alberta's crime rate was the lowest.

SNAPSHOT: Edmonton

The approach to Edmonton from the west is through immense stretches of flat prairie punctuated by oil wells and small hand-hewn churches.

Near the Edmonton airport, around twelve miles outside the city, a sign points to Leduc, where oil was discovered in 1947. Though the city was already well off from its days as a frontier trading post and as the provisioning point for the Yukon gold fields, black gold floated Edmonton to new levels of prosperity. There are now more than ten thousand oil wells within sixty-two miles of the city plus refineries and supply depots.

What is now Edmonton started out as two cities—one called Edmonton, the other called Strathcona—on either side of the North Saskatchewan River and its deeply sculpted valley.

On the north bank of the river, the Hudson's Bay Company and the North West Company founded Fort Edmonton as a trading post in 1795. Natives and French trappers came there with furs that they sold or exchanged for muskets, provisions, blankets, and other supplies. Fort Edmonton Park, Canada's largest living history park, re-creates the look and sound of the Hudson's Bay fort as it was in 1846 and also enables visitors to experience the Edmonton of 1885, 1905, and 1920.

On the south side of the river, Strathcona grew up around the Canadian Pacific Railway, which came through the area in 1891.

Edmonton was incorporated as a city in 1904. A year later, Alberta became a province of Canada and Edmonton became its capital. A bridge between Edmonton and Strathcona had been finished in 1902. In 1912, Edmonton and Strathcona merged.

In order to cope with Edmonton's notoriously cold, snowy winters, climate-controlled walkways have been built under the city's downtown core. Another resource is the huge West Edmonton Mall, with forty-eight city blocks of shopping, dining, and entertainment. Among other things, it has more than eight hundred shops, a five-acre water park with waves and a beach, an amusement park, an eighteen-hole miniature golf course, a sea lion show, a submarine, an ice skating rink, restaurants, a hotel, and a chapel for anyone who wants to get married there.

In conservative Alberta, Edmonton is known for being relatively liberal. One March morning in front of the Saturday market in Old Strathcona, for instance, some women stood in silence, dressed in black, next to a sign that read WOMEN IN BLACK STANDING FOR JUSTICE PEACE NONVIOLENCE.

In its 2003 annual report, the Edmonton Public Library noted that it had held a "Banned Book Cafe" where visitors were invited to read aloud from banned books to celebrate Freedom to Read Week.

Edmonton and Calgary are like twin and sometimes rival stars in the Alberta constellation. Both have a spectrum of cultural and sporting activities, but Edmonton seems to be the more intellectual of the two and the more arts oriented, while Calgary delights in everything physical.

LOCATION In the geographic center of Alberta on the Trans-Canada Yellowhead Highway and on the VIA Rail transcontinental route; 320 miles north of Montana; 795 miles east of Seattle (flying time, less than two hours); 184 miles north of Calgary (flying time, forty minutes). The most northerly of Canada's major cities, on the same latitude as Hamburg, Germany, and Liverpool, England.

Latitude: 53°34' N; Longitude: 113°31' W; Elevation: 2,192 feet above sea level.

GEOGRAPHY Bisected by the North Saskatchewan River, which flows from the Columbia Icefield in Jasper National Park to Hudson Bay. Surrounded by prairie and low hills covered with farms, wetlands, and forests. Edmonton sprawls over a 259-square-mile area, one of the largest cities by area in North America.

CLIMATE Four distinct seasons. Long hours of daylight in spring and summer (up to seventeen hours in June). Snow cover on the ground from November to mid-March. Average January temperatures range from 16°F to –4°F; average July temperatures from 49°F to 78°F.

POPULATION 937,845 (as of 2002; metropolitan area). Edmonton is the sixth largest city in Canada, but because of its large area it has a low population density—only 32 people per square mile (compared with 1,636 people per square mile in Vancouver or 1,399 people per square mile in Montreal).

ETHNIC DIVERSITY In order of frequency, the ancestors of the largest number of Edmontonians were English, Scottish, German, Irish, Ukrainian, and French. Smaller numbers came from Polish, Chinese, Dutch, North American Indian, Norwegian, East Indian, Swedish, Italian, Métis, and Welsh backgrounds. According to the 2001 census, there were 13,405 people living in Edmonton of U.S. descent.

Visible Minorities: 14.6 percent of the population

Religious Affiliations:

Protestant	31 percent
Catholic	29 percent
None	24 percent

HEALTH In 2003, century-old *Maclean's*, one of the more popular magazines in Canada, ranked Edmonton's Capital Health No. 1 out of the 57 regional health authorities it surveyed.

Edmonton has fourteen hospitals. The University of Alberta Hospital was a pioneer in heart transplants and is noted for advanced cardiac treatment.

Average Life Expectancy (2002):

Males, 77.4 years

Females, 82.4 years

These numbers exceed the national average.

ECONOMY Traditionally, Edmonton's economy has been based on the energy and agricultural industries (including oil, gas, and chemicals, meat processing, and grain handling), but today is more diversified. As the gateway to much of northern Canada, Edmonton is a distribution hub. Tourism and entertainment are also important employers and sources of revenue.

Developing industries include advanced manufacturing, agri-food products, information and communications technology, and forest products. Edmonton is trying to foster biomedicine and biotechnology as well as nanotechnology and microsystems.

UNEMPLOYMENT RATE 5.1 percent (2003)

EARNINGS
Average annual earnings for full-time workers (2001): $41,388
Median family income (couples, 2001): $62,663

HOUSING
Average gross monthly payments for rented dwellings (2001): $619
Average monthly payments for owner-occupied dwellings (2001): $833
In 2004, the average value of a dwelling was $179,610.
Two-thirds of the population live in homes that they own. Among renters, 37.2 percent spend more than 30 percent of their household income on shelter. Among homeowners, 14.7 percent spend more than 30 percent of their household income on shelter (2001).

EDUCATION The public school system has 203 schools with an enrollment of 81,200 students. Among the schools are some in which the curriculum is taught in English and up to half the time in American Sign Language, Arabic, Chinese (Mandarin), German, Hebrew, Punjabi, Spanish, or Ukrainian. There is also a K-12 French immersion program in which most of the core curriculum is taught in French.

There are special schools within the public system for the performing and visual arts, sciences, sports, and for Christian education. In addition, there are public schools for students with learning disabilities or other special needs and a K-12 distance-learning program for the homeschooled.

A Catholic school system with 84 schools and around 32,000 students is also supported with public funds. Parents can send their children to any school they want, provided there's room.

The University of Alberta, established in 1908, has 34,000 full- and part-time students. Its students are second only to McGill's in winning Academic All-Canadian awards for excellence in both varsity sports and academics. The university's resources include a medical school and mammoth teaching hospital. Tuition for in-province students is $5,033; for international students, $12,161.

Northern Alberta Institute of Technology, Alberta's largest technical school, has 48,500 students enrolled in technical, vocational, and apprenticeship programs.

Grant MacEwan College, Alberta's largest college, has 57,200 students.

Other colleges and universities include Athabasca University, Concordia University College, Kings University College, Taylor University College and Seminary, and the Edmonton campus of the University of Lethbridge.

The library system has sixteen branches. Relatively low spending on libraries (US $22.4 per capita compared with US $38.1 per capita in Vancouver and US $33.6 per capita in Toronto.)

URBAN TRANSIT Light-rail transit subway; buses; six taxi companies.

CULTURE Edmonton's downtown Arts District includes the Winspear Centre, where the Edmonton Symphony Orchestra plays; the Citadel Theatre, where classic and contemporary plays are performed; and the Edmonton Art Gallery. The Edmonton Opera and the Alberta Ballet Company perform at the Northern Alberta Jubilee Auditorium at the University of Alberta.

Edmonton has thirteen professional theatre companies. In the summer, the city hosts an eleven-day-long International Fringe Theatre Festival with 1,200 performances on thirty stages.

The Royal Alberta Museum (formerly called the Provincial Museum of Alberta and renamed in May 2005 to honor Queen Elizabeth II's centennial visit to the province) is particularly known for its Syncrude Gallery of Aboriginal Culture. The museum is the flagship of over twenty museums in and around the city.

The Odyssium, a science center, has the largest planetarium dome in North America as well as an observatory, interactive exhibit galleries, and an IMAX theatre.

The Muttart Conservatory of botanical specimens from all over the world is a city landmark with its four glass pyramids, three of them sheltering different climatic environments, with the fourth one for seasonal floral displays.

FESTIVALS Edmonton calls itself the "Festival City" with thirteen major festivals during an eleven-week period each summer. Among Edmonton's festivals are: Canadian Birkebeiner Ski Festival (cross-country) (February); Jazz City International Music Festival (June-July); River City Shakespeare

Festival (June-July); International Street Performers Festival (July); Edmonton's Klondike Days/A Taste of Edmonton (July); Edmonton Heritage Festival (July-August); Folk Music Festival (August); Caribbean Arts Festival (August); International Fringe Theatre Festival (August); Labatt Blues Festival (August); Symphony Under the Sky Festival (September); International Film Festival (October); Canadian Finals Rodeo and Edmonton's River City Roundup (November); Edmonton New Year's Eve Downtown Festival (December).

SPORTS *Professional Sports Teams:* Edmonton Oilers (National Hockey League) and the Edmonton Eskimos (Canadian Football League). A regular stop on pro golf's Canadian tour. Thoroughbred harness horse racing from early March to mid-June. Each November, the city hosts the Canadian Finals Rodeo.

Seventy golf courses are located within a one-hour drive of city center, including the oldest municipal golf course in Canada. Canoeing, snowmobiling, snowshoeing, and cross-country skiing (in or near the city). Edmonton has more than 1,000 facilities for recreation and amateur sports.

The city is four hours' drive (229 miles) from Jasper National Park in the Canadian Rockies, which offers skiing, hiking, fishing, whitewater rafting, camping, horseback riding, birding, wildlife viewing, dogsledding, and skating. It is a half-hour drive from Elk Island National Park for bird watching, hiking, and wildlife viewing.

The North Saskatchewan River Valley park, with seventy-six miles of trails, is the longest stretch of urban parkland in North America.

MEDIA Two newspapers (*Edmonton Sun* and *Edmonton Journal*); fifteen radio stations; six television stations

PUBLIC SAFETY Edmonton had shown a 10.3 percent increase in crimes between 2002 and 2003, giving the city one of the higher crime rates in the country. Overall, there was a slight increase in crime between 2003 and 2004, with one category of crime balancing another.

There were 28 homicides in 2004, an increase of 56 percent over the previous year, 11 attempted murders, an increase of 267 percent, and 6 percent more motor vehicle thefts (9,053 in 2004 compared with 8,577 in 2003). But the number of robberies went down by 15 percent, as did sexual and nonsexual assaults (declines of 8 percent and 10 percent, respectively).

SNAPSHOT: Calgary

Calgary was already on the map as an important cattle center when oil was discovered just south of the city in 1914. More oil turned up north of the city in 1947, making it the oil center of Canada. American investors brought money and technology to help get the petroleum business started. Many stayed, and Calgary is considered the most American of Canadian cities today.

Since the 1970s, because of oil and natural gas, Calgary has become the commercial center of Alberta; it has the second largest concentration of corporate head offices in Canada.

Fort Calgary was built in 1875 at the junction of the Bow and Elbow Rivers as a barracks for the North-West Mounted Police. The Mounties had been sent to western Canada to put a stop to illegal whiskey trading and to keep the peace in what was then the Northwest Territories. Blackfoot, Sarcee, and Assiniboine Indians had long lived in the area and traded with white trappers who came in the 1700s.

The Canadian Pacific Railway reached Calgary in 1883, and the government's offer of free land drew settlers as it had in Manitoba. Many came from the United States. Calgary was incorporated as a town in 1884 and as a city in 1893.

Many large ranches developed in the area, and Calgary became the center of Canada's meatpacking industry. In 1912 four Calgary ranchers backed an American-born trick roper named Guy Weadick who had an idea for a rodeo. They called it the Calgary Stampede. The Calgary Exhibition and Stampede has become a world-famous annual event featuring bull riding, steer roping, parades, music and dance performances, fireworks, livestock exhibitions, street fairs, and handicrafts.

Today, Calgary has a compact inner city dominated by the 626-foot-tall Calgary Tower. To mitigate the city's cold winters, enclosed walkways, called "Plus 15s" because they are fifteen feet above street level, connect nearly half the downtown buildings. There are underground walkways as well.

In warmer weather, the Stephen Avenue Mall, lined with turn-of-the-last-century sandstone buildings, is a bustling pedestrian retail strip with outdoor cafes, shoppers, street performers, and nightclubs.

In the 1970s and '80s the city spent millions of dollars on urban renewal projects in the downtown area. A Convention Center opened in 1974 and the EPCOR Centre for the Performing Arts in 1985. An indoor arena, the Olympic Saddledome, was built in 1983 for the Calgary Flames of the National Hockey League and was used for the 1988 Winter Olympic games, which were held in Calgary. It was renamed the Pengrowth Saddledome in 2000.

LOCATION On the prairie just east of the Rocky Mountain foothills in southwest Alberta, at the junction of the Bow and Elbow Rivers. The Trans-Canada Highway and the Canamex Corridor, which runs from northern Canada to Mexico, cross in Calgary. By plane Calgary is 1.5 hours from Seattle, two hours from Salt Lake City, and 2.5 hours from Denver, Minneapolis, and San Francisco.

Latitude: 51°6' N; Longitude: 114°1' W.

CLIMATE Average January temperature, 16°F; average July temperature, 63°F. Average annual precipitation, 17.5 inches. More than 2,000 hours of sunshine a year.

POPULATION (2001 census) 878,866 (city); 951,395 (metropolitan area) The youngest population of any city in Canada, with an average age of 34.

ETHNIC DIVERSITY About half the people in Calgary have some British ancestry. Immigrants from Europe after World War II included Dutch, French, Germans, and Scandinavians. Immigrants constitute 19.8 percent of Calgary's population.

Visible Minorities: 16.1 percent of Calgary's population. People of Chinese descent are the largest nonwhite ethnic group. There are also South Asians, Filipinos, blacks, and other minorities. Some 900 Sarcee Indians live on the Tsuu Tina reserve southwest of the city.

ECONOMY Calgary's economy is based on oil, natural gas, coal, cattle, and wheat. It is also a center for technology and manufacturing. There are many engineering, geological, geophysical, and surveying consultant firms in Calgary, and most Canadian banks have western headquarters in the city.

Calgary has more small businesses than any other major city in Canada.

EARNINGS
Average annual earnings for full-time workers (2001): $48,805
Median household income (all households, 2001): $57,879
Median family income (couples, 2001): $70,411
Calgary residents have the highest average personal income in Canada.

UNEMPLOYMENT RATE 4.1 percent (one of the lowest rates in Canada)

HOUSING The average price of a house in Calgary in 2004 was $222,860.

The average rent for a three-bedroom apartment in 2003 was $786.

In 2001, more than 70 percent of Calgary residents lived in owner-occupied dwellings. Of these people, 17.4 percent were spending 30 percent or more of their income on shelter compared with 36 percent of the renters.

EDUCATION Calgary has more than 200 public schools and more than 80 parochial schools. Both are supported by public funds.

The public library system has fifteen branches, but spends only U.S. $20.2 per capita, per year. That's less per capita than many cities with fewer economic resources than Calgary.

Sixty-two percent of the people who live in Calgary have a postsecondary education.

The University of Calgary is noted for its engineering, architecture, medicine, social work, and science programs. Tuition for Alberta residents is $5,127; for international students it's $12,032.

The Mount Royal College and Southern Alberta Institute of Technology are also in Calgary.

HEALTH
Average Life Expectancy (2001):
Males, 78.1 years
Females, 82.4 years

MEDIA Two daily newspapers: *The Calgary Herald* and *The Calgary Sun*, plus seven radio stations (one French), and a half dozen TV stations, including Global TV.

TRANSPORTATION More than twenty passenger airlines use the Calgary International Airport. U.S. nonstop destinations include Chicago, Dallas, Denver, Detroit, Houston, Los Angeles, Minneapolis, Salt Lake City, Las Vegas, San Francisco, Seattle, and Phoenix.

The Canadian Pacific Railway has its headquarters in Calgary. The nearest VIA rail stations are in Jasper and Edmonton.

URBAN TRANSIT Bus and light-rail rapid transit (the latter is free in the center of town). Transportation for the physically and mentally disabled is available through Handi-Bus within the city limits.

CULTURE The Calgary Philharmonic Orchestra performs in the EPCOR Centre for the Performing Arts, which is part of the Olympic Plaza Cultural District—home to many of Calgary's other visual, theatre, music, and dance groups. The Alberta Ballet Company performs in the Southern Alberta Jubilee Auditorium, which also hosts classical music, pop, opera, and rock concerts. The Honens International Piano Competition is held in Calgary every three years

Museums: The Glenbow Museum, western Canada's largest, is noted for its First Nations exhibits. Also, the Olympic Hall of Fame and Museum; Calgary ace to win Chinese Cultural Centre; Family of Man Museum; Naval Museum of Alberta; Calgary Science Center; Museum of the Regiments (one of North America's largest military museums); Calgary Aero Space Museum.

Heritage Park Historical Village, on sixty-six acres shows life in the region as it was, pre-1914.

The highly regarded Calgary Zoo, Botanical Garden, and Prehistoric Park has a collection of over 1,000 animals and more than 4,000 ornamental plants.

SPORTS The Calgary Stampeders (Canadian Football League); Calgary Vipers (Northern Baseball League); Calgary Flames (National Hockey League); Roughnecks Lacrosse Club (National Lacrosse League).

Four major equestrian events are held annually at Spruce Meadows. Auto races take place at Race City Speedway. Professional and amateur rodeos are held throughout the year.

Recreational Sports: Skiing at Canada Olympic Park, which has facilities for luge, bobsledding, ski jumping, snowboarding, and mountain biking. Ice skating at Olympic Plaza in downtown Calgary and many other locations, including the Olympic Oval, built for the 1988 Olympic Winter Games. Golfing on more than forty courses in and around Calgary. Climbing at the University of Calgary's Outdoor Recreation Centre. Soccer at the Calgary Soccer Centre, North America's largest indoor soccer facility.

More than 21,000 acres of parkland within the city limits offer canoeing, swimming, skating, and cross-country skiing. The rivers are bordered by 342 miles of pathways for biking, walking, jogging, and rollerblading.

The Devonian Gardens, a 2.5-acre enclosed tropical roof garden on top of a downtown shopping complex, has nearly a mile of paths, a sculpture garden, and a playground.

Banff National Park is slightly more than one hour's drive away from Calgary.

PUBLIC SAFETY Calgary showed an increase in crime rate of 2 percent between 2002 and 2003. In 2003, there were 1.1 homicides, 116 robberies, 841 break-ins, and 537 motor vehicle thefts (all figures per 100,000 population). Calgary's crime rate was lower than other large prairie province cities, but still much higher than the crime rates in Toronto, Quebec, and other major metropolitan areas in eastern Canada. (Toronto, for instance, had an increase in crime of 0.01 percent between 2002 and 2003, with a total of 5,304 criminal offenses per 100,000 population, compared with Calgary's 7,251 criminal offenses per 100,000 population.)

SNAPSHOT: SASKATCHEWAN

On September 1, 1905, Saskatchewan became a province of Canada, along with its neighbor Alberta. They were the eighth and ninth provinces to join Canada. The vast plains of southern Saskatchewan have become Canada's breadbasket, producing more than half of the wheat grown in Canada and exporting wheat to many parts of the world. Saskatchewan farmers also raise beef cattle and grow barley, canola, flaxseed, oats, and rye. The forested north has most of the province's rivers and lakes and some of the best hunting and fishing in North America.

In 1944, following years of depression and drought in the prairies, Saskatchewan elected the first socialist government in North America when it gave a landslide victory to Tommy Douglas and his Co-operative Commonwealth Federation (CCF) party. Douglas remained in power until 1961 and helped bring paved roads and sewage systems, among other things, to farmers, but he is remembered and revered today as the father of Canada's Medicare.

Universal health care, or "socialized medicine," began in Saskatchewan over the protest of the province's doctors, who went on strike for three weeks, but, by 1967, the year of Canada's Centennial, the entire country had universal health care. The provincial motto is "From Many People Strength!"

Another towering political figure of that period is also associated with Saskatchewan, where he lived for much of his life. As prime minister of Canada from 1957 to 1963, John G. Diefenbaker argued for a national bill of rights. In 1960, he saw this vision realized when Canada's first Bill of Rights was adopted.

Saskatchewan's human history begins with the First Nations who are known to have lived in this region for at least six thousand years. Wanuskewin Heritage Park near Saskatoon is on the site of a place used by the Plains

Indians for meeting and hunting. Trails in the three-hundred-acre park link a buffalo jump, medicine wheel, and seventeen other prehistoric sites used for thousands of years. Southwest of Saskatoon, near Herschel, petroglyphs at the Ancient Echoes Interpretive Centre depict prehistoric Aboriginal life.

Fur traders built trading posts on the Saskatchewan River, but it wasn't until the late 1850s that reports of the good farming land, in what would become central Saskatchewan, encouraged European settlers to move there. The earliest homesteaders went to the valley of the North Saskatchewan River. In 1876, the town of Battleford became the capital of the Northwest Territories.

As the railroad pushed into the west (it reached what is now Saskatchewan in 1882–1883), settlers began to arrive in large numbers. The first contingent of the North-West Mounted Police, dressed in red tunics to resemble British soldiers, rode ahead of the railroad to keep the peace. They became today's Royal Canadian Mounted Police and, in the summer of 2005, celebrated the 125th anniversary of their march west with a horseback ride along the Red Coat Trail (Highway 13).

The arrival of the railroad was threatening to the Métis, descended from the Plains Indians and French fur trappers, who feared losing their lands to settlers. Led by Louis Riel, the Métis had confronted the federal government over similar issues in Manitoba in 1869 and 1870. When the government did not respond to their petitions, the Métis set up a temporary government at Batoche, on the South Saskatchewan River, in March 1885. Negotiations with Ottawa broke down, and the ensuing North-West Rebellion was crushed by federal troops sent out from Ontario.

Settlement was rapid in the 1890s. Americans frequently went north from Minnesota and the Dakotas to what is now Manitoba and on to Saskatchewan and Alberta. From 1899 to 1904, almost one hundred and sixty thousand Americans moved into Canada. Many more followed in the years leading up to World War I. Many of them were, or became, farmers.

Grasslands National Park of Canada, one of two national parks in Saskatchewan, preserves some of the last untouched prairie in North America. The six-hundred-acre park, 233 miles southwest of Regina, is the only place in Canada where once numerous black-tailed prairie dogs can still be found in their natural habitat.

LOCATION Saskatchewan is in the middle of Canada's Prairie provinces (see map on pages xviii–xix). The province's southern border touches the states of Montana and North Dakota.

GEOGRAPHY 760 miles from north to south, Saskatchewan covers more than a quarter million square miles. It has four major river systems: the North and South Saskatchewan Rivers and the Assiniboine and Churchill Rivers.

The fertile southern half of the province is crisscrossed by neatly gridded roads. The forested, lake-studded northern regions are almost uninhabited. Many places are accessible only by air, including the Athabasca Sand Dunes Provincial Park, the most northerly expanse of sand dunes in the world.

Saskatchewan is the only Canadian province with entirely manmade boundaries. Like its neighbor, Alberta, it was carved out of the Northwest Territories.

CLIMATE Average January temperature, 0°F; average July temperature, 64°F. Saskatchewan has an average of 2,500 hours of sunshine annually. Average yearly precipitation, 15 inches.

PROVINCIAL CAPITAL Regina

POPULATION 992,995 (est., Oct. 2005). The population of Saskatchewan has decreased since 1991, when it was 1,002,686.

Most people live in the lower part of the province, more than half in cities and towns.

POPULATION DENSITY 1.04 people per square mile

ETHNIC DIVERSITY About 95 percent of the province's population was born in Canada, with most of the remainder born in the United States, Great Britain, Europe, and Asia. Germans, Ukrainians, and French are among the Europeans. Some 45,000 have First Nations roots. About half of them live on reserves.

Visible Minorities: The largest number of visible minorities in the province are in Regina and Saskatoon, where they represent 4.4 percent and 4.7 percent, respectively, of the population. Among the visible minorities, the largest number are Chinese.

HEALTH See Appendix, page 216, for details on Saskatchewan's health care coverage and how to apply for it.

In 2003–2004, Saskatchewan spent $2.527 billion on health care, with most of this money going for regional health services. Health accounts for 44 percent of provincial program spending. Despite the large sum of money invested in health care, the province has some special problems in health care delivery because of its size and the remoteness of many communities, and because in Saskatchewan, the proportion of people 65 and older is greater than in Canada as a whole (14.8 percent and 13.0 percent, respectively).

With significant budget overruns in previous years, the province has been forced to make some changes in health care delivery, including administrative cut-backs, facility closures or conversions, and reductions in long-term bed numbers.

At the same time, additional money is being spent to reduce the backlog of patients waiting for non-life-threatening surgery, to expand diagnostic testing capacity, and to provide more money for chemotherapy treatments and renal dialysis (among other measures).

Average Life Expectancy (2001):
Males, 76.2 years
Females, 81.8 years
Infant Mortality Rate: 5.5 per 1,000 live births (2001)

ECONOMY Chief industries: agriculture, mining, manufacturing, and tourism. Saskatchewan produces more than 54 percent of the wheat grown in Canada, 70 percent of the barley, and around half of the oats, rye, flaxseed, and canola—all major export crops. The province yields about 15 percent of Canada's petroleum. Large oil fields were discovered in Saskatchewan in the 1950s as well as uranium and potash. Potash mining has become a major industry since that time. Saskatchewan is one of the world's leading producers of potash, used in fertilizers. The southern part of Saskatchewan has deposits of salt and natural gas.

Thirty-six percent of the population works in community, business, and personal services while 16 percent works in wholesale and retail trade; 13 percent works in agriculture. The United States is Saskatchewan's largest trading partner. The province exported $6.9 billion worth of goods to the United States in 2002.

EARNINGS Average earnings of the population, 15 and over, for holders of a university certificate, diploma, or degree (2001): $40,279 (compared with $50,069 in Alberta, a neighboring Prairie province)

UNEMPLOYMENT RATE 4.9 percent (Dec. 2005). The national average for that month was 6.1 percent.

HOUSING Compared with other parts of Canada, housing continues to be affordable in Saskatchewan as measured by shelter costs relative to income.

(The neighboring province of Manitoba has seen sharp increases in housing affordability recently, while Saskatchewan's western neighbor, Alberta, is the most affordable province in Canada for homeowners. While home prices tend to be higher in Alberta than they are in Saskatchewan, incomes are also higher.) In Saskatchewan, homeowners spend, on average, 27.7 percent of their pretax income for mortgage payments, utilities, and property taxes.

In 2001, the Regina neighborhood of Wascana Plains and Southeast Saskatoon were the most expensive areas in the province. In Wascana Plains, the average dwelling cost $171,191, while in Southeast Saskatoon, it cost $179,469.

EDUCATION Saskatchewan children from age 7 to 15 must attend school. The province's public schools are governed by local boards of education. There are also parochial and Protestant schools and French-language schools, all of which receive provincial funds.

Regina is home to the University of Regina and its affiliated colleges, Campion and Luther. The First Nations University of Canada, an Indian-run college, is also affiliated with the University of Regina.

The University of Saskatchewan and St. Thomas More College are in Saskatoon.

The Saskatchewan Institute of Applied Science offers skills training at four campuses (Saskatoon, Regina, Moose Jaw, and Prince Albert). The province has nine regional colleges and Canada's largest interactive distance learning network.

TAXES Most items and services for sale in Canada are subject to a 7 percent goods and services tax (GST). In addition, Saskatchewan levies a 7 percent sales tax—the lowest of any province that charges this tax.

GOVERNMENT Premier: Lorne Calvert (New Democratic Party). Legislative Assembly is a one-chamber legislature with fifty-eight members.

Political Parties: The major political parties of Saskatchewan are the Liberal Party, the New Democratic Party (NDP), and the Saskatchewan Party. The NDP was formed in 1961 from the Co-operative Commonwealth Federation (CCF) and several labor unions. The Saskatchewan Party was established in 1997 by a number of Liberals and Progressive Conservatives. Several months later the Progressive Conservatives voted to be inactive.

TRANSPORTATION There are major rail centers in Moose Jaw, Regina, Saskatoon, and Weyburn and airports in Regina and Saskatoon, with several small airlines providing transportation to remote areas of the province. Paved two-lane highways link most of the major cities of southern Saskatchewan.

CARS AND AUTO INSURANCE Automobile insurance is compulsory and is automatically purchased from Saskatchewan Government Insurance (SGI) when a vehicle is licensed. SGI offers the lowest rates in Canada, with rates based solely on the applicant's personal driving record. A minimum of $200,000 third-party liability coverage is required. Collision and comprehensive insurance are voluntary. Additional insurance can be purchased from private brokers.

Cars purchased in the province are subject to the provincial sales tax (PST) on the market value above $3,000. Cars brought into Saskatchewan from another province must be registered within ninety days.

ATTITUDES TOWARD GAYS In 2004, as a result of a court case and a judicial decision, Saskatchewan recognized marriage between same-sex partners. Nevertheless, many people in the province remained opposed to the idea, including some marriage commissioners who threatened to resign if they were forced to officiate. Saskatchewan justice minister Frank Quennell said that the definition of marriage and who could marry was under federal jurisdiction and that while churches could choose to marry people or not, marriage commissioners derived their authority from the province and were obliged to follow its laws.

CULTURE Numerous First Nations powwows take place in Saskatchewan, especially during July and August. Typically, they're three-day events with dancing, drumming, crafts, and native food. Two of the major powwows are the Home Coming-Meewasin A Pekiwiwin Powwow in Wanuskewin (June) and Standing Buffalo Indian Powwow at Fort Qu'Appelle (August).

Regina and Saskatoon both have theatres, art galleries, and musical venues (see pages 115 and 118).

There are four Western Development Museums in Saskatchewan. The one in Moose Jaw (forty-four miles west of Regina) focuses on transportation and houses memorabilia of the Snowbirds, Canada's air demonstration team. In Saskatoon, the museum re-creates early twentieth-century life in western Canada. The museum in North Battleford depicts a 1920s farming village. The Yorkton Western Development Museum focuses on the immigrants who came to western Canada.

FESTIVALS Vesna in Saskatoon (Ukrainian music, food, and crafts, May); Cathedral Village Arts Festival in Regina (May); Saskatchewan Jazz Festival in Saskatoon, Regina, and North Battleford (June–July); Regina Mosaic Folk Festival (July); Saskatchewan Air Show in Moose Jaw (early July); Ness Creek Music Festival in Big River (July); Saskatchewan Festival of Words in Moose Jaw (July); Saskatoon Shakespeare on the Saskatchewan (July–August); Regina Dragon Boat Festival (September); Saskatoon Fall Fair (November); Prince Albert Winter Festival (February).

SPORTS More than 420 Saskatchewan players have played in the National Hockey League, more than any other province, American state, or European country. Winter: curling, ice hockey, snowmobiling, dogsledding, and snowshoeing. Summer: golfing on 250 courses, tennis, soccer, lacrosse, horseback riding, and canoeing. Saskatchewan has fifty-eight documented wilderness canoe routes. Stock car racing and horse racing are also popular.

Prince Albert National Park, 143 miles north of Saskatoon, offers hiking, cycling, and camping in almost one million acres of grassland, wooded parkland, and dense forest. In addition, there are 34 provincial parks and 101 regional parks.

PUBLIC SAFETY In 2003, and again in 2004, Saskatchewan had the highest crime rate of any province. Homicides increased from 27 in 2002 to 41 in 2003. There were 2,057 violent crimes and 6,613 property crimes in 2003, with slight decreases in 2004.

SNAPSHOT: Regina

Princess Louise, daughter of Queen Victoria and wife of the then governor-general of Canada, did not think much of Pile O' Bones as a name for a town, much less a territorial capital. In 1883, when the railroad reached this former Indian campsite on the prairie that was about to go on to greater things, the princess intervened. She named the new capital of the Northwest Territories in honor of her mother.

When Saskatchewan was created in 1905, Regina graduated from territorial to provincial capital. In 1912 a tornado destroyed the city. Today's downtown area was built in its aftermath.

Regina is the major financial and marketing center of Saskatchewan, second in size only to Saskatoon. It is a green oasis, planted with more than three hundred thousand trees, its tall buildings rising like a mirage out of the prairie.

Location has been a major reason for the city's growth. Regina is on the main rail line linking eastern and western Canada and is also on the Trans-

Canada Highway. An airport in Regina is served by AirCanada, Northwest, WestJet, and other airlines.

Besides being the capital of the province, Regina, in the heart of Canada's richest wheat-growing region, is the headquarters of the Saskatchewan Wheat Pool, one of the largest marketing co-ops in the world. The city is also home to the Royal Canadian Mounted Police Training Academy.

The city has a rich artistic and multicultural tradition. The stream that wandered through the Pile O' Bones campsite today goes through the center of Regina. Southeast of the downtown area, a dam created Wascana Lake, which is surrounded by Wascana Centre, one of the largest urban parks in North America. Within the park are the Legislative Building, the University of Regina, the Royal Saskatchewan Museum, and the Saskatchewan Centre of the Arts.

LOCATION
Latitude: 50°27' N; Longitude: 104°37' W; Elevation: 1,894.35 feet above sea level.

In south-central Saskatchewan, about 100 miles north of the United States border. Winnipeg, Manitoba, is 357 miles away, and Calgary, Alberta, 471 miles.

CLIMATE Average January temperature, 2°F; average July temperature, 67°F. The temperature is above freezing for only five months of the year. Average annual rainfall and snow amount to 14 inches, with most of it falling as summer rain. Regina is the sunniest capital in Canada, with an average of 2,365 hours of sunshine annually.

POPULATION (2001 census) 178,225; 192,800 in the metropolitan area

POPULATION DENSITY 580 per square mile

ETHNIC DIVERSITY 92 percent of the population is Canadian-born.
Visible Minorities account for 6 percent the population.

ECONOMY Regina has more than 250 manufacturing plants. Products include cement, fertilizer, and steel. The petroleum pipeline linking the Alberta oil fields with ports on the Great Lakes goes through Regina. The oil fields of southern Saskatchewan have helped make Regina, with its oil refineries, an important oil center.

The city's location on the cross-country highway and rail lines makes it a trade and distribution center for the region. Nearly 25 percent of its workers have jobs in wholesale and retail trades. Many others work for the city, provincial, and federal governments.

Major nonmanufacturing industries include insurance, financial, and data management services; telecommunications; film and video production; and call centers.

EARNINGS
Average earnings, working full year, full-time (2001): $41,147
Median family income (couples with families, 2001): $58,889

HOUSING The average cost of a house in Regina was $111,869 in 2004.
Average monthly rental for a three-bedroom apartment in 2003: $689.
In 2001, 41.1 percent of renters spent 30 percent or more of their household income on shelter. Only 10.7 percent of people who owned their housing spent 30 percent or more of their household income on shelter. Seventy percent of Regina's residents own their own homes.

EDUCATION Both the Regina Public School Board and the Regina Catholic School Board are supported by property taxes. There are 75 English-language elementary schools and 14 English-language high schools in the two systems. In addition, there is a French-language school, Monseigneur de Laval, that goes from kindergarten through grade 12.

More than half of each dollar that the city collects in property taxes goes to finance the school system and the public library. The Regina Public Library, which has nine branch locations, is rated among the top systems in Canada in terms of its facilities and per capita spending.

The University of Regina awards bachelor's, master's, and doctoral degrees. Undergraduate tuition for Saskatchewan students is $4,998 to $5,191. International students pay $8,653. Regina is also home to the First Nations University of Canada, which is affiliated with the University of Regina and is administered by the country's Native peoples. Campion and Luther colleges are also affiliated with the University of Regina.

The Saskatchewan Institute of Applied Science and Technology offers full-time and part-time training at its Wascana campus.

HEALTH The Regina Health District cares for residents of the city and supplies acute care to other communities in south Saskatchewan where comparable expertise and facilities are not available. The services provided to Regina residents include acute care, rehabilitation, long-term institutional support, mental health, home and community-based services, and public health services.

Serious budget overruns that began in 1998 and grew worse the following year led to a necessary overhaul of the district's offerings and administration, which are still going on. However, in addition to the need to balance the budget, the city and the province are committed to delivering good health care. In 2004, for instance, the province allocated $2 million to buy a new magnetic resonance imaging machine for Regina, which is enabling the city to do five to six thousand more MRIs annually.

Average Life Expectancy (2001):

Males, 76.4 years

Females, 81.9 years

MEDIA One daily newspaper, the *Leader-Post,* and nine radio stations (eight English-language stations and one in French). There are three English-language television stations and one in French.

URBAN TRANSIT Regina has a public bus system, but it offers limited service. During peak hours, Monday through Friday, buses run every twenty minutes, but during off-peak hours weekdays and all day on weekends, they run every thirty minutes or every hour. There is no bus service on holidays.

CULTURE The Saskatchewan Centre of the Arts, part of the Wascana Centre, includes the Centennial Theatre Concert Hall, where the Regina Symphony (Canada's longest continuously operating orchestra) plays, and Hanbidge Hall, a convention facility. The Globe Theatre, in the old City Hall, is home to Regina's professional acting company.

The MacKenzie Art Gallery in the T. C. Douglas Building houses paintings and sculpture, the Saskatchewan Science Centre's Kramer IMAX Theatre presents science and nature films, and the Royal Saskatchewan Museum features galleries devoted to First Nations, earth sciences, and life sciences, among others.

Two major agricultural exhibitions take place in the city each year: the Western Canada Farm Progress Show in June is a showcase of farming equipment and technology. The Canadian Western Agribition in November is the second largest cattle show in North America.

SPORTS Saskatchewan Roughriders (Canadian Football League).

Recreational Sports: Swimming (in an Olympic-sized pool), ice hockey, curling, tennis, lacrosse, cricket, rugby. A paved pathway almost five miles long runs along Wascana Creek and is used for biking, jogging, walking, and cross-country skiing. Six golf courses or clubs. Regina has what is said to be the best lawn-bowling green in Canada.

More than a hundred parks. The largest, Wascana Centre, has 2,300 acres.

PUBLIC SAFETY In 2003, Regina had one of the highest homicide rates in Canada. There were 5.1 homicides for every 100,000 people. In addition, there were 230 robberies, 2,071 break-ins, and 1,355 motor vehicle thefts per 100,000 residents. The total increase in crime between 2002 and 2003 was 4.8 percent.

Public buses in Regina, which, as noted above under Urban Transit, run on a limited schedule, have a "Safebus" program whereby anyone in distress can flag them down and get help.

SNAPSHOT: Saskatoon

Members of an Ontario Temperance Colonization Society settled Saskatoon on the banks of the South Saskatchewan River in 1883. While they did not succeed in keeping alcohol out of the community in the long run, they chose a good place for what would become Saskatchewan's largest city. The settlers saw that the river was ideal for ferry and steamboat traffic. In addition, like Regina, Saskatoon grew as a marketing and trade center with the arrival of the Canadian Pacific Railway.

The city gets its name from a wild berry the settlers found growing on the banks of the river. The Cree Indians called the berries "misaskquatoomina." Saskatoon pie is a traditional treat in Saskatchewan.

Saskatoon, which was incorporated as a city in 1906, straddles the river. Seven bridges connect the two parts of the city.

The depression and dust storms of the 1930s hit Saskatchewan hard, but potash mining north of Saskatoon in the '50s and new factories helped provide jobs in the city. In the mid-1970s, the Canadian government built an oilseed and grain development center at the University of Saskatchewan, which was founded in Saskatoon in 1907.

LOCATION Saskatoon is 161 miles northwest of Regina and just over 186 miles north of the U.S. border. Situated in the center of the major highways of the region. Near the western edge of the Saskatchewan Plain.

Latitude: 52°7' N; Longitude: 106°38' W; Elevation: around 310 feet above sea level.

CLIMATE Four distinct seasons, with dramatic changes in temperature and unpredictable weather. Average January temperature, −0.5°F; average July temperature, 65.1°F. On the coldest days of the year, however, the temperature can dip to −22°F, while in summer, temperatures can exceed 90°F. Average annual precipitation is 13.7 inches. Saskatoon is one of the sunniest cities in Saskatchewan.

POPULATION 232,807 in the metropolitan area (2004)
91% of the population is Canadian-born.
Visible Minorities: Constitute 6 percent of the population.

ECONOMY The University of Saskatchewan is the largest employer in Saskatoon. Leading industries are farming, food processing, and the development of computer systems and electronic equipment. Potash and uranium are mined north of the city.

UNEMPLOYMENT RATE 5.5 percent (2003)

EARNINGS
Average earnings, working full year, full-time (2001): $39,465
Median family income (couples with families, 2001): $60,815

HOUSING In 2004, the average price of a house in Saskatoon was $132,549.
In 2001, 62 percent of Saskatoon residents lived in owner-occupied dwellings for which their average monthly payments were $769. The average gross monthly payments for rented dwellings was $580.
In 2001, 38.5 percent of renters reported spending 30 percent or more of their household income on shelter. Only 11.5 percent of people who owned their housing spent 30 percent or more of their household income on shelter.

EDUCATION Saskatoon's public school system operates forty-four elementary and seven high schools, serving approximately 22,000 students. The school system provides special education support for those who need it; educational psychologists; transportation for special needs, French immersion, and out-of-area students; before- and after-school care programs; an outdoor school; work education programs; and a range of extracurricular activities.
More than 15,000 students are enrolled in the Saskatoon Catholic School system, which has thirty-four elementary schools, five high schools, and two associate schools. Kindergarten classes are offered in English, French, and Ukrainian.

With a main library and six branches, Saskatoon spends more on libraries than most other Canadian cities (U.S. $31.2 per capita).

The University of Saskatchewan has produced two Nobel laureates in chemistry and seventy Rhodes scholars. A research leader in agriculture, medicine, and sciences, it is establishing a worldwide reputation in biotechnology. The Canadian Light Source synchrotron allowing researchers to study atomic structures, one of Canada's largest science projects, is in a campus building the size of a football field.

Tuition for Saskatchewan students, $4,803 to $5,373. International students pay $11,811. Students are covered by provincial health insurance at no charge.

HEALTH Three hospitals and a number of long-term care facilities.

URBAN TRANSIT Public transportation includes buses and taxis. Bus fares are among the lowest in Canada, with unlimited usage monthly passes for adults cost $57, with discounts for seniors and students. Seniors (age 65 and over) can purchase annual passes that allow unlimited travel on all regular services of the transit system.

MEDIA The daily newspaper *The Saskatoon Star Phoenix* has a weekend edition called *The Saskatoon Sun*. Six radio stations.

CULTURE Five theatres and many open-air concerts in summer. The Saskatchewan Symphony and touring shows perform at Centennial Auditorium. Saskatchewan Place has rock concerts, trade shows, and hockey and other sporting events.

The Mendel Museum, the city's main art gallery, features local, national, and international artists. Other museums reflect the pioneer days of the province and the Ukrainian heritage of the area.

There are several museums on the University of Saskatchewan campus, including Natural Sciences, the Museum of Antiquities and the Diefenbaker Canada Centre, a museum, archive, gallery, and research center for Canadian studies.

SPORTS Saskatoon Blades (Western Hockey League). University of Saskatchewan teams include football and basketball. There's also stock car and horse racing.

Recreational Sports: Boating and fishing. The twenty-five-mile-long Meewasin Valley Trail runs along both banks of the South Saskatchewan River and is used by bikers and joggers.

PUBLIC SAFETY In 2003, Saskatoon had one of the highest crime rates in Canada, with a 16.5 percent increase from the previous year. Per 100,000 of the population, there were 3.3 homicides, 306 robberies, 2,083 break-ins, and 744 motor vehicle thefts.

SNAPSHOT: MANITOBA

Manitoba is located at Canada's geographic center. French fur traders worked the area during the seventeenth century, building forts and trading posts. Many mixed-blood descendants of these men, the French-speaking, Catholic Métis, were living in the Red River Valley in 1869 when the Hudson's Bay Company ended two hundred years of company "privileges" in what was then known as Rupert's Land and the Northwest Territories (today's provinces of Manitoba, Saskatchewan, and Alberta plus the Northwest Territories and Nunavut). Most of the land was returned to Great Britain. The new Dominion of Canada wanted to open it to settlers.

The Métis, led by the charismatic Louis Riel, fearing the loss of their culture and their lands, confronted government surveyors. The Métis captured Fort Garry (near the site that would become Winnipeg) and held several government officials prisoner during the winter of 1869.

By the summer of 1870, an agreement was negotiated giving the Métis some land and allowing Manitoba to become Canada's fifth province, which it did on July 15, 1870. But one of the prisoners held at Fort Garry had been tried for insubordination and executed by Riel's provisional government. Riel found it expedient to go to the United States. In 1874, he was elected to Parliament from a Manitoba district and managed to sneak into the House of Commons to be sworn in, but as a fugitive with a price on his head, he was not able to take his seat. His fellow MPs expelled him. Ten years later, Riel returned to Saskatchewan to lead the Métis in a second rebellion. Government troops defeated them in 1885. Riel was captured, tried as a traitor in Regina, and hanged.

Manitoba was open for settlement by 1877 and immigrants were encouraged by governmental ads for "free land." A $10 registration fee was all that settlers had to pay for 160 acres, so long as they built a house (of log or sod) and lived on or cultivated the land for the following three years.

Many small towns developed in the province, and Winnipeg exploded in a land boom in the early 1880s, when the Canadian Pacific Railway confirmed it would run its main line through the city. By 1887, Winnipeg had become the center of Canada's grain trade and the financial and commercial center of the plains.

In 1912, Manitoba's northern boundary was extended to the Hudson Bay; it is larger than Japan and twice the size of the U.K.

LOCATION Manitoba is the easternmost of the three Prairie provinces. (See map on pages xviii–xix.) North Dakota and Minnesota are to the south.

GEOGRAPHY Manitoba is rocky in the north, with forests and plains in the south. A small part of the extreme north is Arctic tundra. The province has four main land regions. They are (from northeast to southwest): the Hudson Bay Lowland, the Canadian Shield, the Manitoba Lowland, and the Saskatchewan Plain. Rivers and lakes cover almost a sixth of Manitoba's 250,946 square miles. Large rivers include the Red, the Saskatchewan, the Winnipeg, the Nelson, the Churchill, and the Hayes.

Churchill on Hudson Bay is the only seaport in the Prairie provinces. Manitoba has four hundred miles of coastline.

CLIMATE Average January temperature, −4°F; average July temperature, 66°F. Average annual precipitation, 20 inches.

PROVINCIAL CAPITAL Winnipeg

POPULATION 1,119,583 (2001 census); 1,178,109 (est., Oct. 2005)

POPULATION DENSITY Four people per square mile province-wide; however, 72 percent of the population lives in urban areas.

ETHNIC DIVERSITY Manitobans have British, German, Ukrainian, French, and Irish roots. There are also First Nations people, and people of Polish, Dutch, Filipino, Icelandic, Russian, Swedish, and Italian descent. The province has the largest Icelandic population outside of Iceland and the largest French-speaking population outside of Quebec.

Visible Minorities: 7.9 percent of the population. Filipinos are the largest visible minority group (30,490 in 2001), followed by South Asians (12,875), blacks (12,820), and Chinese (11,925).

Religious Affiliations:

Protestant	43 percent
Catholic	29 percent
None	19 percent

In 2001, there were 13,035 Jews living in the province, 5,745 Buddhists, and 5,095 Muslims.

HEALTH See Appendix, pages 212–213, for details on Manitoba's health care coverage and how to apply for it.

Average Life Expectancy (2001):

Males, 75.7 years

Females, 81.1 years

This is less than the Canadian national averages for that year of 77.0 years for men and 82.0 years for women.

Infant Mortality Rate: 7.0 per 1,000 live births (2001)

This was the highest rate in the Prairie provinces and one of the highest rates in Canada.

Health Care Satisfaction: In 2003, Manitobans responded to questions about the quality of the health care they had received in the previous twelve months (Statistics Canada, Canadian Community Health Survey, 2003). They were more satisfied with their family doctor care than Canadians as a whole but less satisfied with hospital care and with their overall health care services.

ECONOMY $30 billion economy. The province has a diversified economy, a highly skilled workforce, low business costs, and a strategic geographic location. Natural resources include its large supply of freshwater, fertile farmland, rich metal and mineral deposits, hydroelectric energy, forests, and abundant fish and wildlife.

Chief products are agricultural: pork, beef, wheat, canola, milk, oats, potatoes. Manufacturing: food products, transportation equipment, chemicals, clothing, electronics, and wood products. Mining: large deposits of nickel, copper, and zinc. Recently prospectors have been searching for diamonds.

Service industries, concentrated in Winnipeg, employ the greatest number of Manitobans. These include such activities as education, health care, legal services, tourism, and repair shops, as well as finance, insurance, and real estate. Wholesale and retail trade are also important employment sectors.

EARNINGS

Average earnings, working full year, full-time: $36,729 (2001)

Median family income (couples): $55,885 (2001)

Average earnings of the population, 15 and over, for holders of a university certificate, diploma, or degree (2001): $41,856 (compared with $50,069 in Alberta, also a Prairie province.)

UNEMPLOYMENT RATE 4.1 percent (Dec. 2005). One of the lowest unemployment rates in Canada. Only Alberta is were lower.

HOUSING The average cost of a house in Manitoba in 2003 was $97,670. A house in Winnipeg averaged $121,925 in 2004 and one in Brandon averaged $103,490. By 2005, however, Manitoba housing prices were going up, with the benchmark price of a detached bungalow up 10.8 percent from the year before. The average rent for a three-bedroom apartment in Winnipeg in 2003 was $777.

EDUCATION Most children begin school in Manitoba at age five. Instruction is in English, French, or both. There are also English-German, English-Hebrew, and English-Ukrainian schools and private schools.

Manitoba has universities in Brandon, Winnipeg, and St. Boniface.

Proportion of the population, age 25 to 54, with one or more postsecondary degrees: 50.6 percent (2001). (The overall proportion for Canada was 55.7 percent in 2001.)

TAXES Manitoba gets about 55 percent of its revenue from taxes, mostly on income and retail sales. Corporate income taxes and taxes on gasoline, liquor, and tobacco also provide income for the province. Also, there is some income from license fees. The provincial sales tax is 7 percent.

GOVERNMENT *Premier:* Gary Doer (New Democratic Party). Manitoba has a one house Legislative Assembly with fifty-seven members.

Political Parties: The major political parties of Manitoba are the Progressive Conservative Party, the New Democratic Party, and the Liberal Party.

Manitoba elects fourteen members to the federal House of Commons in Ottawa and sends six senators to the Canadian Senate.

LAWS In 1985 the Supreme Court of Canada ruled that Manitoba's laws, which were written only in English, had to be translated into French.

TRANSPORTATION The Winnipeg International Airport links Winnipeg to large cities in other provinces and to the United States, with numerous flights to hubs in Chicago, Denver, and Minneapolis. Smaller lines connect to Brandon, The Pas, Thompson, Churchill, and other communities. Main rail lines run east and west as well as north to Churchill. The Trans-Canada Highway runs through Winnipeg and Brandon. Major roads link Flin Flon and Winnipeg with North Dakota and Winnipeg with Thompson. Winnipeg is 145 miles from Grand Forks, North Dakota, and 434 miles from Minneapolis, Minnesota.

Greyhound Bus Lines offers scheduled and chartered service throughout Canada and the United States. Grey Goose and Beaver Bus Lines run within the province of Manitoba.

CARS AND AUTO INSURANCE Manitoba has the most comprehensive basic auto insurance coverage in Canada. Rates for the average family passenger vehicle are under $800 a year. Rates have remained stable in Manitoba while increasing on average 21 percent elsewhere in Canada (2003 statistic).

Basic insurance is compulsory. When a vehicle is registered in Manitoba, the registration and insurance fees are sold as a package called Autopac. Insurance rates vary depending on the type and year of a vehicle and the insured's driving record. People who live in rural communities pay less for insurance than those in urban areas.

Winter driving in Manitoba is difficult because of the cold temperatures and salt on the roads. Cars must have block heaters and defrosters.

A driver's license from another country is good in Manitoba for three months. Then the driver must obtain a Manitoba license by taking both a written test and a road test.

CULTURE The Royal Winnipeg Ballet and the Winnipeg Symphony Orchestra and other musical groups draw visitors to the capital city. The Manitoba Museum of Man is also a major attraction.

FESTIVALS Winnipeg International Children's Festival (June); Manitoba Summer Fair (held in Brandon, June); Jazz Winnipeg Festival (June); Dauphin Countryfest (June and July); Manitoba Highland Gathering (July); Winnipeg Folk Festival (July); National Ukrainian Festival in Dauphin (July); Winnipeg Fringe Theatre Festival (July); Manitoba Stampede and Exhibition (July); Manitoba Sunflower Festival (July); Steinbach Pioneer Days (July and August); Islendingadagurinn (Icelandic Festival of Manitoba) in Gimli (late July-early August); Folklorama in Winnipeg (late July-early August); Opaskwayak Indian Days (August); Morden Corn and Apple Festival (August); Winnipeg Festival du Voyageur (February).

SPORTS See listings under Winnipeg, page 127.

Recreational Sports: Skiing, snowboarding, fishing, boating, and horseback riding. More golf courses per capita than any other province in Canada.

Parks: Riding Mountain National Park (1,150 square miles). Also, twelve provincial parks. The International Peace Garden, commemorating the friendship between the United States and Canada, spills over the border with 1,451 acres in Canada and 888 acres in the United States. More than 150,000 flowers bloom each year in the formal gardens that mark the boundary.

PUBLIC SAFETY Criminal Code offenses in Manitoba increased by 10.7 percent between 2002 and 2003 and again by 1.5 percent between 2003 and 2004, the second highest crime rate of any province. In 2003, violent crimes were down 0.7 percent (1,626 per 100,000 population), but property crimes increased by 12.4 percent (per 100,000 population). In 2004, there were 1,602 violent crimes and 5,699 property crimes (per 100,000 in population).

SNAPSHOT: Winnipeg

"Winnipeg is like an island," says U.S.-born Kay Stone, who has lived there since 1969 and is now a Canadian citizen. "Our closest big city is Minneapolis, which is an eight-hour drive away. So Winnipeg is self-contained. Anything you want to find here, you can find on some level—amateur and professional."

More than half the population of Manitoba lives in Winnipeg, yet Kay says, "It's still small enough to be friendly."

Winnipeg, situated at the fork of the Assiniboine and Red Rivers, has long been a commercial center. In 1738, the French-Canadian fur trader Sieur de La Vérendrye built Fort Rouge on the site. During the early 1800s there was a rivalry between the fur trading companies in the area, which was settled in 1821 when the Hudson's Bay Company absorbed its competitor. Meanwhile, Scottish and Irish farmers settled along the Red River. In 1870, when Manitoba joined the Dominion of Canada, the Red River settlement was renamed Winnipeg and became the capital of the province. It was incorporated as a city in 1873.

The Canadian Pacific Railway came to Winnipeg in 1881 and the government's offer of free land drew settlers from the east and elsewhere in the following years. Many Europeans settled in the area in the early 1900s, and Winnipeg became western Canada's manufacturing center. In 1905 it was the fastest growing city of its size in North America and increasingly famous for its architecture.

However, what Winnipeg may be most famous for is a bear. In 1914, at the start of World War I, Winnipeg native and army captain Harry Colebourn took a black bear to England with him as a mascot for his regiment. When he was ordered to France, he gave the bear to the London Zoo. A. A. Milne's son Christopher was so enamored of it that his father wrote the Winnie the Pooh stories.

The depression of the 1930s, and beyond, in Canada hit Winnipeg hard, as it did the prairies in general. But World War II generated renewed demand for livestock, lumber, and other products of the province, boosting the city's economy once again. Another literary connection with the city was made in World War II. William Stephenson (the man called Intrepid) was the inspiration for Ian Fleming's 007 character. Stephenson was a Winnipeg native.

In 1972 Winnipeg and its suburbs were combined into a single municipality, which greatly increased the city's population. A new convention center opened in 1975 along with a system of enclosed walkways over the streets.

With the new century, the city is once again undergoing an architectural renaissance, and there is much excitement about its new Waterfront Drive.

LOCATION Winnipeg covers 180 square miles (the metropolitan area covers 1,603 square miles) at the junction of the Red and Assiniboine Rivers in southern Manitoba. It's about sixty miles north of the U.S. border and almost midway between the Atlantic and Pacific Oceans.

Latitude: 49°54' N; Longitude: 97°14' W; Elevation: 784 feet above sea level.

CLIMATE Average January temperature, −2°F; average July temperature, 68°F. Average annual precipitation, 21 inches. The amount of snow that falls on Winnipeg is not significantly more than what falls on Milwaukee, Wisconsin; however, the colder weather in Winnipeg keeps it from melting until well into springtime. The cold in Winnipeg is legendary. "Usually when it's below freezing in November, that's it until sometime in March," says Kay Stone. "The worst for me, I found, was not the cold, because you can just not go out if you want. It's the length of days. When it hits sunrise at nine and sunset at four thirty, I'm not happy. When the sun rises at three thirty or four A.M. and stays up until ten thirty or eleven at night, I like that."

POPULATION 619,544; metropolitan area: 671,274 (2001 census)

ETHNICITY More than 80 percent of Winnipeg's residents were born in Canada and are of mixed European ancestry. About one-third have British ancestors. The next largest group is French, then German and Ukrainian. There are also a large number of Métis.

ECONOMY The Winnipeg Commodity Exchange, Canada's only agricultural futures market, is in the city. The Canadian Wheat Board and many grain companies have their headquarters here, and the Winnipeg Stock Exchange helps make the city an important financial center. Major national trucking companies also have their headquarters in the city. It is the home of the Royal Canadian Mint.

UNEMPLOYMENT RATE 5.3 percent (2003)

EARNINGS
Average earnings, working full year, full-time (2001): $38,876
Median household income (all households, 2001): $43,385
Median family income (couples, 2001): $60,520

HOUSING The average price of a house in Winnipeg in 2004 was $121,925, but home prices are rising. Since 1999, the average Winnipeg house price has increased by 24.5 percent. "Still, it's an incredible bargain by Canadian standards, let alone by New York standards," says Dan Stone, who teaches history at the University of Winnipeg.
Average rent for a three-bedroom apartment (2003): $777.

EDUCATION There are 255 elementary and high schools in the city's public school system, which is funded chiefly through local property taxes. There are also 40 parochial and private schools in the city.
The University of Manitoba, founded in 1877, is the oldest university in western Canada. It has graduated more Rhodes scholars than any other university in western Canada. In-province tuition, $3,592; $6,847 for out-of-province students.
Also, there is the University of Winnipeg. In-province tuition, $3,130 to $3,554; out-of-province students, $5,407.
Other colleges in the city: Red River College, Red River Community College.

HEALTH
Average Life Expectancy (2001):
Males, 76.0 years
Females, 81.2 years

MEDIA Two daily newspapers, the *Winnipeg Sun* and the *Winnipeg Free Press*. The Canadian Broadcasting Corporation has three radio stations in the city, one of which is French. The CBC has two televisions stations and the Canadian Television Network has one. There is also a Manitoba Television Network cable channel.

Aboriginal Peoples Television Network, headquartered in Winnipeg, is the first national Aboriginal network in the world.

TRANSPORTATION The Trans-Canada Highway and Manitoba's main highways connect at Winnipeg. VIA Rail and a U.S. railway provide passenger service to and from the city. The Winnipeg International Airport is the only major international airport between Toronto and Calgary.

URBAN TRANSIT Winnipeg's bus service is called Winnipeg Transit. Children, students, seniors and people who buy tickets in advance of boarding get discounts.

A new bridge, the Esplanade Riel Bridge, links downtown Winnipeg with the French Quarter.

CULTURE The Royal Winnipeg Ballet is internationally recognized. The Winnipeg Art Gallery has the world's largest collection of contemporary Inuit art. The Manitoba Museum, considered one of the best in Canada, presents the history of the province. Other museums: Children's Museum, Jewish Heritage Centre of Western Canada, Ukrainian Cultural and Educational Centre, Costume Museum of Canada.

The Manitoba Theatre Centre is Canada's oldest English-language regional theatre, while Le Cercle Molière is Canada's oldest continuously operating French theatre.

There are many historic sites, including the Riel House that belonged to Louis Riel's mother. A museum explains the history of the Métis resistance and the Riel family. The Saint Boniface Museum, built in 1846–51, was the first convent and hospital in western Canada. Louis Riel is buried in the cemetery of the ruined St. Boniface Cathedral, which was destroyed by fire. Winnipeg has a rich architectural heritage, dating to the beginning of the nineteenth century.

Winnipeg's Folklorama (August) is North America's largest multicultural festival. Festival du Voyageur (February) is the largest winter festival in western Canada.

SPORTS Manitoba Moose (American Hockey League), Winnipeg Goldeyes (Northern League baseball) and Winnipeg Blue Bombers (Canadian Football League).

Assiniboine Park, the largest urban forest park in Canada, has a zoo and facilities for cross-country skiing, ice skating, and tobogganing. There are more than forty golf courses in the city or within an hour's drive.

PUBLIC SAFETY The Winnipeg crime rate jumped 10.5 percent between 2002 and 2003, with a total of 11,864 criminal code offenses (per 100,000 population). This was one of the highest crime rates in Canada.

In 2003, there were 2.6 homicides, 235 robberies, 1,162 break-ins, and 1,493 motor vehicle thefts (all figures, per 100,000 population).

SNAPSHOT: Brandon

For those who seek small-town warmth with big-city amenities, Brandon is a place to consider.

Manitoba's second largest city is much smaller than Winnipeg, but serves an extensive agricultural region. Two-thirds of Manitoba's farmland is within eighty-one miles of Brandon. It is the education, health, retail, service, and entertainment center of the region.

The Canadian Pacific Railway reached what is now Brandon in 1881, bringing an influx of new inhabitants. The railroad continues to be an important link between Brandon and eastern and western Canada.

A supply center for farmers who came to the area, Brandon is home to the Agriculture and Agri-Food Canada Research Centre, which researches land resource management in western Canada. Brandon University, with 3,224 students (a significant number in a city with a population of around 40,000 people), contributes to the city's cultural life. Dr. Wilfred Bigelow, inventor of the pacemaker, and Tommy Douglas, former Saskatchewan premier and father of Canada's Medicare, were Brandon graduates.

Brandon's Keystone Centre, with almost ten acres under one roof, is one of the largest convention, entertainment, agriculture, and recreation complexes in Canada. Concerts, fairs, national curling and figure skating competitions, wrestling, and other events take place there.

LOCATION On the Assiniboine River, west of Winnipeg along the Trans-Canada Highway and about two-thirds of the way from Winnipeg to the Saskatchewan border.

Latitude: 49°52' N; Longitude: 99°59' W; Elevation: 1,300 feet above sea level.

CLIMATE Mean January temperature, −4°F. Mean July temperature, 66°F. Average of 46 inches of snow annually.

POPULATION 39,716 (2001 census); 43,000 (est., 2004).

ETHNIC DIVERSITY

Visible Minorities: Only 2.4 percent of Brandon's population belongs to a visible minority group, with the largest numbers Chinese, black, and South Asian.

Religious Affiliations:

Protestant	53 percent
None	22 percent
Catholic	20 percent

HEALTH The Brandon Regional Health Centre provides care to a large part of southwestern Manitoba. Brandon has a wide array of dental clinics, chiropractors, and other specialized health care professionals.

ECONOMY Brandon is a service and distribution center for surrounding farm areas. Manufacturing and service industries are the fastest growing sectors of the Brandon economy. Most residents work in health care, education, retail, and government jobs. Food processing and chemical and fertilizer manufacturing are also large employment sectors.

EARNINGS

Average annual earnings for full-time workers (2001): $34,588

Median family income (couples, 2001): $55,649

HOUSING The average price of a house in 2004 was $103,490

Average gross monthly payment for rented dwellings (2001): $543

Average monthly payments for owner-occupied dwellings (2001): $677

EDUCATION The Brandon School Division has around 7,500 students enrolled in twenty-three schools that go from elementary through senior high school.

Brandon University, founded in 1899, is internationally known for its music faculty. Almost a third of the students are of Aboriginal origin. Tuition is $3,119 for Manitoba students; $5,249–$5,779 for international students.

Also in Brandon, Assiniboine Community College and technical schools.

URBAN TRANSIT The Brandon Transit bus system serves the city but notes that "schedule times may vary due to the road, weather, or traffic conditions." Discounts for seniors, students, and multiple-use passes.

CULTURE The Art Gallery of Southern Manitoba emphasizes contemporary Manitoban art in a regional, national, and international collection. Offers art classes and lectures.

The Western Manitoba Centennial Auditorium is a venue for ballet, classical concerts, festivals, music recitals, and plays.

Musical performances at Brandon University. Also in Brandon are the B.J. Hales Museum of Natural History; the Brandon Allied Arts Center; the Commonwealth Air Training Plan Museum.

SPORTS The city of Brandon's Sportsplex houses racquetball courts, an ice arena, an Olympic-sized swimming pool with a 104-foot water slide, and a track and field facility. The Recreation and Sports Centre has a golf course, tennis courts, curling ice, tobogganing, cross-country ski trails, and a snowmobiling staging area. In and near Brandon, mountain biking, canoeing, kayaking, curling, tobogganing facilities, and snowmobiling are available as well as six local golf courses.

Parks: The Assiniboine Riverbank Trail system runs along more than ten miles of the river. The Eleanor Kidd Gardens in the river corridor have a performance plaza and seating area for community arts performances set among annual and perennial flower beds.

PUBLIC SAFETY There were fewer violent crimes and property crimes in Brandon in 2004 than there were in 2003. The rate of violent crimes decreased by 6 percent, while the rate of property crimes decreased by 24 percent, from 4,130 in 2003 to 3,148 in 2004.

SNAPSHOT: ONTARIO

U.S. companies have invested heavily in Ontario, both with money for new businesses and by establishing branches of existing U.S. corporations. This investment has fostered the province's industrial preeminence within Canada.

Ontario is Canada's most populous province and the heart of the Canadian economy. Most Ontarians live in what is called the "Golden Horseshoe," which extends from the western end of Lake Ontario through Toronto and Hamilton to the Niagara River.

In 2004, 45.6 percent of Ontarians lived in the Greater Toronto region.

In a report prepared in February 2005, Ontario's Ministry of Finance estimated that the population of the province would increase by 1.6 million people between 2004 and 2014, with 1.1 million of that increase being due to migration into the province—and the bulk of that due to foreign immigration.

Around half of Canada's manufactured goods are produced in Ontario, which has ready access to raw materials, a skilled workforce, inexpensive hydroelectric power, and proximity to export markets in the United States. The close economic connection between the United States and Ontario is somewhat ironic considering past differences. In the aftermath of the American Revolution, thousands of United Empire Loyalists fled the United States for Canada. Many of them settled in what is now Ontario, where they were given generous land grants.

The Constitutional Act of 1791 created Upper Canada (part of present-day Ontario) and Lower Canada (now Quebec Province). The first capital of Upper Canada was Newark (renamed Niagara-on-the-Lake), but it was moved to York (now called Toronto) out of fear of an American invasion. The United States finally did invade during the War of 1812, burning the parliament buildings of Upper Canada in 1813.

The American Civil War again caused alarm on the Canadian side of the border. As that war drew to a close, another American invasion seemed possible or even probable. The British North America Act of 1867, which created the Dominion of Canada, was a partial result. Britain didn't want the expense of defending the Canadian colonies, and so set them partially adrift.

Canada East was renamed Quebec, and Canada West became Ontario, joining in confederation with Nova Scotia and New Brunswick to create the nucleus of a new country.

Over the years, the United States has been a catalyst—sometimes an enemy and at other times an ally. Ontario has experienced both aspects of this mercurial relationship.

LOCATION Southernmost province of Canada. (See map on pages xviii–xix.) Ontario borders Minnesota and also has almost contiguous borders with New York State in the east and Michigan in the south, separated only by narrow bodies of water. (Windsor, Ontario, is on the south side of the Detroit River, just across from Detroit, with a suspension bridge and tunnel connecting the two cities. Niagara Falls are partly in Ontario, and partly in New York State.) Point Pelee, in southern Ontario, is at the same latitude as northern California.

GEOGRAPHY Second largest province in area (415,598 square miles). Lakes and rivers make up one-sixth of the province (around 250,000 lakes with an area of around 70,000 square miles). Forests cover almost three-quarters of Ontario.

From east to west, the province is 1,012 miles long and from north to south, 1,047 miles—about the same distance as from New York City to Omaha, Nebraska. The prairie was shaped by glaciers.

The St. Lawrence Seaway connects Lake Superior on part of Ontario's southern flank with the Atlantic Ocean.

The three main geographic areas of the province are the mineral-rich Canadian Shield, which runs through the center; the swampy and, in some cases, permanently frozen, Hudson Bay Lowlands to the north; and the Great Lakes–St. Lawrence Lowlands in the south. This is the region where most of the population lives and the center of most agriculture and industry. Except for a high ridge of limestone cliffs running 250 miles north of Niagara Falls (the Niagara Escarpment), the Great Lakes Lowlands are rolling plains that were once thickly forested.

The highest point in the province is the Ishpatina Ridge (2,274 feet above sea level) in the Canadian Shield.

CLIMATE The Great Lakes Lowlands tend to have a more moderate climate than the north (though it can get very cold in Toronto in winter and even in early spring). In the southernmost part of the province, at Point Pelee, the January mean temperature is 24°F (compared with −12°F at Hudson Bay). The average July temperature at Point Pelee is 74°F; at Hudson Bay, it is about 57°F. Precipitation in southern Ontario is 30 inches a year.

PROVINCIAL CAPITAL Toronto

POPULATION 12,589,823 (est., Oct. 2005)

POPULATION DENSITY 35 people per square mile (2005). However, 90 percent of the population lives in less than 10 percent of the land area, with much of the Canadian Shield unoccupied.

MAJOR CITIES In addition to Toronto and Ottawa, Ontario's largest cities are Mississauga, Hamilton, London, Windsor, and Kitchener (twinned with Waterloo, though they are separate municipalities). Most are manufacturing and industrial centers. Hamilton is an important port on Lake Ontario and Canada's steel capital. Kitchener was first settled by Swiss-German Mennonites from Pennsylvania around 1800 and still has many German-speaking residents. In the more northern part of the province, Thunder Bay, on Lake Superior, is the world's largest freshwater port, with a mix of forty-two nationalities and the largest Finnish population outside of Finland.

ETHNIC DIVERSITY Immigrants were 26.8 percent of the population in 2001. (Many live in Toronto, where they were 49.4 percent of the population.)

Visible Minorities: More than half of the visible minorities in Canada live in Ontario. Visible minorities were 19.1 percent of the population in 2001. Within the visible minority group of 2.2 million people in 2001, the breakdown was:

South Asians	26 percent
Chinese	22 percent
Blacks	19 percent

Religious Affiliations:

Protestant	35 percent
Catholic	35 percent
None	16 percent
Muslim	3 percent

LANGUAGES English is the primary language of Ontario, with French the second language; however, because of the highly diversified immigrant population, more than fifty languages are widely used and understood, which has been helpful to the province in pursuing international business.

HEALTH See Appendix, pages 214–215, for details on Ontario's health care coverage and how to apply for it.

In June 2005, the provincial government announced new funding of at least $1.75 billion to Ontario hospitals over a three-year period beginning in 2005. The money will be used for operating expenses.

There are more than two hundred hospitals in the province, ranging from community emergency facilities to specialty and research hospitals.

Health Care Satisfaction: In 2003, Ontarians responded to questions about the quality of the health care they had received in the previous twelve months (Statistics Canada, Canadian Community Health Survey, 2003). They were less satisfied with their hospital and family physician care than Canadians as a whole.

Average Life Expectancy (2001):
Males, 75.4 years
Females, 79.5 years
Infant Mortality Rate: 5.4 per 1,000 live births (2001)

ECONOMY Ontario has the largest and most diversified economy of any province, with the highest income per capita. Agriculture, mining, oil and gas extraction, forestry, manufacturing, and tourism are among the important sectors of the Ontario economy. The province owns 88 percent of Ontario's forests and issues licenses for timber harvesting, recreation, and tourism uses. Ontario's mines are more productive than those anywhere else in Canada, employing around fifty thousand people. The mines yield gold, nickel, copper, zinc, cobalt, silver, and platinum.

Approximately one-quarter of Ontario's workforce is employed in government, education, health care, the arts, culture, and recreation. Slightly less than a quarter works in manufacturing and construction. The manufacture of motor vehicles and parts for motor vehicles is a huge industry in the province. Ontario's chief exports are motor vehicles and parts, machinery and mechanical appliances, electrical machinery, nonferrous metals and allied products, and pulp and paper.

Around 25 percent of Canada's farms are in Ontario, primarily producing corn, lamb, fruit, soybeans, nursery plants and flowers, poultry, eggs, and vegetables. Beef cattle, hogs, winter wheat, and dairy are other important products. Agricultural employment was up in May 2005, as were jobs in mining, and oil and gas extraction. The number of manufacturing jobs continued to decline.

EARNINGS
Average earnings, working full year, full-time: $47,299 (2001)
Median family income (couples): $66,476 (2001)
Average earnings of the population, 15 and over, for holders of a university certificate, diploma, or degree (2001): $53,525 (This was higher than the Canadian national average of $48,648.)

UNEMPLOYMENT RATE 5.5 percent (Dec. 2005). (The national average for that month was 6.1 percent.)

HOUSING Province-wide, 41.9 percent of renters spent 30 percent or more of their income on shelter in 2001. Among homeowners, that figure was 17.3 percent. More rental apartments were available in Ontario in 2004 than in 2003.
Average value of dwelling: $199,884 (2001)
Average gross monthly payments for renters: $753 (2001)
Average monthly payments for owner-occupied dwellings: $964 (2001)

EDUCATION Under the British North America Act of 1867, some religious schools were guaranteed public support if they had received it prior to the passage of the act. As one of the original four provinces in Confederation, Ontario qualifies. Hence it has two publicly funded school systems—one public and the other Roman Catholic. Schools in both systems are supervised by the provincial Ministry of Education.

School attendance is compulsory between the ages of 6 and 16. Ontario parents who choose to send their children to private schools receive a tax credit which, in 2006, will be 50 percent of tuition up to a maximum of $3,500 per child.

Proportion of the population, aged 25 to 54, with one or more postsecondary degrees: 57.3 percent (2001). (The overall proportion for Canada was 55.7 percent in 2001.)

Universities and Colleges: University of Toronto, Queens University in Kingston, McMaster in Hamilton, University of Waterloo in Waterloo, Brock University in St. Catharines, Carleton University in Ottawa, Lakehead University in Thunder Bay, Laurentian University in Sudbury, Nipissing University in North Bay, Ontario College of Art and Design in Toronto, Royal Military College in Kingston, Ryerson University in Toronto, Trent University in Peterborough, University of Guelph in Guelph, University of Ontario Institute of Technology in Oshawa, University of Ottawa, University of Western Ontario in London, University of Windsor in Windsor, Wilfrid Laurier University in Waterloo, and York University in North York.

GOVERNMENT *Premier*: Dalton McGuinty (Liberal Party). The Legislative Assembly has 106 members. Ontario's main political parties are the Liberal Party, the Progressive Conservative Party, and the New Democratic Party.

The province elects 106 members to the federal House of Commons. The federal government appoints 24 members to the Senate.

LAWS Provincial laws are posted on-line at www.e-laws.gov.on.ca within two business days of being enacted or amended.

TRANSPORTATION There are sixty airports throughout the province, including the Lester B. Pearson Airport in Toronto, which is Canada's busiest airport. The province's extensive railway system (8,296 miles) carries both passengers and freight. VIA Rail runs intercity rail service. Within the Golden Horseshoe, GO Transit provides commuter trains and buses. There are 45,000 miles of paved roads and highways within the province.

CARS AND AUTO INSURANCE Automobile insurance is compulsory and is regulated by the Financial Services Commission of Ontario, an arm's-length agency of the Ministry of Finance.

Between the first quarter of 2002 and the first quarter of 2003, auto insurance rates went up an average of 19.09 percent. Complaints about the rising cost caused the provincial government to institute cost-containment reforms, with the savings passed on to consumers. At the end of the first quarter of 2005, rates were 7.46 percent lower than they had been during the first quarter of 2004.

ATTITUDES TOWARD GAYS Same-sex marriage has been legal in Ontario since June 2003. In February 2005, the provincial legislature passed a bill that changed the definition of marriage to accommodate same-sex marriage. The lesbian, gay, bisexual, and transgendered population of Toronto is the third largest in North America. Gay Pride is celebrated in August with a major festival.

CULTURE Toronto and Ottawa are flourishing arts centers.

The Stratford Festival in Stratford, Ontario, offers renowned productions of Shakespeare's plays as well as plays by other authors, concerts, and musicals between May and November. The equally renowned Shaw Festival in Niagara-on-the-Lake features the work of George Bernard Shaw and his contemporaries from April through November.

The government-backed Ontario Arts Council spends around $25 million annually to fund individual artists and art groups. Film and documentary production are supported by the Ontario Film Development Corporation.

FESTIVALS More than three thousand annual festivals and events in Ontario. Among them are maple syrup festivals in Elmira, Paisley, Vanier, Delta, and Perth, all in April; the Valley Festival in Pembroke—classical music concerts (April to September); Folklore Festival in Thunder Bay (April); Guelph Spring Festival—classical music (April–May); Festival of Birds in Leamington (May); Thousand Islands Jazz Festival in Brockville (May); Toronto Distillery District Jazz Festival (May); Canadian Tulip Festival in Ottawa (May); Waterloo County and Area Quilt Festival (May); Dundas Buskerfest (June); Blind River's White Pine Cultural Festival (June–August); Ottawa International Jazz Festival (June and July); Toronto International Carnival (late July); Owen Sound Celtic Festival (September); Toronto Cabbagetown Festival (September); Kitchener-Waterloo Oktoberfest (October); Niagara Icewine Festival (January).

SPORTS For professional sports teams see the Toronto and Ottawa listings.

Recreational Sports: Canoeing, sailing, kayaking, cricket, golf, tennis, hockey, horseback riding, cross-country and downhill skiing, dogsledding.

Parks: Five National Parks: Bruce Peninsula, at the northern end of the Niagara Escarpment and the largest remaining area of natural habitat in southern Ontario; Georgian Bay Islands, in Lake Huron, accessible only by boat, with hiking and camping; Point Pelee, thirty miles southeast of Windsor, known as a viewing point for bird and monarch butterfly migrations; Pukaskwa, the wild northern shore of Lake Superior and the only wilderness national park in Ontario; and St. Lawrence Islands in the Thousand Islands of Lake Ontario—the tops of a submerged mountain chain—and Canada's smallest national park.

There are 272 provincial parks, many of them open year-round. The largest and oldest is Algonquin Park, 170 miles north of Toronto.

PUBLIC SAFETY Counterfeiting incidents nearly doubled in Ontario in 2003; however, the overall crime rate remained virtually unchanged between 2002 and 2003. Between 2003 and 2004, total criminal code offenses dropped 5.1 percent. In 2003, Ontario reported the lowest crime rate of any province for the first time since statistics began to be collected in 1962 a trend that continued in 2004. In 2003, incidents of impaired driving decreased by 9 percent from their 2002 levels.

In 2003, there were 784 reports of violent crime in Ontario per 100,000 population, down 5.4 percent from 2002. There were 3,241 property crimes per 100,000 population, up by 0.2 percent. In 2004, there were 755 violent crimes and 3,013 property crimes per 100,000 in population.

SNAPSHOT: Toronto

At 1815 feet, Toronto's landmark CN Tower is the tallest freestanding structure in the world. Riding its exterior glass elevators up to the observation deck at 1,136 feet takes a strong stomach, but for those below, the tower serves as an excellent point of reference. It's difficult to get lost in the core of Toronto. The tower is south, and beyond it is Lake Ontario. Take it from there.

Between the SARS epidemic, which crippled Toronto's tourism and convention business, and painful cuts to social services, Toronto went through a bad patch in the first years of the twenty-first century but is now trying to reposition itself as one of the great cities of North America.

Several important cultural structures are being enlarged, including the Royal Ontario Museum, the Art Gallery of Ontario, the Royal Conservatory of Music, and the Gardiner Museum of Ceramic Art. Toronto's first opera house, the Four Seasons Performing Arts Centre, is under construction.

Toronto is the most ethnically diverse city in Canada, with colorful Chinese, Irish, Greek, Italian, Ukrainian, and Polish neighborhoods (and many more). For foodies, the Kensington and St. Lawrence markets are an exciting reflection of the city's diversity. One of the repeated lessons of history has been that crosscultural fertilization produces strong new ideas—and Toronto certainly has a multiethnic population second to none. Out of this "mosaic," as Canadians prefer to call it (differentiating themselves from the American "melting pot"), may come great things.

LOCATION On Lake Ontario, the easternmost of the Great Lakes. One and a half hours by air from New York City, Philadelphia, Hartford, Boston, and Chicago. It's around seventy-five miles to Niagara Falls and the New York State border, and ninety-six miles to Buffalo, New York.

Latitude: 43°41' N; Longitude: 79°38' W; Elevation: 567 feet above sea level.

CLIMATE Average January temperatures, 18°F to 30°F; average July temperatures, 63°F to 81°F. An average of three inches of rain falls in July. Average annual precipitation is 30.1 inches.

Spring, summer, and fall are pleasant in Toronto. Winter is not. It can be bitterly cold. Toronto has a seven-mile-long underground city with places to eat, shops, banks, medical offices, and theatres because there are times when many people would prefer not to be outside.

POPULATION (2001 census) 2,481,494 (city of Toronto); 4,682,897 (metropolitan area)

ETHNIC DIVERSITY Toronto residents come from almost two hundred different countries. More than half the city's population was born outside of Canada, with large numbers from China, Italy, the Philippines, India, the United Kingdom, Jamaica, Hong Kong, and Sri Lanka. Between 70,000 and 90,000 immigrants and refugees settle in Toronto every year.

Mass is said in thirty-five different languages in the Roman Catholic Archdiocese of Toronto.

Visible Minorities:

Chinese	25 percent
South Asian	25 percent
Black	20 percent
Other	30 percent

Religious Affiliations:

Catholic	34 percent
Protestant	24 percent
Hindu	4 percent
Christian Orthodox	4 percent

Half of Canada's Jewish population lives in Toronto (164,510 people). The city also has 254,115 Muslims and 90,590 Sikhs (all figures for the Toronto metropolitan area).

ECONOMY Government, health care, financial services, education, and a broad array of manufacturing and service industries are major employers. Growing industries include information and communications technologies.

UNEMPLOYMENT RATE (2003) 8.7 percent (city of Toronto)

EARNINGS

Average annual earnings for full-time workers (2001): $51,112 (Toronto metropolitan area)

Median family income (couples, 2001): $70,079 (Toronto metropolitan area)

HOUSING

Average price of a house (2004): $315,266

Average rent for a two-bedroom apartment (2004): $1,052 (the highest average monthly rent in Canada)

Average gross monthly payments for rented dwellings (2001): $870 (Toronto metropolitan area)

Average gross monthly payments for owner-occupied dwellings (2001): $1,171 (Toronto metropolitan area)

In Toronto, 42.7 percent of renters spent 30 percent or more of their income on shelter in 2001. Among homeowners, that figure was 22.2 percent.

In December 2004, the vacancy rate for apartment rentals in Toronto was 4.3 percent.

EDUCATION Toronto has 560 public schools, 222 Catholic schools, and 377 private schools.

The University of Toronto has 56,979 full-time students and 11,353 part-time students. Tuition is $4,954 for Ontario residents and $12,045 for international students. Ryerson University has 23,439 students, with 11,213 full-time undergraduates and 12,068 part-time students. York University has 39,578 students, with 27,761 undergraduates.

Toronto colleges include Centennial, George Brown College, Humber College, Seneca College, and Sheridan College. They offer both a full-time undergraduate curriculum and part-time continuing education. Total enrollment for these colleges is around 223,000 students (2002 figures).

In 2001, 26 percent of Toronto's population held a university degree (compared with 15.8 percent for Canada as a whole).

Toronto has the largest public library system in Canada, with ninety-eight branches. The University of Toronto has the largest academic library in the country.

HEALTH

Average Life Expectancy (2001):
Males, 78.2 years
Females, 83.3 years

MEDIA *The Toronto Star* is the largest newspaper in Canada. The nationally distributed *Globe and Mail* and *National Post* are headquartered in Toronto. *The Toronto Sun* is another major daily newspaper. There are dozens of weekly and monthly foreign-language newspapers, as well as free newspapers with entertainment listings. Biweekly papers serve the gay and lesbian communities. A number of regional and national TV and radio networks have head offices in Toronto including the CTV network, CanWest Global, and CityTV. There are many foreign-language cable channels. The Ontario provincial government runs an educational TV network from Toronto.

TRANSPORTATION Lester B. Pearson International Airport is Canada's busiest, with around a thousand flights daily to other parts of Canada, the United States, and elsewhere in the world. City Centre Airport on the Toronto Islands serves small commuter planes. Buses connect Toronto with many parts of Canada and the United States. (From Detroit, the trip takes five hours; from Buffalo, it's two to three hours.) VIA Rail connects Toronto to most major cities in Canada. Amtrak runs daily trains to Toronto from Chicago and New York City.

URBAN TRANSIT Toronto has both a subway system and a bus and streetcar system. Unlimited-ride one-day passes and multiple-trip passes offer substantial discounts.

CULTURE The City of Toronto gives $11 million annually in grants to the arts. It operates six community art centers.

Among major museums are the Royal Ontario Museum (art, archaeology, and science); the Ontario Science Centre; Art Gallery of Ontario; Bata Shoe Museum; George R. Gardiner Museum of Ceramic Art.

Toronto ranks as the third largest theatre center in the English-speaking world, after New York and London, with two hundred professional theatre and dance companies.

The Toronto Symphony Orchestra and the Toronto Mendelssohn Choir (founded in 1894) perform at Roy Thomson Hall. The Elgin and Winter Garden Theatres, former vaudeville houses restored to early twentieth-century splendor, are venues for plays, concerts, and musicals. The Hummingbird Centre for the Performing Arts is the home of the Canadian Opera Company and the National Ballet of Canada. (They will be moving to the Four Seasons Performing Arts Centre, now under construction.) Venerable Massey Hall has near-perfect acoustics and is used for concerts. Broadway musicals play the Canon Theatre, the Princess of Wales, and the Royal Alexandra.

The Distillery District, a complex of forty-four buildings on thirteen acres in downtown Toronto, houses artists, art galleries, boutique shops, restaurants, performance spaces, and a theatre school.

PARKS Toronto has 18,147 acres of parkland divided among more than 1,450 parks. Birds, fish, wildlife, and rare plants live in 399-acre High Park, part of which is still in its natural state. The park also has historic buildings, playgrounds, sports fields, an outdoor ice rink, landscaped gardens, a zoo, a museum, and an open-air theatre. More than one million people use the park each year.

The Toronto Islands in Lake Ontario have more than 550 acres of parkland.

The paved Martin Goodman trail runs for almost fourteen miles between The Beaches and the Humber River and is used by cyclists, in-line skaters, and joggers.

SPORTS *Professional Sports Teams:* Toronto Maple Leafs (National Hockey League), Toronto Blue Jays (American League, baseball), Toronto Argonauts (Canadian Football League), Toronto Rock (National Lacrosse League), Toronto Raptors (National Basketball Association), Toronto Lynx (United Soccer League).

Skydome, where the Blue Jays play, is a city landmark with an eight-acre retractable roof. (The stadium is also used for rock concerts, conventions, and trade shows as well as for basketball, football, tennis, and track.)

Golf: Hundreds of courses in and around Toronto, including the Glen Abbey, where the Canadian Open is played.

The Woodbine Racetrack is Canada's leading thoroughbred racing venue.

PUBLIC SAFETY In 2003, Toronto had one of the lowest crime rates of any major city in Canada. There were 1.9 homicides, 112 robberies, 541 break-ins, and 372 motor vehicle thefts, for a total of 5,304 criminal code offenses per 100,000 people. The increase in crime between 2002 and 2003 was a statistically negligible 0.1 percent.

SNAPSHOT: Ottawa

Tulips are to Ottawa what cherry blossoms are to Washington, D.C., cause for an annual spring festival and parades, a major tourist attraction, and a gift from another country. Ottawa's tulips are from the Netherlands to thank Canada for protecting the Dutch royal family, who fled there during World War II. They also recognize Canada's important role in freeing the Netherlands from German occupation.

Ottawa is the nation's capital and has a tight inner-city area easily negotiated on foot. Canada's Parliament buildings dominate the skyline, their somber Gothic stone and tall spires evoking European capital buildings of the nineteenth century. The Peace Tower, honoring Canadian war dead, guards the entrance to the Parliament buildings and a Centennial Flame burns in front as a symbol of Canada's nationhood.

Nearby are Canada's Supreme Court and National Arts Centre. The Centre, surrounded with sculpture and flower gardens, is Ottawa's main concert and theatre hall. A short ride away on Sussex Drive is Rideau Hall, or Government House, which is also surrounded by attractive gardens. This is the residence of the governor-general, the British Crown's representative in Canada.

Lt. Col. John By, of the British Royal Engineers, supervised the construction of the Rideau Canal system, which linked the Ottawa River with Lake Ontario in the nineteenth century. Unfortunately, there were cost overruns (even then!), and the canal took longer to build than the government thought it should. By was sent home to England, unappreciated, unemployed, and penniless. Nevertheless, the town that developed around his construction site was called Bytown until 1855, when the name was changed to Ottawa—a name that derives from the Outaouak, Algonquin Indians who settled there and traded furs with the British. Today the 125-mile-long canal system is a popular boating area and, in winter, allows many Ottawans to ice-skate to work.

In 1858 Queen Victoria chose Ottawa over Montreal, Toronto, Kingston, and Quebec City to be the capital of a united Upper and Lower Canada. (At the time, one dissident quipped that it was "a sub-Arctic village converted by Royal Mandate into a cock-fighting pit.") Upper Canada, now called Ontario, and Lower Canada, now Quebec Province, joined New Brunswick and Nova Scotia nine years later on July 1, 1867, to become the Canadian Confederation.

Ottawa is a government town and the embassies and their staffers from around the world make it a cosmopolitan city. Bordering on Quebec Province, it is also a bicultural city, with government phones answered in French and English. While the government is the largest employer in Ottawa, many residents also work in high-tech industries, in health care, and in tourism. High-tech was hit hard in 2000, but there are signs of a recovery.

In 2001, Ottawa absorbed twelve surrounding municipalities to become a single city under one mayor and one city manager.

LOCATION On the south bank of the Ottawa River, where it meets the Rideau and Gatineau Rivers. The Ottawa River marks the boundary between Ontario and Quebec Provinces. The capital region actually lies in both, with the city of Ottawa on one side of the river and the city of Gatineau on the Quebec side.

Latitude: 45°19' N; Longitude, 75°40' W.

Ottawa is 127 miles from Montreal to the east and 249 miles from Toronto to the west. It is one hour's drive to Ogdensburg, New York.

POPULATION 774,072, with 1,063,664 in the metropolitan area (2001 census).

Ottawa is the fourth largest city in Canada, after Toronto, Montreal, and Calgary. The city is growing rapidly, particularly in its urban centers of Kanata and South Nepean.

ETHNIC DIVERSITY Most of the people living in Ottawa were born in Canada, but many also come from the Far East, Western Europe, and the United States. There is a vibrant Italian section that celebrates its heritage for a week every June.

In 2001, there were 166,750 immigrants living in Ottawa. In order of frequency, their countries of origin included the United Kingdom, China, Lebanon, the United States, India, Italy, Vietnam, Germany, and Poland.

Religious Affiliations:

Catholic	54 percent
Protestant	22 percent
None	13 percent

In addition, in 2001 there were 41,725 Muslims living in Ottawa-Hull and 11,325 Jews.

CLIMATE Average January temperature, 20°F; average July temperature, 69°F. Ottawa proudly claims to be one of the coldest capitals in the world (along with Moscow and Ulan Bator, the capital of Mongolia).

ECONOMY The federal government and Nortel Telecommunications are the largest employers in Ottawa. Ottawa's hospitals and universities are also major employers.

UNEMPLOYMENT RATE 6.9 percent (2003)

EARNINGS
Average household income, private households (2001): $75,351
Median household income: $62,130

HOUSING By most measures, Ottawa is the third costliest place to live in Canada (after Vancouver and Toronto). Monthly mortgage payments in Ottawa for an average priced home are $1,267.

In the second quarter of 2004, the cost of buying a starter house ranged from $210,000 to $265,000 and an executive detached two-story house ranged from $248,000 to $335,000.

Many in Ottawa, as in Montreal, rent apartments, with the average rent for a two-bedroom apartment, $932.

In 2001, approximately three-fifths of the city's population lived in owner-occupied dwellings. Of these people, 11.9 percent were spending 30 percent or more of their income on shelter, compared with 37 percent of the renters.

HEALTH Five hospitals, many local community service centers, nineteen long-term care facilities, and medical care clinics in most shopping centers.

There are sixty-four retirement homes or communities, some of which provide long-term care.

Average Life Expectancy (2001):
Males, 78.3 years
Females, 82.5 years

EDUCATION Ottawa has around 280 elementary and secondary schools about half of which are public and the other half Roman Catholic. One highly competitive high school caters to the performing arts, with admission by audition. Usually seven students apply for every position available.

The University of Ottawa, North America's oldest and largest bilingual university, has more than 25,000 students. Tuition is $4,589 a year for Ontarians and $12,176 for international students. Carleton University has more than 18,000 students. Annual tuition at Carleton is $4,672 for Ontario residents and $11,438 for foreign students. Ottawa is also home to St. Paul University, the Dominican College of Philosophy and Theology, Algonquin College, La Cité collegiale, and the Université du Quebec à Hull.

URBAN TRANSIT The City of Ottawa is served by Ottawa City Transpo buses and by five taxicab fleets. A multimillion-dollar light-rail project is partially completed and will open up downtown Ottawa to the suburbs.

TRANSPORTATION Flights daily between Ottawa, Boston, Chicago, New York City, and Washington, D.C. Daily trains to Montreal and Toronto and beyond. Two intercity bus lines taking passengers throughout Canada and to the United States.

MEDIA Two daily newspapers in English, the *Ottawa Citizen* and the *Ottawa Sun*, and one in French, *Le Droit*. Sixteen radio stations; fourteen broadcast in English, two in French. Of the city's four TV stations, three broadcast in English, the fourth in French.

CULTURE The National Arts Centre in downtown Ottawa is Canada's largest showcase for the performing arts. The National Arts Centre Orchestra under Pinchas Zukerman performs there throughout the year, along with opera, dance, major theatrical companies, and entertainers from around the world. The city boasts an active Chamber Music Society as well as a variety of dance and theatre companies.

The National Gallery of Canada, designed by Moshe Safdie, who created

Habitat in Montreal at the time of Expo there, has the largest collection of Canadian art in the country and important European works as well. Stellar traveling exhibitions come to this popular gallery.

The Canadian Museum of Civilization features a reconstructed Pacific Coast Indian Village in its Grand Hall and the stories of the earliest Canadians and immigrant cultures. (This museum is actually in Gatineau, directly across the Ottawa River from Parliament Hill.)

Commemorating the sixtieth anniversary of the end of World War II in Europe, a new Canadian War Museum opened in Ottawa in the spring of 2005. The collection includes tanks and airplanes as well as smaller artifacts.

SPORTS Ottawa Senators (National Hockey League), Ottawa Renegades (Canadian Football League), and the Ottawa Lynx (minor league baseball).

More than 7,980 acres of parks and playgrounds and many beautiful gardens.

PUBLIC SAFETY In 2003, there were 5,604 violent crimes reported in Ottawa, including 10 homicides, 15 attempted murders, and 4,310 assaults. That year, there were 36,674 crimes against property, including theft, breaking and entering, and fraud. As a point of comparison, Washington, D.C., in that year recorded 249 homicides, 4,596 aggravated assaults, and 32,678 property crimes. In 2003, the U.S. capital's population was 563,384, far less than that of Ottawa.

DUTCH SOIL IN CANADA

The tulips that blanket parts of Ottawa each spring are there in part because of the birth of a princess. Magriet Francisca was born on January 19, 1943, to Princess Juliana, heir to the Dutch throne, who had fled to Canada in 1940 when the Netherlands fell to German invaders. So that Juliana's child could be born on Dutch soil, an act of Parliament declared the Princess's Ottawa hospital room to be completely out of Canadian jurisdiction. A Dutch flag flew over the Peace Tower on Parliament Hill to celebrate Magriet's birth.

After the Netherlands were liberated in 1945, the Dutch royal family returned home. In gratitude, the people of the Netherlands sent Ottawa 100,000 tulip bulbs. The next year, Princess Juliana sent another 20,000. Every year since then, the Netherlands has sent 10,000 tulip bulbs to Ottawa.

SNAPSHOT: QUEBEC PROVINCE

In the long history of human warfare, few battles stand out as decisive. The battle between the English and the French that took place on September 13, 1759, on Quebec City's Plains of Abraham is an exception. In less than twenty minutes, British troops under Gen. James Wolfe defeated French forces led by Gen. Louis-Joseph, the Marquis de Montcalm. Wolfe died on the battlefield, Montcalm, the next day. In those hellish twenty minutes, 1,300 men were killed or wounded, and the French empire in the New World was no more.

The French made a few more desperate attempts to salvage the situation, but their fate was sealed. The Treaty of Paris, signed in 1763, legally ceded New France to Great Britain; what would ultimately be the country of Canada became a largely English-speaking nation.

In 1760, the French gentry left Quebec, taking with them their possessions and their cannon (only two French-made cannon are still known to be in Quebec City). But common French folk—the tradesmen, the laborers, the trappers, the fishermen—couldn't afford to leave. The Quebec Act of 1774 was a practical document that acknowledged a fact: The French had lost the war but they were still living on the land. Anglican British granted them the right to maintain their old forms of land ownership and their civil laws and to practice their Roman Catholic religion. In 1791, the British Parliament went further, creating a new constitution for its North American colonies whereby Quebec (Lower Canada) and Ontario (Upper Canada) would each have its own legislative assembly.

Quebec is different from the rest of Canada. It always has been different, and it remains resolutely and sometimes pugnaciously different. Despite the fact that many Canadian prime ministers have come from Quebec, despite the fact that two Quebecers wrote "O, Canada," which has become the country's national anthem, Quebecers still wonder if they belong and if they want to belong to the rest of the country. Quebec refused to sign the Canadian Constitution of 1982 and the Charter of Rights and Freedoms. In 1995, a referendum on separating from the rest of Canada was narrowly defeated. (One result of that contretemps was to impel many panic-stricken anglophones to move from Quebec Province to Toronto.) The issue isn't dead.

"Quebecers feel that they're a nation," said Montreal immigration attorney David Cohen. "The real challenge in all of this is for Canada to find a way—and for Quebec to find a way—so that Quebec can remain a part of Canada and still have a feeling of nationhood. There's a saying here that we want an independent Quebec within a strong Canada."

LOCATION In the eastern part of Canada. (See map on page xviii–xix.)

Quebec Province shares borders with New York State, Vermont, New Hampshire, and Maine.

GEOGRAPHY Quebec is Canada's largest province, with a total area of 656,000 square miles. (To put that in perspective, it is almost three times the size of France.) It is one-sixth of Canada's total landmass.

There are said to be one million lakes and rivers in Quebec Province, which has been largely shaped by the glaciers of advancing and retreating Ice Ages. Half of the province is covered with forests.

Most of the province rests on the mineral-rich Canadian Shield—the eroded roots of an ancient, forested mountain range, studded with lakes and largely uninhabited. Swift rivers run from the edge of the shield into the neighboring lowlands, where the St. Lawrence River flows to the Atlantic Ocean. Most of the population lives along the St. Lawrence, which is one of the world's longest navigable waterways. It is 746 miles long and 62 miles wide at its mouth.

Quebec City and Trois Rivières are on the north bank of the river. Montreal is on an island farther south and west, with the city of Laval on another nearby island. Two smaller cities of importance, Jonquière and Chicoutimi, where sawmills, paper mills, and aluminum smelting are the main industries, are on a St. Lawrence tributary, the Saguenay.

The area south of the St. Lawrence is part of the Appalachian Mountain chain that runs down much of the eastern seaboard of North America, with a mixture of deciduous forests and valleys suitable for agriculture. Sherbrooke, settled in 1800 by immigrants from Vermont, is the principal city of this region. Also on the south of the St. Lawrence, the Gaspé peninsula extends into the Gulf of St. Lawrence. It has a relatively temperate climate, with fishing villages along the rocky north coast and farming and forestry predominant in the south.

The Laurentian Mountains are less than an hour's drive north of Montreal. They are more than a billion years old, and are among the oldest mountains in the world. The highest peak, Mont Tremblant (3,175 feet), is beloved by skiers.

CLIMATE Extreme fluctuations in temperature, with cooler temperatures going north. Summers, particularly in the southern part of the province, can be hot and humid. Montreal gets an average of between seven and eight feet of snow in the winter, but Sept-Iles on the north shore of the St. Lawrence and farther east, gets an average of fourteen feet.

PROVINCIAL CAPITAL Quebec City

POPULATION 7,616,645 (est., Oct. 2005)

POPULATION DENSITY Almost 80 percent of the population lives in the south, along the St. Lawrence River. The province has a demographic density of 11 people per square mile.

ETHNIC DIVERSITY Boosted by the large immigrant population in Montreal, there is considerable ethnic diversity in the statistics for the province. However, outside of the Montreal area, most Quebecers are of French descent, with an admixture of Scottish, Irish, and Welsh. In Montreal, for instance, visible minorities constituted 21.1 percent of the population in 2001, but in Quebec City, they were only 1.7 percent. Montreal reported an immigrant population of 27.6 percent in 2001. In Quebec City, only 3 percent of the population was immigrant. A large number of Quebec Province's French-speaking population descends from settlers who arrived in the sixteenth and seventeenth centuries.

First Nations people constitute an important minority in the province. There are 78,000 people who belong to one of ten Amerindian nations or to the Inuit. In 1985, Quebec became the first province in Canada to recognize Native peoples as nations with the right to autonomy.

LANGUAGE In 1974, the National Assembly made French the official language of Quebec Province. Business, government, and most education are conducted in French. French is the native language of 83 percent of the population. Native English-speakers number 11 percent, while the remainder of the population speaks other languages at home, primarily Italian, Spanish, Arabic, Chinese, Greek, Vietnamese, and Portuguese. Over 40 percent of the Quebec Province population speaks both English and French, though knowledge of English declines in the more remote regions. Even in Quebec City, which attracts many English-speaking tourists, it is not unusual to find people with a limited knowledge of English.

The bulk of Quebec Province's anglophones (an estimated 600,000) live in or near Montreal.

HEALTH See Appendix, pages 215–216, for details on Quebec Province's health care coverage and how to apply for it.

The province has 474 public and private institutions providing health and social services, nearly 1,000 medical clinics, and 3,954 community-based agencies. A third of the provincial budget goes for health and social service expenses.

Average Life Expectancy:
   Males, 76.3 years
   Females, 81.9 years
Infant Mortality Rate: 4.8 per 1,000 live births

ECONOMY Much employment in Quebec Province centers on the aerospace, biotechnology, information technology, agriculture, forestry, and mining industries. Quebec's mines yield copper, iron, zinc, silver, and gold. Asbestos is mined in the far north and in the Appalachian Highlands.

Historically, fur trapping and manufacture and fishing have also been important. In Quebec City, the government is a large employer. Tourism also contributes significantly to the economy.

Quebec's aerospace industry accounts for 55 percent of Canadian production, employing more than 42,000 people. Prime contractors include Bell Helicopter Textron, CAE Electronics, Bombardier-Aerospace, Pratt & Whitney Canada, and Rolls-Royce Canada.

The province's biotechnology industry is the largest in Canada in terms of revenue. The major research areas are human and animal health, agriculture, biofood, and forestry and the environment.

More than 100,000 people are employed in the information technology sector, which includes telecommunications, multimedia, computer services and software, e-business and e-media, microelectronics and components, and computer equipment.

In more traditional industries that rely on Quebec's vast natural resources, forestry is of prime importance. The province accounts for one-third of Canada's pulp and paper production. Half of the newsprint produced in Quebec is exported to the United States.

Shipping on the St. Lawrence Seaway is also important. The Seaway, which opened in 1959, employs a series of locks to raise and lower water levels between the Atlantic Ocean and Lake Ontario. This enables ships to transport cargo such as grain and iron ore to and from the Midwest. The Seaway cemented Montreal's importance as a port and an industrial center.

With Quebec Province's large numbers of rivers and lakes, the province is a major producer of hydroelectricity. Some of this powers the province's own industries, while the rest is exported to other Canadian provinces and to the United States.

The United States is Quebec Province's main economic partner. Approximately 80 percent of Quebec's exports go to the United States, and around 45 percent of the province's imports come from there.

EARNINGS In 2001, a worker with a university certificate, diploma, or degree living in Quebec Province had average earnings of $45,834. The average for all workers in the province, 15 years old or over, was $29,385.

UNEMPLOYMENT RATE 8.3 percent (Dec. 2005). (Higher than the national average for that month of 6.1 percent.)

HOUSING In 2001, there were 1,246,745 people in the province living in rented private housing, and 1,703,705 living in private housing that they owned. Among the renters, 35.7 percent were spending more than 30 percent of their household income on housing. This was true of 14.1 percent of the homeowners. These statistics indicate that shelter costs in Quebec Province were less expensive than the national average as a percentage of household income.

The average price of a house in Quebec City in 2004 was $129,149. The average price of a house in Montreal in 2004 was $188,289.

Average monthly rents can range from $493 to $720 for a three-bedroom apartment. There are no brokers' fees or security deposits.

EDUCATION Quebec Province has both publicly funded and private schools. In the public sector, where schooling is free through the end of high school, most teaching takes place in French. If they wish, students can attend English-language schools if one of their parents was educated in an English-language school in Canada. Because of a decision by the Supreme Court of Canada in March 2005, Quebec may be obliged to extend that right to others, including the children of English-speaking immigrants. It remains to be seen how the Supreme Court decision is carried out.

Tuition fees for postsecondary education, including university studies, are among the lowest in North America. Almost 40 percent of the population has postsecondary education of some kind.

Quebec's universities, research institutes, and higher learning centers are located in Montreal, Quebec City, and Sherbrooke. In addition, the Université du Québec has campuses in several other cities in the province.

TAXES Residents pay progressive income taxes to the Canadian and Quebec governments, with a maximum tax rate of 48.22 percent. Income from all sources is taxed. Exemptions are allowed for dependents and for taxes paid to foreign governments. Deductions can be claimed for some work-related expenses; rental investment, or business income; and investments in retirement plans, Registered Retirement Savings Plans (RRSPs), and some stock purchase plans. (See pages 69–70 for more on RRSPs.)

Tax examples: In 2002, a single person earning $50,000 in Quebec Province would have paid $7,164 in provincial taxes and $6,240 in federal taxes, for a total tax rate of 26.81 percent. A married couple with one salary and two children, ages 6 and 11, with income of $50,000 in 2002 would have paid $3,568 in provincial taxes and $5,374 in federal taxes for a combined tax rate of 17.88 percent.

GOVERNMENT *Premier:* Jean Charest (Quebec Liberal Party). Quebec has a National Assembly with 125 members, each representing a constituency or riding.

The two main parties are the Parti Québécois and the Quebec Liberal Party.

Right to Vote: Citizens 18 years old or older who have lived in the province for at least six months are eligible to vote.

LAWS Quebec is the only Canadian province with a civil code based on French law. The legal system in the rest of the country derives from British common law. The civil code governs civil rights, relations between citizens, and property matters. The province's criminal code is based on the British model.

Quebec's judicial system has two levels: the lower courts (municipal courts, Quebec Court, and the Superior Court) and the Court of Appeal. The Quebec Court, whose judges are appointed by the provincial government, has jurisdiction over certain civil, criminal, and penal matters. Superior Court judges, who handle penal appeals and matters outside the jurisdiction of other courts, are appointed by the federal government, as are judges of the Court of Appeal—the province's ultimate arbiter.

PROVINCIAL HOLIDAY June 24 (Saint-Jean-Baptiste Day). Near the summer solstice, this holiday was first celebrated in New France around 1638. St. John the Baptist was the patron saint of French Canada. Quebec is the only province that observes this holiday. Typically, the celebration includes parades, bonfires, and performances by prominent entertainers.

TRANSPORTATION Roads link most parts of the province. All regions are accessible by air. Montreal and Quebec City have airports capable of servicing international flights. Public transportation systems exist in Montreal, Quebec City, Hull, and Sherbrooke.

CARS AND AUTO INSURANCE Quebec Province has a public, no-fault insurance program.

ATTITUDES TOWARD GAYS Quebec Province has laws that specifically prohibit discrimination based on sexual orientation. In July 2002, the province passed a civil union law giving gay or straight couples the same rights as married couples, including the right to adopt children. Public opinion polls about same-sex marriage have consistently shown that 60 percent of the province supports it—the largest percentage in Canada. On April 1, 2004, the first same-sex marriage in the province took place at Montreal's Palais de Justice.

Montreal in particular has a thriving gay "scene." Each July, Montreal hosts the Gay and Lesbian Pride Festival, and in October, the Black and Blue Festival, with dancing, culture, art, sports, and food. In July 2006, the city hosted the Gay Games.

CULTURE People in search of art museums, symphony orchestras, and the like should look in Montreal and Quebec City. In addition, Quebec proudly points to writers, artists, musicians, and others who have come from the province (particularly to singer Céline Dion) and to the innovative Cirque du Soleil, which originated in Montreal.

Among Quebec writers, Mordecai Richler (*The Apprenticeship of Duddy Kravitz*) and Mavis Gallant (*Collected Stories*) are known to many English-speaking readers. Nevertheless, the culture is pervasively French, and anglophones must look beyond the printed or spoken word to see what Quebec is about.

In part, it's a sense of style—a lace curtain in a window flanked by shutters, with a flower box in front; a carved, wooden door with a silver doorknob; thick, stone walls; a steeply pitched roof. In part, it's a sense of priorities: the preparation of food is an art form and meals can last for hours. In part, it's the continual questing for place, identity, and recognition by a province that was once a nation, and not just a nation, but an empire extending from the Hudson Strait through eastern Canada and down the Mississippi River, which, in 1673, was explored by the Quebec-born, Louis Joliet, whose house can still be seen in Quebec City's Lower Town.

FESTIVALS Major festivals include the Canadian Tulip Festival in Gatineau (May), Le Grand Rire Bleue (comedy festival) in Quebec City (June), Les

Feux d'Artifice de Montreal (fireworks festival, June and July), the Montreal International Jazz Festival (June and July), the Quebec City Summer Festival (July), the Festival Internationale de Lanaudière (classical music festival—the largest in Canada, July and August), the Just for Laughs Festival in Montreal (July), SAQ New France Festival in Quebec City (August), and the Quebec Winter Carnival (January and February).

SPORTS *Recreational Sports:* Fishing, rafting, skiing, snowmobiling, dogsledding, boating, golfing, horseback riding, rock climbing.

The Rivière Rouge in the Laurentians is considered one of the best rivers for rafting in North America. People also head to the Laurentians for downhill and cross-country skiing, which is deemed excellent in the Eastern Townships (Les Cantons de l'Est) and around Charlevoix, not far from Quebec City.

The province has an extensive network of cross-country ski trails that are patrolled and furnished with heated cabins. Snowmobiling is another popular winter sport. There are more than 263 local snowmobiling clubs, all members of the Fédération des Clubs de Motoneigistes du Québec, which maintains 15,538 miles of marked trails, also provided with heated cabins and repair services.

More than 300 golf courses, most of them located in or near the Eastern Townships, Laurentians, Mauricie-Bois-Francs, and Outaouais.

Bicycling, which is popular in many parts of the province, reaches a zenith of popularity in Montreal, which has 217.5 miles of bike paths on the 310-square-mile island. Cyclists can leave the island by bridge, subway, or ferry, and once on the south shore of the St. Lawrence, connect to a 2,500-mile-long network of cycling routes through the Monteregie and Eastern Townships regions of the province. An annual bicycling event, the Tour de l'Ile, brings more than 45,000 bicyclists onto Montreal's streets, just to ride together and have a good time.

Three national parks (Forillon, La Mauricie, and the Mingan Archipelago) and eighteen provincial parks, plus nature reserves, game sanctuaries, and municipal parks.

PUBLIC SAFETY In 2003, there were 479,688 crimes committed in Quebec Province (excluding traffic). The rate of 6,407 offenses per 100,000 people puts Quebec well below Canada's national average of 8,132 crimes per 100,000 people. Of the crimes reported in Quebec, 53,373 were crimes of violence. Most of the remainder were crimes against property.

VALUES Beginning in 1960 with what is now called "The Quiet Revolution," Quebec changed from a socially conservative province dominated by the Roman Catholic church to one of the most liberal—if not the most liberal—provinces in Canada. Extensive alterations in the structure of government and in the provision of social services occurred with unprecedented rapidity. Quebec embarked on an idealistic course of equality and tolerance with a social safety net for all from which it has not looked back.

In December 1986, Quebec formally adopted a Declaration on Interethnic and Interracial Relations that supported the rights outlined in Canada's Charter of Human Rights and Freedoms. Basically, these documents guarantee the right to life and freedom and prohibit discrimination in all forms. Quebec's Charter of Human Rights and Freedoms was adopted in 1975.

SNAPSHOT: Quebec City

Encircled by massive stone walls, a turreted, castlelike hotel dominating its skyline, Quebec City is often described with the words "romantic" and "quaint." But in former days Canada's oldest city, founded in 1608 as a French trading post on the St. Lawrence River, was anything but quaint. The capital of New France from 1664 to 1763 and of Lower Canada from 1791 to 1841 was the nerve center of a vast territory, bustling with politicians, merchants, artisans, sailors, fur traders, farmers, clerics, and others who had business in the New World.

Such a fine and strategically situated city was a tempting prize. Quebec's now-picturesque walls were built for defensive purposes. Some decidedly unquaint battles took place within them and near them. The decisive battle of the Seven Years' War between the British and the French occurred on the Plains of Abraham, now a tranqil park in which more than a thousand soldiers are buried. In addition, there were repeated skirmishes with the Iroquois and a bitter battle with the Americans, who attacked Quebec City on December 31, 1775.

That was long ago and long forgiven. Now Quebec is on friendly terms with the United States, the province's largest trading partner. With a specific goal to double the number of immigrants who choose to live there, the city would undoubtedly welcome Americans these days, especially if they are experienced with computers, telecommunications, engineering, or the sciences.

Immigrants to Quebec will find a tolerant, liberal, idiosyncratic society. "We are very stubborn," explains Richard Séguin, who works with Quebec City tourism. "We wanted to survive as a French country in North America, and for that we had to have for all those years a very strong will not only to survive but to enjoy life."

Some people characterize the Quebec lifestyle as more European than life in other parts of North America. "There's more living for today," says Montreal immigration attorney David Cohen. "In Toronto people say, 'TGIM'—'Thank God it's Monday!' Here, we're less driven."

Quebec City has been recognized as one of the best cities in Canada in terms of quality of life issues such as affordable housing, high-quality, low-cost child care, maternity leave, and per capita spending on parks, recreation areas, museums, and festivals.

On January 1, 2002, Quebec City merged with twelve surrounding municipalities of the Communauté Urbaine de Québec to form one large city with eight boroughs. It is the capital of Canada's largest province.

LOCATION Situated on Cap Diamant, a rocky promontory facing the St. Lawrence River and its tributary, the St. Charles. Quebec City is approximately 150 miles northeast of Montreal (around three hours by train, or two-and-a-half hours by car).

Latitude: 46°50' N; Longitude: 71°15' W.

GEOGRAPHY At Quebec City, the St. Lawrence River narrows, which gave the city its name. "Kebek" is an Algonquin word for "narrow passage." The oldest part of the city is next to the river, with the walled Upper Town on the cliff above. Twenty-five steep staircases and a funicular connect the two. The walled area of the city is only four square miles. Outside the walls are modern commercial and residential areas.

CLIMATE Summers can be hot and humid. Winter can begin as early as November, with heavy snow through March and even a few flurries in April. Average January temperature ranges, 18°F to 1°F. Average July temperature ranges, 55°F to 77°F.

POPULATION 697,753 (2002)

ETHNIC DIVERSITY Most of the population is French-speaking and at least nominally Roman Catholic.

The immigrant population is around 3 percent of the total.

HEALTH
> *Average Life Expectancy* (2002):
> Males, 76.5 years
> Females, 82.0 years

ECONOMY In Quebec City, the government is the major employer. Other major employers are Laval University and Caisses Populaires Desjardins (a bank). The city has a deep seaport capable of receiving large cargo vessels as well as cruise ships, including the *Queen Mary 2,* the largest passenger ship in the world. In former times, the river, which is salty and subject to twenty-two-foot-high tides even though eight hundred miles from the Atlantic Ocean, used to freeze in the winter. Now it is kept open for navigation.

UNEMPLOYMENT RATE 11.7 percent (2003)

EARNINGS
> Average annual earnings for full-time workers (2001): $37,264
> Median family income (couples with families, 2001): $50,806

HOUSING The average price of a house in Quebec City in 2004 was $129,149. The average rent for a three-bedroom apartment was $656 in 2003. Housing costs in Quebec City are among the lowest in Canada relative to income.

EDUCATION Two universities, Laval and the Université du Québec, plus several community colleges. The history of Université Laval goes back to 1663 when Monseigneur François de Laval, the first bishop of New France, founded the Séminaire de Québec with the authorization of King Louis XIV. Laval currently has almost 29,000 undergraduate students and around 7,200 who are pursuing graduate studies. Tuition at Laval is $2,101 for Quebec residents and $4,834 for those from outside Quebec.

URBAN TRANSIT The upper and lower towns of Quebec City (within the walls and below them, in the Old Port) are very walkable, but there is a public bus system and taxis are plentiful. Two bridges and a ferry connect Quebec City with the south shore of the St. Lawrence.

CULTURE Many museums including the Musée National des Beaux-Arts du Québec with an outstanding collection of Quebec artists and interesting changing exhibitions. The Musée de la Civilisation, designed by Moshe

Safdie, the architect of Montreal's famous Habitat, has permanent exhibits about Quebec's history and the province's aboriginal nations. The city's many art galleries exhibit the work of local artists and others. Throughout the year, there are dance, theatrical, and musical performances. The city is home to the Orchestre Symphonique de Québec, the Violons du Roy, and the Opéra de Québec.

SPORTS Two professional sports teams: the Remperts (Junior hockey) and Quebec City Capitales (minor league baseball). Université Laval has a football team.

Winter: Snowmobiling and cross-country and downhill skiing (the Mont Sainte-Anne ski resort is nearby as is the Massif de la Petite-Rivière-Saint-François, which has the highest vertical drop east of the Rockies), however, Quebec City's most unusual winter activity may be ice climbing and ice sliding at Montmorency Falls. At 274 feet, the falls are one and a half times higher than Niagara, and the mist generated freezes into a tall cone, while parts of the falls turn into sheets of climbable ice.

Summer: Boating, rafting, fishing, golfing—all within the city or close by.

MEDIA Three French-language newspapers in Quebec City, *Le Soleil, Le Journal*, and *Voir*, and one English-language newspaper, *The Chronicle-Telegraph*.

PUBLIC SAFETY Statistics for 2004 indicated that Quebec City had one of the lowest crime rates in the country. There were a total of 4,997 criminal code offenses that year. By comparison, Regina in Saskatchewan, a much smaller city, recorded a total of 15,430 criminal code offenses—the highest number in Canada in 2004. The homicide rate in Quebec City in 2004 was 0.8 per 100,000 people compared with 5.0 per 100,000 people in Regina.

SNAPSHOT: Montreal

People who are used to mountains such as the Rockies scoff at Montreal's "Royal Mountain" ("Mont Real" as it was named by explorer Jacques Cartier, who climbed it in 1535.) It's a mere 764 feet high, but whether called a mountain or a hill, it's a prominent landmark on the 310-square-mile island that forms the core of the city. Anyone who walks up the steep streets on Mont Royal's flanks will speak of it with respect—especially in winter when it's covered with ice and snow.

Montreal, which is the second largest metropolitan area in Canada (after Toronto), is a city that welcomes immigrants. More than one in four residents was born outside of the country. Nevertheless, it is also decidedly French in its language of choice—Montreal is the second largest French-speaking city in the world after Paris. Business is conducted primarily in French (though 53 percent of the population is bilingual). The French influence is also present in the city's sense of style and in its love affair with food.

Diners can sample more than eighty kinds of national and regional cuisines in the city's more than five thousand restaurants. As for taking a two-hour lunch, though Montreal is a financial, shipping, and industrial center, people don't apologize for lingering over their petit fours. Colleagues and customers will certainly understand and may well be similarly occupied.

As a fashion center, Montreal is preeminent in Canada. Around 49,000 people work in Montreal's clothing industry. Possibly inspired by the city's cold winters—temperatures between December and March are consistently well below freezing—four-fifths of the fur coats manufactured in Canada are made in Montreal.

The church steeples that punctuate Montreal's skyline are a reflection of the city's French Catholic heritage, but though most residents are nominally Catholic, church attendance on a regular basis is down, and many churches have been closed or converted to other uses.

Nevertheless, many Montrealers will have their children baptized and will marry in the church and, when they die, will have themselves buried in a church cemetery. The Catholic Cimetière Notre Dame-des-Neiges on Mont Royal is the city's largest, with the graves of more than a million people in a lovely, parklike setting. Nearby is Mount Royal Cemetery, a nondenominational Protestant cemetery, which is laid out like a landscaped garden. A small Jewish cemetery is also situated on the mountain.

Perhaps of more daily interest to the living is Montreal's other underground city—one of the world's largest. Almost twenty miles of pedestrian walkways link 10 downtown subway stations, 89 office buildings, 8 hotels, 2,727 apartments, 350 restaurants and food courts, 1,700 boutiques, 22 movie theatres and exhibition halls, 4 universities and a college, 6 bus depot and train stations, 3 skating rinks, 9 fitness centers, and 3 medical and dental clinics.

This underground city is decorated with artwork and lined with shops and restaurants. People who carefully plan where they live, work, eat, and play might never have to go outside unless they want to.

LOCATION

Latitude: 45°28' N (the same latitude as Venice, Geneva, Lyons, and Milan); Longitude: 73°45' W.

Montreal is forty-five miles from the U.S. border (about an hour's drive from New York State and Vermont). It is a two-and-a-half hour drive from Quebec City (three hours by train, which makes a few stops along the way).

GEOGRAPHY The core city of Montreal is located on an island thirty-two miles long and eleven miles wide. The Montreal region is an archipelago of more than four hundred islands at the confluence of the St. Lawrence and Ottawa Rivers. On January 1, 2002, all the municipalities of the island merged with those of surrounding islands to create the new City of Montreal, which consists of twenty-seven boroughs.

CLIMATE Mean January temperature, 13.4°F; mean July temperature, 67.6°F. Mean annual rainfall, 29 inches. Average annual snowfall, 84.3 inches.

POPULATION (2001) 1.81 million (city); 3.57 million (metropolitan area)

POPULATION DENSITY 1,399 people per square mile (In North America, only New York and Los Angeles are more densely populated than Montreal.)

ETHNIC DIVERSITY Twenty-eight percent of Montreal's residents were born outside of Canada (compared with 49 percent in Toronto and 38 percent in Vancouver). Seventy-seven percent of the immigrants to Quebec Province settle in Montreal. Although more than half of Montreal's people have French ancestry, more than eighty ethnic groups are represented in the Montreal metropolitan area, including Italian, Irish, English, Scottish, Haitian, Chinese, and Greek. As of 2001, most new immigrants to Montreal came from Algeria, China, France, and Haiti. Montreal has the largest Arab community in Canada. As of 2001, there were 56,000 Arabic-speaking people in the Montreal area. Blacks constitute the largest visible minority (139,305 people, according to the 2001 census), followed by Arabs, South Asians, and Latin Americans.

HEALTH

Average Life Expectancy (2003):
   Males, 75 years
   Females, 81.1 years

ECONOMY Seventy-eight percent of Montreal's economy is in service industries and 20 percent in manufacturing.

High-tech and finance are major employers. Four Canadian banks and six foreign banks have their head offices in Montreal as do ten out of Canada's twenty-five largest companies. Half of the Canadian biopharmaceutical industry is located in Montreal.

Because of its strategic location on the route to the Great Lakes, Montreal has the largest container port on the East Coast and the closest international port to the industries and raw materials of the Midwest.

In 2003, Montreal was seventh in job growth among the twenty-five largest metropolitan areas in North America.

UNEMPLOYMENT RATE 7.5 percent (2001)

EARNINGS
Average earnings for full-time workers: $41,792
Median family income (couples): $59,465

HOUSING Housing in Montreal tends to be less expensive than in other large metropolitan areas of Canada. In 2004, Montreal residents paid 31.2 percent of pre-tax household income for monthly housing compared with 47.3 percent in Vancouver and 37.2 percent in Toronto.

Most people (60 percent) lease a place to live compared with 46 percent in Vancouver and 38 percent in Toronto.

Many leases begin on July 1 (Canada Day), which is moving day for an estimated hundred thousand families each year.

Average gross monthly payments for rented dwellings: $568
Average monthly payments for owner-occupied dwellings: $845
The average price of a house in Montreal in 2004 was $188,289.

EDUCATION Montreal has four universities—two French-language (Université de Montreal and Université du Québec à Montreal) and two English-language (McGill and Concordia). With a total enrollment of 158,000 students, Montreal has more university students per capita than any other city in North America.

For residents of the province of Quebec, the cost of attending these universities is relatively modest, around $2,880 a year for McGill, for instance, not including books, health insurance, and housing. Students from other parts of Canada would pay $5,613 to attend McGill, while international students would pay around $13,461 per year.

There are five school boards on the island of Montreal, three French and two English. Unless a parent was enrolled in an English-speaking school in Canada, the children of immigrants who wish to attend a public (government-subsidized) school must go to a French-language school.

URBAN TRANSIT The subway system (known as the metro) has sixty-five stations spread out over four subway lines. Also, Montreal has a fleet of 1,600 city buses. Commuter trains link municipalities to the west, northwest, and southwest of Montreal Island. In addition, the city has 4,447 taxis.

According to the 2001 census, most people who work outside the home drive to work.

ATTITUDES TOWARD GAYS Montreal is home to one of the largest gay communities in the world. Gay life in Montreal centers on an area known as the Village (east of Rue Amherst), where there are saunas, bars, restaurants, hotels, and clothing stores that cater to a gay clientele. In 2006, Montreal hosted the Gay Games.

MEDIA Three French-language daily newspapers and one in English. There are thirty-three radio stations, of which fourteen are in English and three are multilingual. The city's seventeen regular television stations include six that broadcast from the United States.

CULTURE Montreal has 60 theatre stages, 171 movie screens, and more than 100 English and French theatre companies.

The city is home to the Orchestre Symphonique de Montréal, L'Opéra de Montréal, and more than thirty other musical organizations, including the Orchestre Metropolitan and the Orchestre Symphonique de Laval.

The Musée des Beaux-Arts de Montréal (the Montreal Museum of Fine Arts) is one of the city's preeminent museums, with a strong permanent collection and a series of important temporary exhibits. However, there are many other museums in Montreal dedicated to specialized topics, from the life of a saint (Marguerite Bourgeoys, for instance) to history (the fine and extensive McCord Museum of Canadian history).

SPORTS Although the Montreal Expos have decamped to Washington, D.C., the city still has three professional sports teams—the Montreal Canadiens (National Hockey League), the Impact soccer team (United Soccer League First Division), and the Alouettes (Canadian Football League).

The Grand Prix of Canada, the first Formula 1 race in North America, is held annually at the Circuit Gilles-Villeneuve. This is a wildly popular event that causes Montreal's hotels to be booked months in advance.

Recreational Sports: Downhill and cross-country skiing, hockey, curling. More than one hundred golf courses in the Greater Montreal area.

The city has more than a thousand parks and green spaces.

PUBLIC SAFETY The crime rate in Montreal has dropped dramatically in the last decade. In 2002, for instance, there were sixty-six homicides in the metropolitan region, which has a population of 3.57 million.

SNAPSHOT: NEW BRUNSWICK

The Mi'kmaq, Passamaquoddy, and Maliseet, or Malecite, Indians were the first to live in this region of dense inland forests, swiftly flowing rivers and streams, and ragged coastline where the sea teems with fish. Next came the French, some of them Acadians who had been driven out of Nova Scotia by the British in the 1750s.

Then, in 1776, the first Americans decided to move to Canada. At the end of the American Revolution, they were followed by about 14,000 colonists who remained loyal to England. They found refuge along the coast of New Brunswick and in other parts of British North America.

Many, who settled along the Atlantic coast, became involved in shipping and were instrumental in having the region declared a separate province in 1784.

In 1785, St. John, where many of the Loyalists had settled, was the first city incorporated in what is now Canada. It is the largest city in the province today. A coastal village, St. Andrews, was another Loyalist settlement. In 1783, Loyalists from Castine, Maine, dismantled their homes and floated them to St. Andrews on barges. St. Andrews is now a resort town with a pronounced British feel to it.

New Brunswick was named for the British Royal family of Brunswick-Luneburg (the House of Hanover). Along with Quebec, Ontario, and Nova Scotia, it was one of the original four provinces of Canada.

With its unique French and English (and American!) heritage, New Brunswick is Canada's only officially bilingual province, and Moncton is the country's only officially bilingual city. As required by the Official Languages Act (passed by the Canadian parliament in 1969 and amended in 2002), all provincial government business must be transacted in either language. In

New Brunswick, schoolchildren are entitled to be educated in the language of their choice.

Approximately 35 percent of New Brunswick's population speaks Acadian French as their first language.

Textile and iron industries replaced the province's early sailing ship industry. By 1890, two national railway systems linked New Brunswick with Montreal, and St. John became a chief winter port on the east coast. New Brunswick's pulp and paper industry grew in the 1920s and '30s and, after World War II, expanded greatly. Shipbuilding became important in the St. John area.

Deposits of copper, lead, silver, and zinc were discovered in the Bathurst-Newcastle region in the 1950s, and hydroelectric plants were built to get additional power for mining and manufacturing. The largest oil refinery in Canada was built in St. John in 1960.

In 1970, North America's first deepwater terminal for oil tankers opened near St. John. The next year, a terminal opened to handle ship-transported cargo packed in large wooden containers. Both of these developments were a boost to St. John's economy. Then, in 1982, the first nuclear power plant in Canada's Atlantic Provinces began operations at Point Lepreau, near St. John. Half of the electricity it generates is exported to the United States.

The world's highest tides occur in the Bay of Fundy, off the southern coast of New Brunswick. Campobello, summer home of U.S. president Franklin Delano Roosevelt's family, is located in the bay. It is now known as the Roosevelt-Campobello International Peace Park and is administered jointly by the U.S. and Canadian governments.

LOCATION South of Quebec Province's Gaspé Peninsula. Bordered on the east by the Gulf of St. Lawrence and the Northumberland Strait, which lies between New Brunswick and Prince Edward Island. The Isthmus of Chignecto connects New Brunswick with Nova Scotia, which lies to the southeast, separated from New Brunswick by the Bay of Fundy. On the west, New Brunswick shares a 318-mile-long border with the state of Maine.

GEOGRAPHY 28,355 square miles, including 520 square miles of inland water; 1,410 miles of coastline. Highest elevation, Mount Carleton (2,690 feet). The province is 250 miles from east to west and 230 miles from north to south.

Part of the ancient Appalachian Mountain region that runs down the eastern coast of North America as far as Georgia. Heavily forested in the interior. Shaped by glaciation that covered the area with sandy, acidic soil and created swamps and lakes in the lowlands. An extensive network of rivers. St. John River, the largest (450 miles long), has a famous reversing falls caused by the enormous force of the huge tides rolling in from the Bay of Fundy.

The rivers provided access to the province's forested interior and were formerly used for logging and steamboat transportation. Now they are important for fishing, boating, and hydroelectric power. All of New Brunswick's major cities are located on rivers.

CLIMATE Average January temperature, 14°F; average July temperature, 64°F. Average yearly precipitation, 45 inches.

PROVINCIAL CAPITAL Fredericton. Population, 47,560 (2001 census).

Originally a Loyalist settlement named for the second son of George III, Prince Frederick.

St. John is the largest city and chief industrial and shipping center. Population, 69,661 (2001 census).

Moncton is also a rail and shipping center with some high-tech and service industries (such as call centers). It is the fastest growing city in New Brunswick. Population, 61,046 (2001 census).

POPULATION 751,726 (est., Oct. 2005), down about one percent from the 1996 census

POPULATION DENSITY 26 people per square mile, double the density of most of the other Canadian provinces. Half live in urban areas. Most live near the coast and in the southern part of the province.

ETHNIC DIVERSITY The New Brunswick population primarily descends from French, English, Irish, Scottish, German, Acadian, North American Indian, Dutch, and Welsh forebears (in order of frequency). In the mid-1800s, many Irish people moved to New Brunswick, particularly to St. John, because of the potato famine in Ireland. In 2001, there were 3,925 people in the province who said that their ancestors were American (from the United States), representing 0.01 percent of the population. About 97 percent of New Brunswick residents were born in Canada.

Visible Minorities: The visible minority population of the province is very small (0.01 percent). Of these, the largest number are black (3,850 people in 2001), followed by Chinese and South Asians.

About two-thirds of the population speaks English and one-third speaks French as their native language. People in the south and west of the province are mostly English-speaking. The north and east have more Acadians, who speak French.

Religious Affiliations:

Catholic	54 percent
Protestant	37 percent
None	8 percent

In 2001, there were 1,275 Muslims in the province, and 670 Jews.

HEALTH See Appendix, page 213, for details on New Brunswick's health care coverage and how to apply for it.

Average Life Expectancy (2001):

Males, 76.1 years

Females, 81.8 years

Infant Mortality Rate: 4.3 per 1,000 live births (2001). This was the lowest rate in the Atlantic provinces and the second lowest rate in Canada.

ECONOMY Agriculture, fishing, forestry, mining, and manufacturing are the main industries. The manufacture of paper products is the leading manufacturing activity. Food and beverage processing is second. Potatoes are the province's leading cash crop. As in most other provinces, service industries provide the largest portion of New Brunswick's gross domestic product ($22 billion in 2001). Community, business, and personal services employ 38 percent of the people, wholesale and retail trade 16 percent, transportation and communication 10 percent, and government 7 percent. Port St. John has the biggest oil refinery in Canada.

EARNINGS

Average earnings of the population, 15 and over, for holders of a university certificate, diploma, or degree (2001): $40,375. (Compared with $48,648 average in Canada.)

High rates of poverty among children and the elderly.

UNEMPLOYMENT RATE 9.1 percent (Dec. 2005). The national average for that month was 6.1 percent. Young people, women, and Aboriginal people are particularly likely to be unemployed or underemployed.

HOUSING The average price for a house in the Fredericton area in 2004 was $119,191. In St. John it was $116,836.

Province-wide:

Average gross monthly payments for rented dwellings: $507 (2001)

Average monthly payments for owner-occupied dwellings: $583 (2001)

In St. John:

Average gross monthly payments for rented dwellings: $481 (2001)

Average monthly payments for owner-occupied dwellings: $666 (2001)

EDUCATION There are around 135,000 students in New Brunswick's public school system. Students can choose to be educated in English or French.

In 1996, the province abolished all local and district school boards. Schools are run at the local level by parents who are elected, and these parents appoint district councils from among their numbers. There are two provincial school boards, one English, and the other French. Members are district council and ministerial appointees. The province funds the school system from general revenues and creates the district budgets. The cost of public education is one of the largest items in the provincial budget. Though homeschooling is permitted, schooling is compulsory from the age of 5 until the age of 18 or the completion of high school.

The University of New Brunswick has campuses in Fredericton and St. John. It offers liberal arts courses as well as science, computer, and engineering programs. The university was founded in 1785 as the Provincial Academy of Arts and Sciences and was renamed in 1859. Its historical buildings include the first astronomical observatory in Canada, which is on the Fredericton campus. Tuition for an in-province student at the University of New Brunswick, $5,091; for international students it's $9,713.

The University at Moncton is Canada's only French-language degree-granting university outside Quebec Province. It is a research center for Acadian studies.

Mount Allison University in Sackville was established by Wesleyan Methodists in 1839, but has been run by the government since 1960. It has graduated forty-five Rhodes scholars. Most students are in arts or sciences, with international relations the fastest growing program. The Owens Art Gallery, on the Mount Allison campus, has a permanent collection of more than 2,500 European and North American artworks. Tuition for in-province students at Mount Allison is $6,001; international tuition is $11,811.

St. Thomas University in Fredericton is affiliated with the Roman Catholic Church.

There are five regional public library systems in the province.

TAXES New Brunswick gets about half its income from provincial taxes on income, property, and gasoline. The provincial sales tax is 8 percent. There is revenue sharing with the federal government, too, and money comes from taxes on government-controlled liquor sales and from license and permit fees.

GOVERNMENT *Premier:* Bernard Lord (Progressive Conservative Party). The Legislative Assembly has fifty-five elected members.

The political parties represented in the provincial legislature are the Liberal Party of New Brunswick, the Progressive Conservative Party of New Brunswick, and (a distinct minority to the other two) the New Democratic Party. Since the late nineteenth century, all the governments have been formed by either the Liberals or the Progressive Conservatives.

In the late 1960s, the Liberal government of Premier Louis Robichaud, the first Acadian premier of New Brunswick, took over the operation of all provincial courts, schools, and health and welfare institutions in an effort to equalize the disparities in service between the province's urban and rural areas.

The provincial government collects local taxes and administers education, health, welfare, and legal matters. Municipalities (incorporated cities, towns, and villages) and local service districts in the unincorporated areas of the province are responsible for fire and police protection, water service, and, where applicable, street maintenance and sewers.

The province elects ten members to the federal House of Commons. The federal government appoints ten members to the Senate.

TRANSPORTATION National and regional airlines link Fredericton, Moncton, and St. John with cities in Canada and the United States. Railroads connect the province to major cities in Quebec and Ontario. New Brunswick has highways running along the coastal areas and toward Fredericton. The Trans-Canada Highway goes along the St. John River and through Moncton. The Confederation Bridge links New Brunswick and Prince Edward Island. Transatlantic ships dock at St. John even during winter.

CARS AND AUTO INSURANCE The high cost and lack of availability of auto insurance have been inflammatory topics in the province. To help keep premiums under control, legislation was enacted in 2003 capping payment for nonpermanent minor injuries at $2,500, while other laws addressed discriminatory underwriting practices, including those based on age and gender. A consumer advocate was hired as ombudsman for New Brunswick drivers.

ATTITUDES TOWARD GAYS Same-sex marriages had not been legalized in New Brunswick at the time that federal legislation was passed in June 2005 making them legal throughout Canada.

MEDIA There are five daily newspapers in the province, including a French daily paper. Some thirty radio stations broadcast in the province, and the CBC sends programs overseas from its shortwave transmitter in Sackville. There are four major TV stations, including one broadcasting in French. Cable television and Internet service are available in most of the province.

CULTURE The cultural life of the province is a mixture of Acadian, Celtic, Aboriginal, and traditional, European-derived art forms.

The late English newspaper publisher and political figure Lord Beaverton was born in New Brunswick and endowed some of its important cultural institutions. The Beaverbrook Playhouse is the home of the New Brunswick Symphony Orchestra; the Beaverbrook Art Gallery in Fredericton has important works by British and Canadian painters.

Theatre New Brunswick stages several plays annually at the Playhouse in Fredericton and also tours the province. The Atlantic Ballet Theatre Company of Canada performs in Moncton.

The New Brunswick Museum in St. John was founded in 1842 and has collections pertaining to heritage, history, fine arts, humanities, and natural science.

The Acadian Historical Village near Caraquet reconstructs Acadian life from 1780 to the early 1900s. Fort Beausejour near Sackville is on the site of an eighteenth-century French fort to which the Acadians retreated when they were being attacked by the British. The King's Landing Historical Settlement, a re-created village in Prince William, shows how Loyalist settlers in the region lived from 1784 to 1890. Shippagan has an Aquarium and Marine Center, and Doaktown, an Atlantic Salmon Museum. St. Andrews has the Huntsman Marine Science Centre and Aquarium.

New Brunswick has had its share of important poets and novelists writing in both English and French about life in the province. It also has produced painters, sculptors, and musicians who are well known in Canada.

FESTIVALS Still mindful of its Loyalist beginnings, St. John has an annual Loyalist Heritage Festival (July). Among New Brunswick's other festivals (numbering more than 160) are: Festival Jazz et Blues d'Edmundston (June); Campbellton Salmon Festival (late June-early July); Kings County Covered Bridge Festival (July); Baie des Chaleurs International Chamber Music Festival (July); Shediac Lobster Festival (July); New Brunswick Highland Games and Scottish Festival held in Fredericton (July); Lameque International Festival of Baroque Music (July); Atlantic Seafood Festival in Moncton (August); Miramichi Folk Song Festival (August); Festival Acadien de Caraquet (August); Harvest Jazz and Blues Festival in Fredericton (September); Kedgwick Fall Festival (October).

Annual Aboriginal Festivals: Metepenagiag Trout Derby (May); St. Anne's Festival, Kingsclear First Nation (July); St. Anne's Festival, Burnt Nation First Nation (July); Tobique Labour Day Festival (September).

At powwows from June through September, New Brunswick's First Nations drum, dance, and sell crafts and Native food.

SPORTS Hunting, tennis, boating and other water sports, birdwatching, horseback riding. More than ninety sandy beaches and the warmest waters north of Virginia. Skiing in Campbellton and elsewhere.

Fishing: Atlantic salmon spawn in the province's rivers, particularly in the Miramichi.

Golf: Kingswood Golf Course in Fredericton is considered one of the best in Canada. Many other golf courses in the province.

New Brunswick has two national parks: Fundy National Park and Kouchibouquac National Park. There are a number of provincial parks, as well. The Herring Cove Provincial Park has a nine-hole golf course.

PUBLIC SAFETY New Brunswick's crime rate increased by 6.4 percent between 2002 and 2003. There were a total of 7,117 criminal code offenses (per 100,000 population). There were 991 violent crimes and 3,034 property crimes (per 100,000 population).

Double-digit increases in vehicle theft were reported. However, instances of impaired driving decreased by 11 percent, the largest decrease of any province.

One Moncton resident said, "We lock our garages but we don't lock our doors."

ST. STEPHEN, NEW BRUNSWICK, AND CALAIS, MAINE

Calais, Maine, and St. Stephen, New Brunswick, are just across the river from each other. Residents routinely cross Ferry Point Bridge to shop in the other country, friends and families travel back and forth to visit, and ambulances and fire departments of both towns rush to each other's aid.

Each year since 1974 the communities have joined together to celebrate their international friendship with a week of parades, pageants, and popcorn. Flags of the United States and Canada fly side by side as representatives from the two countries meet on the bridge for the International Friendship Handshake Ceremony that kicks off the festival.

Locals on both sides like to tell the story of the War of 1812, when the British military provided St. Stephen with gunpowder for protection against the enemy Americans in Calais. When the Fourth of July rolled around and the St. Stephen town fathers learned that their American neighbors lacked enough gunpowder for a proper celebration, they quietly sent over a supply.

—Karen Hammond
South Bristol, Maine
From an article, "Three Nation Vacation"
released by the Travel Acts Syndicate

SNAPSHOT: NOVA SCOTIA

Nova Scotia is a small province—the second smallest in Canada—but it is packed with varied landscapes that range from wild, sea-buffeted cliffs to a placid, fertile valley.

Halifax, the capital city, has one of the finest harbors in the world, which has made it a shipping center, a military stronghold, and, sometimes, the scene of dramatic events.

After the loss of the *Titanic* in April 1912, some of the bodies were brought back to Halifax and are buried there. Artifacts from the *Titanic* are on display at the Maritime Museum of the Atlantic.

During World Wars I and II, Halifax was a naval base and headquarters of the Allied convoys bound to and from Europe. On December 6, 1917, the *Mont Blanc,* a French munitions ship collided in Halifax harbor with a

Norwegian relief ship, the *Imo*. The resulting explosion killed more than 1,700 Haligonians, injured 4,000, and damaged much of the city.

Halifax is to Canada what Ellis Island in New York harbor is to the United States—the storied entry point to the nation. Between 1928 and 1971, one million people came into Canada through Pier 21 in Halifax. A large number of Canadians are descended from these immigrants.

In more remote times, the search for a Northwest Passage to Asia led several explorers in the fifteenth and sixteenth centuries to what is now Nova Scotia, or New Scotland. The French settlement at Annapolis Royal marked its four hundredth anniversary in 2005. It was one of the first European settlements on the North American continent.

France and England battled over what the French called Acadia for a hundred years. Finally, in 1713, under the Treaty of Utrecht, the French retreated to Cape Breton and the British got the main peninsula of Nova Scotia. But each country continued to prepare for war and build large forts. The French built Fort Louisbourg on Cape Breton Island overlooking the Gulf of St. Lawrence; the British built theirs in 1749, in the place they named Halifax. It became Nova Scotia's capital that year.

The Treaty of Utrecht made the French who lived in Nova Scotia British subjects. In the early 1750s, British colonial troops from New England began to drive out the Acadians who refused to swear allegiance to Britain. Some went to the French colony Louisiana, where their descendents are still called Cajuns. Others fled to Prince Edward Island, Quebec, and other colonies. Some returned later and settled in fishing villages on the coast.

Britain offered land deals to encourage New Englanders to come and settle on the Acadian lands, and they did. In 1760, more than twenty shiploads of New Englanders arrived. The American Revolution brought thousands more who were called Loyalists. Some of the Loyalists were blacks who had been promised their freedom in Nova Scotia. More blacks came during the War of 1812. Settlers were also coming in large numbers from the British Isles. In 1848, Nova Scotia became the first part of Canada to gain self-government and was one of the four original provinces in Confederation in 1867.

Historically, the sea fueled the Nova Scotian economy and colored its way of life. Fishing and shipping were paramount. In the late 1890s, steel and coal were also thriving industries.

Today, coal mining in Pictou County and on Cape Breton Island have shut down, and overfishing has severely damaged the province's cod fishery, each dealing a blow to the provincial economy. Nova Scotia has the second highest per capita debt in the country. Only Newfoundland has more. But there is new oil production around Sable Island and 38,000 jobs have been created in the province since 1999.

A modern network of roads, including the Nova Scotia section of the Trans-Canada Highway, was built in the 1950s, and the Canso Causeway, which links Cape Breton Island and the mainland, was completed. Tourism has been growing. Nova Scotia has more historic sites than any other province except Quebec.

The Nova Scotia–built schooner *Bluenose* won the International Fisherman's trophy five times between 1921 and 1938 and appears on the Canadian dime. A replica based in Lunenburg on the Atlantic shore of Nova Scotia offers summertime cruises. Like its predecessor, it was built in Nova Scotia, where people still know a thing or two about the sea.

LOCATION The Atlantic Ocean, the Gulf of St. Lawrence, the Northumberland Strait, and the Bay of Fundy all but surround Nova Scotia, which is connected to New Brunswick by a narrow isthmus. (See map on page xix). Mainland Nova Scotia is linked to Cape Breton Island by a causeway over the Strait of Canso.

GEOGRAPHY Nova Scotia is five hundred miles long from tip to tip. Cape Breton Island lies off its northeastern end. The Atlantic Plateau, the Northern Highlands, and the Lowlands are the three main geographic regions. Maximum elevation on the mainland is 689 feet above sea level. (On Cape Breton Island, the maximum elevation is 1,745 feet.) The coastline is 4,750 miles long, including islands. (No place in Nova Scotia is more than thirty-five miles from the ocean.) The Mersey and St. Mary's Rivers are the longest in the province, both seventy-two miles long, and there are more than four hundred lakes. The largest lake is Bras d'Or Lake on Cape Breton Island. It is a saltwater lake and covers 360 square miles. The highest recorded tide in the world—fifty-three feet—was recorded in the Bay of Fundy.

CLIMATE The sea surrounding Nova Scotia keeps the climate from becoming too extreme. Average January temperature, 23°F; average July temperature, 64°F. The coolest place in summer is the Atlantic coast, which is also the mildest in winter. Fog is common along the Atlantic and Fundy coasts in spring and early summer, sometimes causing airport closures.

PROVINCIAL CAPITAL Halifax. Population, 359,183 (2001 census)

POPULATION 908,007 (2001 census); 938,116 (est., Oct. 2005). Nova Scotia's population has tended to remain flat or to decrease slightly in recent years. A booklet published by the province in January 2005, *Nova Scotia's Immigration Strategy,* says, "We are facing a number of demographic and economic challenges—slow population growth, an aging population, low birthrate, out-migration of young people, urbanization, low immigration numbers—all of which may lead to labour shortages, slowing demand for goods and services, increasing fiscal pressures in the years to come." The booklet states that Nova Scotia is actively seeking immigrants.

POPULATION DENSITY 42 people per square mile

ETHNIC DIVERSITY Most Nova Scotians identify themselves as Canadians, but those who specify ethnic origins list Scottish, English, Irish, French, German, Dutch, North American Indian, Welsh, Italian, and Acadian in that order, and with smaller numbers from other parts of the world. In the 2001 census, 4,385 people claimed some U.S. ancestry.

Immigrants represent 4.6 percent of the population, the highest percentage among the Atlantic Provinces but still much lower than many other provinces in Canada. (In Ontario, for instance, immigrants represent 26.8 percent of the population.)

Visible Minorities: Visible minorities constituted 4 percent of the population in 2001. Blacks were the largest single group (19,670 people) followed by Arab and West Asians (4,000 people), Chinese (3,290 people), and South Asians (2,890 people).

Religious Affiliations:
    Protestant   49 percent
    Catholic   37 percent
In 2003, there were 3,545 Muslims in the province, 2,120 Jews, and 1,235 Buddhists.

LANGUAGE English is definitely the predominant language of Nova Scotia though there are a few French speakers. Interestingly, Gaelic is still spoken in some parts of the province. (In the early nineteenth century, it was the third most common language in Canada.)

HEALTH See Appendix, page 214, for details on Nova Scotia's health care coverage and how to apply for it.

The provincial government's 2005–2006 budget calls for a $214 million increase in health care spending to improve access to care and shorten waiting times for services. Special funding was authorized for autism programs, diabetes-related costs, stroke care, and mental health. The total health care budget for the province is $2.5 billion.

Average Life Expectancy (2001):

Males: 76.2 years

Females: 81.3 years

Infant Mortality Rate: 5.6 per 1,000 live births (2001)

ECONOMY Service industries employ more Nova Scotians (41 percent) than any other sector. These include education, health care, government, engineering, hospitality, finance, insurance, and real estate.

Paper products, processed foods, tires, and transportation equipment are manufactured in the province. Milk, hogs, chicken, and eggs are among Nova Scotia's chief agricultural products. Lobster, scallops, crab, shrimp, haddock, and herring are staples of the fishing industry.

Nova Scotia has two large deposits of gypsum, at Windsor and East Millford. There are underwater natural gas and oil deposits around Sable Island.

The provincial government states that it projects employment growth in oil- and gas-related fields; geology; accounting; sales; industrial; computer information systems; health care (nurses and doctors); and accounting and finance and that there are needs for technicians and engineers and supervisors.

EARNINGS

Average earnings, working full year, full-time: $37,872 (2001)

Median family income (couples): $51,641

Average earnings of the population, 15 and over, for holders of a university certificate, diploma, or degree (2001): $41,146 (compared with the Canadian national average of $48,648)

UNEMPLOYMENT RATE 8.0 percent (Dec. 2005). The national average for that month was 6.1 percent.

HOUSING The average price of a house in Halifax-Dartmouth in 2004 was $175,132; in Cape Breton it was $66,419. In Halifax in 2003, the average rent for a three-bedroom apartment was $935.

Province-wide:

Average gross monthly payments for rented dwellings: $590 (2001)

Average monthly payments for owner-occupied dwellings: $633 (2001)

Halifax:
Average gross monthly payments for rented dwellings: $657 (2001)
Average monthly payments for owner-occupied dwellings: $823 (2001)

EDUCATION The Provincial Education Act governs public schools in Nova Scotia, and locally elected school boards control them. Schools are funded by the provincial and municipal governments, with some help from the federal government. Some parents homeschool their children, and there are private schools, but they must meet provincial standards.

There are ten degree-granting universities in Nova Scotia that are members of the Association of Universities and Colleges of Canada. Picturesque Acadia University in Wolfville is noted for its academics as well as for its champion varsity sports teams. Tuition for in-province residents, $7,824; for international students it's $13,963.

The Université Sainte-Anne at Church Point was founded in 1890 to educate francophone and Acadian students. Students come not only from Nova Scotia, but from other provinces in Canada and from France and francophone Africa. There are 406 full-time students and 92 part-time. Tuition is $5,250 for Nova Scotia residents; $7,460 for international students.

Dalhousie University (undergraduate and graduate) is in Halifax. About half the student body comes from outside Nova Scotia. Tuition for in-province students is $6,121 to $6,871; for international students, the tuition is $10,440 to $11,190.

St. Mary's University in Halifax has the biggest business faculty in the Atlantic provinces and the largest faculty of arts in Nova Scotia. Tuition for in-province students is $5,536 to $5,636; for international students, it's $10,706 to $10,806.

Other universities are the University College of Cape Breton in Sydney, the University of King's College in Halifax, Mount St. Vincent University in Halifax, and the Nova Scotia College of Art and Design in Halifax. The Nova Scotia Agricultural College is in Truro, and St. Francis Xavier University is in Antigonish.

Libraries: The Nova Scotia provincial library is in Halifax, and there are nine regional library systems in Nova Scotia.

TAXES Property taxes are the main source of revenue for municipal services such as fire protection and garbage collection. Each municipal government decides what the tax rate will be, but the provincial government assesses property values.

Tax example: In 2004, a family with an income of $50,000 would have paid $4,606 in provincial taxes if they were living in Halifax, according to a table prepared by Saskatchewan Finance. Provincial income taxes would have accounted for $2,606, with retail sales taxes adding $1,690 to the family's tax bill, and gasoline taxes, $310. This would have made Nova Scotia's provincial tax bill one of the steeper ones in Canada.

The 2005–2006 provincial budget contained no new taxes, and in fact, reduced some taxes for businesses.

GOVERNMENT *Premier*: John Hamm (Progressive Conservative). (Mr. Hamm has announced plans to retire in 2006.) The Legislative Assembly has fifty-two elected members.

Political Parties: The political parties represented in the Legislative Assembly include the Liberal Party, the Progressive Conservative Association of Nova Scotia, and the New Democratic Party. In addition, there are fourth parties such as the Marijuana Party and the Nova Scotia Party. Fourth parties tend to be fleeting, with small constituencies.

The province has eighteen counties, with three regional municipalities and thirty-one towns. Each municipality and town elects a mayor and a council. An elected council governs in each rural municipality, with a leader, called a warden, being chosen from the council. Nova Scotia elects ten members to the House of Commons. Nine representatives of the province are appointed to the Senate by the federal government.

TRANSPORTATION The province's largest airport is in Halifax, but Sydney and Yarmouth also have airports. The largest seaport is in Halifax. Ferries and other ships link coastal towns with ports in Maine, New Brunswick, Newfoundland, and Prince Edward Island. Railways serve the province's cities, linking them to a national system. The main highways run along coastal areas in the western part of the province.

CARS AND AUTO INSURANCE Discriminatory underwriting practices, including the use of age and gender as the basis for a rating, are prohibited by law. A consumer advocate monitors compliance.

Payments for nonpermanent minor injuries are capped at $2,500. A Nova Scotia Insurance Review Board reviews and approves future rate changes.

ATTITUDES TOWARD GAYS Same-sex marriage has been legal in Nova Scotia since September 2004.

MEDIA Eight daily newspapers in Nova Scotia, including the *Royal Gazette,* whose precursor, the *Halifax-Gazette,* dates from 1752 and was the first paper published in Canada. There are twenty radio stations and two television stations. Cable TV service is available in many communities.

CULTURE Nova Scotia has a diverse cultural heritage that is reflected in music, art, and food.

Cape Breton is world renowned for its music, a combination of Scottish, Acadian, and Irish. In addition, there are many other opportunities throughout the province to hear Celtic music, both in concert and informally.

Many of Nova Scotia's museums reflect the province's history and culture: The Art Gallery of Nova Scotia has a collection of regional, national, and international art. Some other museums include Acadian House Museum; Army Museum; Atlantic Canada Aviation Museum; Fisheries Museum of the Atlantic (in Lunenburg); Fundy Geological Museum; Maritime Museum of the Atlantic (in Halifax); Museum of Natural History; Waverly Heritage Museum. Nova Scotia's first Mi'kmaq art gallery, Naguset Native Art Gallery, is in Mahone Bay.

Pier 21 in Halifax is a National Historic Site that recounts the immigrant experience.

In Halifax, Symphony Nova Scotia plays classical music and pops. The Neptune Theatre, Halifax's leading professional theatre, presents plays and musicals.

FESTIVALS Around eight hundred festivals are held annually in Nova Scotia. Among them are: Annapolis Valley Apple Blossom Festival (May); Halifax Celtic Feis (June); Nova Scotia Multicultural Festival in Halifax (June); Stan Rogers Folk Festival in Canso (July); Nova Scotia International Tattoo in Halifax (July); Atlantic Jazz Festival in Halifax (July); Pictou Lobster Carnival (July); Antigonish Highland Games (July); Festival acadien de Clare (late July–mid-August); Halifax International Busker Festival (August); Celtic Colors International Festival (October).

SPORTS The Halifax Mooseheads (Junior A division hockey team). The Moosehead Premium Dry Speedway hosts auto races from May through October. Pro golf tours stop in Halifax.

Summer: Deep-sea fishing, hunting, canoeing, sailing, kayaking, windsurfing, golf, shipwreck diving, tennis. Winter: downhill and cross-country skiing, snowmobiling.

Parks: Two national parks: the Cape Breton Highlands National Park on

Cape Breton Island is known for its dramatic cliffs and its scenic highway, the Cabot Trail; Kejimkujik National Park in southwestern Nova Scotia offers canoeing, camping, and hiking and in the fall a brilliant display of foliage. The province also has nine national historic parks and sites. There are about 120 provincial parks.

PUBLIC SAFETY Nova Scotia experienced an increase in crime of 10.5 percent between 2002 and 2003, the largest increase in the Atlantic provinces. However, Nova Scotia's homicide rate was the lowest in twenty-five years. In 2003, there were 1,199 violent crimes and 3,654 property crimes (per 100,000 population).

BLACKS IN NOVA SCOTIA

According to the Black Cultural Centre for Nova Scotia—a museum, cultural, and educational center in Dartmouth (part of the Halifax Regional Municipality)—Nova Scotia is the birthplace of black culture in Canada.

Around 3,500 free blacks fled the American colonies between 1782 and 1785, seeking refuge in Nova Scotia and New Brunswick, where they thought they would find equality and economic opportunity. For the most part, they were disappointed.

Black immigrants were cheated of land that had been promised to them and forced to work on public projects, the Black Cultural Centre says. Slavery had been practiced in Quebec since 1689, the Centre says, when King Louis XIV of France decreed that it was legal. By 1749, there were slaves in Nova Scotia. Between 1783 and 1784, around 1,232 black slaves were brought to Nova Scotia, Prince Edward Island, and New Brunswick by British masters.

Slaves were as harshly treated in Canada as they were in the United States, according to the Black Cultural Centre. However, slavery did not flourish in Canada, and beginning in the late eighteenth century, British North American law courts ruled against it.

By the time legal emancipation was declared throughout the British Empire on August 1, 1834, most Canadian slaves were already free. The British government set aside money to compensate slave masters for their loss of property, but no one in Canada applied.

Continued on next page

BLACKS IN NOVA SCOTIA

Prior to the U.S. Civil War, many escaped slaves utilized the Underground Railroad of safe houses to make their way to Canada and freedom. There are a number of Nova Scotian communities, including Preston, Guysborough, Lincolnville, Tracadie, and Boylston, whose residents can trace their ancestry to these escaped slaves.

Blacks came to the Maritime provinces, particularly to Nova Scotia, at other times and for other reasons. Jamaicans came in the late eighteenth century, though most of them left for Sierra Leone in Africa in 1800. During the War of 1812, around two thousand U.S. blacks fled to the Maritimes. In the 1920s, hundreds of Caribbean immigrants came north to work in the Cape Breton coal mines and steel factories.

Today, blacks constitute the largest group of visible minorities in Nova Scotia. During February, for instance, people who describe themselves as Black Loyalist Families stage a monthlong celebration of their African heritage.

SNAPSHOT: PRINCE EDWARD ISLAND

Canada's smallest province is the only one completely separated from the mainland of North America, its only tie being the 8.1-mile-long Confederation Bridge that opened on May 31, 1997. The privately owned bridge links Borden-Carleton on Prince Edward Island with Cape Jourimain, New Brunswick. It is the longest bridge over ice-covered waters in the world, built to withstand the pummeling that the Northumberland Strait delivers in the winter. It takes ten to twelve minutes to cross the bridge at normal driving speeds.

For people in search of peace and quiet, Prince Edward Island may be the place. The island lacks the raw materials and power resources that would have allowed it to industrialize. The economy is based on agriculture and fishing, as it has been for years, and more recently, on tourism.

Visitors to the island are attracted by its bucolic beauty—pink sand dunes in Prince Edward Island National Park, ruddy cliffs, small villages, and an interesting mixture of Celtic, Acadian, and Aboriginal culture.

Some visitors come in search of the turn-of-the-last-century way of life that they read about in *Anne of Green Gables*. Lucy Maud Montgomery's red-headed orphan has made Prince Edward Island world famous. The marketing of Anne is an industry in the province. Visitors can see Green Gables where the spunky Anne "grew up" and visit other places mentioned in Montgomery's books as well as the remains of the house where the author grew up. There's *Anne of Green Gables—The Musical* (performed in the province's capital, Charlottetown, during the summer), an Anne of Green Gables Museum at Silver Bush, a three-day "Anne" tour and so on.

Real history is on view here, too. Prince Edward Island was the birthplace of the Dominion of Canada. On September 1, 1864, what is now known as the Charlottetown Conference was convened to discuss Canadian union. Representatives of Nova Scotia, New Brunswick, Upper Canada (Ontario), and Lower Canada (Quebec) attended as well as their P.E.I. hosts.

After two more conferences, Canada became a nation in 1867, ironically without Prince Edward Island, which was flush at the time from shipbuilding and thought there would be no monetary advantage. When some railroad deals went sour six years later and the federal government agreed to help with a bailout, P.E.I. reconsidered, joining the Confederation in 1873.

The human history of Prince Edward Island begins with the Mi'kmaq Indians, who used the island during the summer for fishing, hunting, and some planting. In 1534, Jacques Cartier landed on the northern shore and claimed it for Francis I, king of France. Over the years, it has had various names reflecting its political fortunes: The Mi'kmaq called it "Epekwitk" meaning "resting on the waves." The French called it Ile Saint-Jean. The British acquired it in 1763 with the Treaty of Paris that ended the Seven Years' War and called it St. John's Island. It was named Prince Edward Island in 1799 in honor of Edward, the Duke of Kent and father of Queen Victoria.

Charlottetown was designated the capital city in 1765 and named for Queen Charlotte, the wife of King George III. The king decided to pay off a few debts by parceling out the island to some British nobles. Their absentee ownership was a disaster for the island. Most made no attempt to develop their holdings, but they were also unwilling to sell them. Immigrants had no incentive to settle on P.E.I. However, some Scots arrived in the late-eighteenth and early-nineteenth centuries, and two hundred American Loyalists fled there after the American Revolution.

Today, some Americans are still finding sanctuary on the island. Carol Horne, a P.E.I. native, describes her sister, Sandra, and her sister's New

York–born husband, John. They moved to Charlottetown from Boston a couple of years ago. "I think they wanted a different lifestyle," Carol says. "Now he runs his business from the front room of the house. They look out their back window onto a river. They walk up to the gym every day or walk around the boardwalk in Charlottetown harbor. Nothing is more than about six blocks away and life is simpler."

LOCATION In the eastern part of Canada on the Gulf of St. Lawrence. Separated from Nova Scotia and New Brunswick by the shallow Northumberland Strait.

GEOGRAPHY The island is a little more than 175 miles long and varies in width from 2.5 to 37 miles. Constitutes 0.1 percent of Canada's total land mass. Area, 2,184.76 square miles. Gently rolling farmland, plus cliffs, sand dunes, marshes. Forty-six percent of the island is farmland. The fertile soil is red in color because it contains a lot of iron oxide.

CLIMATE Spring temperatures range from 46°F to 71°F; summer daytime temperatures are usually in the seventies but can go as high as 90°F; autumn temperatures, 46°F to 71°F, with cool evenings; winter, 11°F to 26°F. Average annual precipitation, 44 inches.

PROVINCIAL CAPITAL Charlottetown (population, 32,245)

POPULATION 135,294 (2001 census); 138,278 (est., Oct. 2005)

POPULATION DENSITY 63 people per square mile.
P.E.I. has the highest population density in Canada.

ETHNIC DIVERSITY Most people in P.E.I. have Scottish, English, Irish, or French ancestors (in that order). A much smaller number are of German and Dutch descent.

In 2001, the immigrant population of P.E.I. constituted 3.1 percent of the total.

Visible Minorities: A very small number of visible minorities. Province-wide, they constituted 0.01 percent of the population in 2001. In Charlottetown, just 0.02 percent of the population were visible minorities in 2001, including 140 black residents and 115 Chinese.

Religious Affiliations:

Catholic	47 percent
Protestant	43 percent

In 2001, there were 195 Muslims living in P.E.I., 135 Buddhists, and 55 Jews.

HEALTH See Appendix, page 215, for details on P.E.I.'s health care coverage and how to apply for it.

As of May 2005, P.E.I. is reconstructing its public health system. Regional health authorities are being replaced by a new Department of Social Services—eliminating 180 jobs and generating estimated savings of $9 million.

P.E.I. has an aging population. Women are having fewer children.

Average Life Expectancy (2001):

Males, 75.4 years

Females, 81.7 years

(P.E.I.'s life expectancy figures were lower than the national averages for Canada in 2001, particularly for males, where the national average was 77 years.)

Infant Mortality Rate (2001): 7.2 per 1,000 live births (the highest in the Atlantic provinces and higher than the Canadian national average of 5.2 per 1,000 live births).

ECONOMY The three primary industries are farming, fishing, and tourism.

Potatoes, which are sold throughout Canada and internationally, are the main crop, but P.E.I. farmers also sell tobacco and vegetables, dairy products, cattle, hogs, eggs, hens, chickens, and ranch-raised mink and fox for the fur industry.

High-quality fish come from P.E.I. waters, but the volume of fish such as cod, mackerel, hake, and tuna is relatively small. Lobstering is a major source of revenue in the fisheries sector. The island's Malpeque oysters are world famous, while P.E.I. mussels are served in fine restaurants throughout North America. Most of the catch is exported.

Irish moss, an algae that is processed into an emulsifying and stabilizing agent for beer, ice cream, toothpaste, and other products, is harvested and processed on the west coast of the island.

Tourism accounts for around $350 million in annual revenues.

In 2003, the province's gross domestic product was $3.9 billion.

There are approximately the same number of men and women in the workforce; however, women tend to work in clerical, administrative, and medical or health jobs, many of which pay less than jobs held by men. Most women earn less than $20,000 a year.

EARNINGS

Average earnings, working full year, full time: $33,511 (2001)

Median family income (couples): $50,912 (2001)

Average earnings of the population, 15 and over, for holders of a university certificate, diploma, or degree (2001): $37,063 (compared with $41,942 in Newfoundland and Labrador, a neighboring Atlantic province).

UNEMPLOYMENT RATE 11.3 percent (2004). The national average for 2004 was 7.2 percent. In Dec. 2005, the unemployment rate was 12.2 percent (compared to the national average for that month of 6.1 percent).

HOUSING Most people in P.E.I. live in single, detached houses, which they own. Only 18 percent of the population lives in rented housing.

Province-wide:

Average value of house: $110,815 (2004)

Average gross monthly payments for renters: $543 (2001)

Average monthly payments for owner-occupied dwellings: $605 (2001)

Charlottetown:

Average value of dwelling: $125,367 (2001)

Average gross monthly payments for renters: $580 (2001)

Average monthly payments for owner-occupied dwellings: $734 (2001)

EDUCATION The public school system is administered by the provincial department of education and three school boards—two regional, English-language boards and one French-language board that serves the entire province. Education is compulsory for children from age 7 to 15 but is available from ages 6 through high school graduation or age 20. The public school system begins in grade 1. There are around sixty-five elementary and secondary schools. Prince Edward Island children have not scored well on recent standardized tests of basic math and English.

There are four private schools in Charlottetown (Fair Isle Adventists, Full Circle Cooperative, Grace Christian School, and Immanuel Christian School). Otherwise, the only alternative to the free, public system is home-schooling.

A study found in 1991 that approximately 50 percent of working-age men in P.E.I. and approximately 40 percent of working-age women had not completed high school.

The University of Prince Edward Island, a small liberal arts college, was founded in Charlottetown in 1969 through the merger of St. Dunstan's University and Prince of Wales College. Tuition, $4,757 for provincial residents; $8,357 for international students. The Atlantic Veterinary College is on the university's campus.

Holland College, a public community college, has locations throughout the island.

The Canadian College of Piping and Celtic Performing Arts is one of two full-time bagpiping colleges in the world. Students also study fiddling, drumming, and Highland and step dance.

Libraries: The library system, which has more than twenty branches, is operated by the provincial department of education.

TAXES No provincial sales tax on clothing and footwear. Otherwise, the sales tax is 10 percent.

In March 2004, a family with $50,000 in total income would have paid $4,417 in provincial taxes in Charlottetown, with a breakdown as follows: provincial income tax, $2,848; retail sales tax, $1,289; gasoline tax, $280 (*Source*: Saskatchewan Finance).

GOVERNMENT *Premier:* Pat Binns (Progressive Conservative Party). The Legislative Assembly has twenty-seven elected members. Charlottetown sends five representatives to the assembly and Summerside sends two. The remaining regions of the province send one each.

Since the late nineteenth century, two parties have dominated Prince Edward Island politics, the Liberals and Progressive Conservatives. There have been third parties from time to time, but they have not done well.

Prince Edward Island sends four elected representatives to the federal Parliament in Ottawa. In addition, four senators are appointed by the federal government.

Prince Edward Island is divided into three counties, but there are no county governments. The cities and towns are governed by elected mayors and a council. The seventy-five unincorporated municipalities on the island are run by elected chairpersons and councilors.

PROVINCIAL HOLIDAY In Charlottetown and east, government employees and some in the private sector get a holiday on Gold Cup and Saucer parade day, in mid-August, when a major harness race is held in the capital. This is instead of a day off on the first Monday in August, a commonly observed holiday elsewhere in Canada.

TRANSPORTATION Accessible via the Confederation Bridge linking P.E.I. and New Brunswick. CTMA Ferries run from Souris, P.E.I., to the Magdalen Islands in the province of Quebec. Northumberland Ferries go between Wood Islands, P.E.I., and Caribou, Nova Scotia (from May to late December). Charlottetown has an airport with direct air service to and from Toronto and Montreal and connections through Halifax, Nova Scotia. Trains go to Moncton, New Brunswick, with bus connections to P.E.I. There are no trains on the island. There are around three thousand miles of roads, most of them paved.

CARS AND AUTO INSURANCE P.E.I. has the lowest auto insurance rates in Canada. Discriminatory underwriting practices are prohibited by law. Payments for nonpermanent minor injuries are capped at $2,500. When someone moves to P.E.I. from another country, they must register as a new driver with the Department of Transportation and Public Works. Licenses are valid for three years and expire on the licensee's birthday.

ATTITUDES TOWARD GAYS Before same-sex marriage became legal by federal law, Prince Edward Island did not issue marriage licenses to same-sex couples. Since 2000 there has been a Gay and Lesbian Pride Festival on the island in July.

MEDIA Two daily newspapers, the *Guardian* and the *Journal Pioneer*. Also, eight radio stations, three network TV stations, and cable television. CBC broadcasts a nightly program of Prince Edward Island news.

CULTURE Prince Edward Island attracts one million visitors between May and October—around eight times the resident population—so the island, and particularly its capital, Charlottetown, have cultural offerings that might not be there otherwise. "There are a lot of book clubs and poetry readings and art events and I think more culture than you would expect in a community of 30,000 or even 140,000 for the whole island," says Carol Horne.

Charlottetown has theatres, museums, and art galleries. The Confederation Centre of the Arts, which opened in 1964 for the centennial of the Charlottetown meeting that put Canada on the road to independence, has theatres, an art gallery and museum, a library, and restaurants.

Founders' Hall, a living history museum on the Charlottetown waterfront, presents the story of Canadian Confederation from 1864 to the creation of the territory of Nunavut in 1999.

There are long-running community theatres in Victoria-by-the-Sea and Georgetown.

St. Mary's Church in Indian River is known for chamber music, jazz, Celtic, contemporary, and choral music.

Most typical of Prince Edward Island culture are the numerous places, from pubs to community halls, with traditional Celtic ceilidhs—fiddling, dancing, and singing. During the summer there are ceilidhs almost every night of the week in one community or another.

FESTIVALS Charlottetown Festival (late May–October); Summerside Highland Gathering (June); Celtic Festival (late June–September 1); Atlantic Superstore Festival of Lights (late June–early July); Bluegrass and Oldtime Music Festival (July); Evangeline Bluegrass Festival (July); Summerside Lobster Carnival (July); Rollo Bay Fiddle Festival (July); P.E.I. Potato Blossom Festival (July); Atlantic Fiddlers Jamboree (July); St. Peter's Wild Blueberry Festival (August); L. M. Montgomery Festival (August); L'Exposition Agricole et let Festival Acadien de la Région Evangeline (September); P.E.I. International Shellfish Festival (September).

SPORTS Deep-sea and fly-fishing, clamming, hunting, birdwatching, sea kayaking, canoeing, sailing, windsurfing, horseback riding.

More than twenty-five golf courses in the province. The Links at Crowbush Cove is considered one of the finest courses in Canada.

Renowned for harness racing, which has been a part of island life for more than a hundred years.

The 175-mile-long Confederation Trail, which was developed on abandoned railroad lines, is used for hiking, cycling, and snowmobiling.

Prince Edward Island National Park, on the north shore of the island, presents visitors with a landscape of pink sand dunes, salt marshes, and red sandstone cliffs. Green Gables, the farmhouse owned by Lucy Maud Montgomery's cousins and the setting for her "Anne" novels is in the park. Around thirty provincial parks offer hiking trails and wildlife viewing. Some also offer camping.

PUBLIC SAFETY In 2003, Prince Edward Island had 897 violent crimes, 3,598 property crimes, and 8,619 criminal offenses (all per 100,000 population). This represented an increase in the crime rate of 9.8 percent between 2002 and 2003. Double-digit increases in vehicle theft were reported in P.E.I. While most provinces reported decreases in impaired driving, P.E.I. showed an increase of 11 percent, the largest of any province.

SNAPSHOT: NEWFOUNDLAND AND LABRADOR

Canada begins in Newfoundland and Labrador with Mile One of the Trans-Canada Highway, the road that ends five thousand miles away in Victoria, British Columbia. Cape Spear is the most easterly point on the North American continent, just ten minutes outside of the province's capital, St. John's, which is one of the oldest settlements in North America. It was claimed for Queen Elizabeth I in 1583 by Sir Humphrey Gilbert when he came upon what is now the city's harbor.

"How old is the city?" Lorraine McGrath, a St. John's native, was asked. She paused for a minute to calculate. "Five hundred and eight years," she said. She was figuring from the time when the Italian explorer John Cabot, financed by King Henry VII of Great Britain, entered St. John's Harbor on St. John's Day in 1497.

Canada also begins in Newfoundland and Labrador because of the Vikings. Their only known settlement in North America is at L'Anse aux Meadows, Newfoundland, the windswept tip of the Great Northern Peninsula, where a Norse settlement existed for perhaps ten years around A.D. 1000.

By the late 1500s word of the bountiful fishing off Newfoundland had drawn French, Portuguese, and Spanish fleets to the area. Various English explorers attempted to set up colonies, and England and France battled each other until the Treaty of Paris in 1763 gave Labrador to the English. In 1832, the British government established a legislature for Newfoundland with a governor, a council, and an elected general assembly that could make laws, subject to the approval of the British Parliament.

Newfoundland not only has Canada's oldest European settlement, it is the country's newest province. Though party to the talks of Confederation in the 1860s, it didn't join the Confederation until March 31, 1949. Before then, it was a separate, self-governing part of the British Empire known as the Dominion of Newfoundland.

In 2001 the Canadian Parliament changed the name of the province to Newfoundland and Labrador.

Because of its easterly location, Newfoundland has been the scene of many dramatic events. The first successful transatlantic telegraph cable connecting Valentia, Ireland, to Newfoundland was dropped onto the ocean floor by the steamship *Great Eastern* in 1866. The ship landed at Heart's Content, completing its mission, on July 27 of that year.

A new era of communication began when Guglielmo Marconi received the first transatlantic wireless message at St. John's on December 12, 1901. The Morse code signal came from Poldhu in Cornwall.

Americans will remember Newfoundland for another reason: Gander. On September 11, 2001, after the World Trade Center attacks, American air space was closed and jetliners returning to the United States stopped in Canada. Thirty-eight planes carrying 6,595 passengers and crew were diverted to Gander, whose population is barely 10,000.

"They immediately put up emergency services in their city and all the surrounding areas," said Dan Stone, a history professor at the University of Winnipeg. "People threw open their homes. . . . In addition to services being made available, people just went to the airport and said, 'You're American on that plane? Come. I have a spare room.' There was enormous love and sympathy for Americans in the United States when it was needed."

Indeed, Newfoundlanders are noted for their friendliness. They are also known for being funny. "We have a couple of comedy clubs in St. John's," said Lorraine. "We had a comedian in from Ontario. Afterward, I met him and said, "I hope you had a good show!" He said, "Are you kidding? This is the hardest place in Canada to play. Everybody here's funnier than I am."

LOCATION The most easterly part of North America. (See map on page xix.) Newfoundland is closer to Ireland than it is to Ontario.

GEOGRAPHY 156,648 square miles (40,818 Newfoundland, 115,830 Labrador), the largest of the Atlantic provinces. Newfoundland is an island. Labrador is part of the Canadian mainland. Newfoundland's interior is thickly forested. The deeply indented rocky coastline is 6,000 miles long. The Great Northern Peninsula in Newfoundland is the northernmost visible tip of the Appalachian Mountain chain that runs south along the Eastern Seaboard of Canada and the United States to Georgia. Labrador is part of the Canadian Shield and has a barren interior and a rugged coastline.

The famous Newfoundland banks that yielded a rich harvest of cod and other fish for centuries are large areas of shallow water to the south and east of the province, in the Atlantic Ocean.

The province has a time zone unique in North America, half an hour ahead of Atlantic Time. (Atlantic Time applies in most of Labrador.)

CLIMATE Arctic winds and ocean currents keep it cool. Average January temperature, 19°F; average July temperature, 59°F. Average annual precipitation, 44 inches.

PROVINCIAL CAPITAL St. John's, on the Avalon Peninsula, has been the capital of Newfoundland since 1729 and is also the largest city (population, 2001 census: 99,182). The second largest city is Mount Pearl, with a population of 24,964.

POPULATION 512,930 (2001 census). In 2004, the estimated population was 517,000, dropping to 515,591 in October 2005. Since 1981, the province had been losing population almost steadily. A large proportion of those who left were aged 15 to 29.

POPULATION DENSITY Three people per square mile. In both Newfoundland and Labrador, most people live near the coast.

ETHNIC DIVERSITY Most of the population has an English background, followed by Irish, Scottish, French, and North American Indian. In 2001, there were 1,065 people from the United States living in the province, amounting to 0.02 percent of the population.

Visible Minorities: The number of visible minorities in the total population is small (around 1 percent) according to the 2001 census. Of these, most come from South Asia and the next largest group from China.

Religious Affiliations:

Protestant	60 percent
Catholic	37 percent
None	3 percent

In 2001, there were 630 Muslims in the province, 405 Hindus, 185 Buddhists, and 140 Jews.

LANGUAGE Newfoundlanders are known for their colorful, idiomatic speech, English and Irish in origin, but hewn and honed by local usage. *The Dictionary of Newfoundland English* (published in 1990 by the University of Toronto Press) captures some of its humor and variety. Among some wonderful Newfie words are "asquish," meaning "askew," and "flahoolach" meaning "lavish" or "wasteful." There are many more.

HEALTH See Appendix, page 213, for details on Newfoundland and Labrador's health care coverage and how to apply for it.

Average Life Expectancy (2001):
Males, 75.3 years
Females, 80.5 years

This is less than the Canadian national averages for that year of 77.0 years for men and 82.0 years for women.

Infant Mortality Rate: 4.9 per 1,000 live births (2001)

ECONOMY Oil production and mining, particularly of iron ore, account for around $1 billion each year of the province's revenue. The coastal waters off Newfoundland and Labrador have been fishing areas for hundreds of years, but in modern days they have been overfished and the Canadian government has imposed restrictions. Nevertheless, the province's fish products are valued at more than $4 billion annually. Agriculture, a small part of the economy, includes dairy, poultry, nursery products, and forestry. Pulp and paper products manufactured in the province bring in $300 million annually in export revenue. Seafood products are also manufactured. Tourism has become increasingly important as a source of revenue.

Most workers are in service jobs: community, business, and personal services, finance, government, trade, transportation, and communication. Industry, which employs 32 percent of Newfoundlanders, includes construction, manufacturing, mining, and utilities. Only 3 percent work in agriculture.

EARNINGS
   Province-wide:
      Median family income (couples): $45,253 (2001)
      Average earnings of the population, 15 and over, for holders of a
         university certificate, diploma, or degree (2001): $41,942
   St. John's:
      Average earnings, working full year, full-time: $28,125 (2001)
      Median family income (couples): $59,294 (2001)

UNEMPLOYMENT RATE 15.8 percent (Dec. 2005), the highest in Canada. The national average for that month was 6.1 percent.

HOUSING Average price for a house in St. John's in 2004, $132,993; in central Newfoundland it was $54,342.
   Province-wide:
      Average gross monthly payments for renters: $513 (2001)
      Average monthly payments for owner-occupied dwellings: $534
         (2001)
   St. John's:
      Average gross monthly payments for renters: $555 (2001)
      Average monthly payments for owner-occupied dwellings: $795
         (2001)

EDUCATION Newfoundland and Labrador have a single school system administered by five local school boards of fifteen members each, who are elected. Children in the province are required to go to school from age 6 to 16. Schools are publicly funded. There are also a number of private elementary and secondary schools.

The province has one university, Memorial University, but it is Atlantic Canada's largest degree-granting institution. It is one of the world's leading centers of ocean research and also has a respected folklore department. It has a new $1.2 million Petro-Canada Hall for music students and the community. Its main campus is in St. John's; another campus, the Sir Wilfred Grenell College in Corner Brook, specializes in theatre, visual arts, and environmental studies. Tuition for in-province students is $2,992; international students, $8,950.

The College of the North Atlantic, in Stephenville, has more than fifteen campuses in Newfoundland and Labrador. It offers vocational and technical training and first-year university courses.

TAXES Most of the province's income comes from federal grants and corporation and personal income taxes. Service fees, license fees, and sales taxes on gasoline, alcohol, and other products also provide income, as do royalties on natural resources. The provincial sales tax is 8 percent.

GOVERNMENT *Premier:* Danny Williams (Progressive Conservative Party). The House of Assembly has forty-eight members, each of whom represents one district.

Local governments in St. John's, Corner Brook, and Mount Pearl operate under city acts passed by the House of Assembly. Each of the incorporated towns and communities is governed by a council of five to eleven members, who are elected to serve four-year terms.

Parties represented in the House of Assembly: Liberal Party of Newfoundland and Labrador, New Democratic Party of Newfoundland and Labrador, Progressive Conservative Party of Newfoundland and Labrador.

The province elects six members to the federal House of Commons. The federal government appoints six members to the Senate.

PROVINCIAL HOLIDAY There is no holiday on the first Monday in August as is true in many other provinces; however, Regatta Day is often held on the first Wednesday in August—or the first day thereafter when weather permits. (The St. John's Regatta was first held in 1826 and is the oldest continuously held sporting event in North America.)

TRANSPORTATION The Trans-Canada Highway (Route 1) is the main road on Newfoundland, running between St. John's and Port aux Basques, 565 miles away. Public buses traverse the island along the Trans-Canada Highway. Most secondary roads are paved. St. John's International Airport connects to other places in Canada and within the province. In addition, there are flights to Europe, including a daily nonstop to London. Gander also has an international airport.

There are two ferries connecting Nova Scotia with Newfoundland, one to Port aux Basques (around a five-hour trip) and one to Argentia (around fourteen hours). Ferries also run between Newfoundland and Quebec Province and along the coast of Labrador.

CARS AND AUTO INSURANCE The cost and availability of auto insurance was a big issue in the 2003 Newfoundland and Labrador elections. Legislation in 2004 eliminated ratings based on age, gender, and marital status. Insurance premiums were reevaluated and reduced. Insurance companies were required to inform consumers of their rights in making a claim and a new process was instituted for setting rates.

ATTITUDES TOWARD GAYS Same-sex marriage has been legal in Newfoundland and Labrador since December 2004.

CULTURE English, Irish, French, Viking, and Aboriginal cultures are preserved and explored in ten national historic sites, ten provincial historic sites, three provincial museums, and over 150 museums and interpretation centers.

The Rooms, a provincial cultural facility in St. John's, opened in 2005 as the permanent home for Newfoundland and Labrador artifacts, archival materials, and an art gallery.

The Newfoundland Museum in St. John's has artifacts from the Beothuks, who were living in Newfoundland at the time of the European contact. The last member of the tribe died in 1829. The Arts and Culture Centre near Memorial University exhibits Canadian painting and sculpture and has a library and a theater. Memorial University has a botanical garden.

FESTIVALS More than four hundred festivals and musical events annually. Theatre festivals take place during the summer at Gros Morne, Stephenville, and elsewhere in the province. Corner Brook Winter Carnival (February); Cow Head Lobster Festival (July); Humber Valley Strawberry Festival (late July–early August); Royal St. John's Regatta (August); Ramea

Paddle Festival (August); Newfoundland and Labrador Folk Festival (August); Labrador Straits Bakeapple Folk Festival (August). The biennial Sound Symposium in St. John's brings together musicians from around Canada (and around the world) for a week of concerts, jam sessions, and workshops (July).

SPORTS The St. John's Maple Leafs (American Hockey League) play at Mile One Stadium.

Recreational Sports: Hunting, fishing, mountain climbing, kayaking, canoeing, whitewater rafting, skiing, dogsledding, snowmobiling. Over twenty golf courses.

Parks: Two national parks, Gros Morne on the west coast, with billion-year-old rocks, is twenty times older than the Rockies. It is a UNESCO World Heritage Site. Terra Nova is on the east coast.

There are thirty-one provincial parks and ecological reserves. The largest provincial park, Barachois Pond Park, is near St. George's in the Long Range Mountains. Sir Richard Squires Memorial Park, on the Humber River, is famous for Big Falls. Each spring, Atlantic salmon leap these falls to spawn upstream. The Witless Bay Ecological Reserve is the largest Atlantic Puffin sanctuary in North America.

PUBLIC SAFETY Total criminal code offenses decreased in St. John's by 6.4 percent between 2002 and 2003. For the province as a whole, they increased by 3.6 percent in that period. In 2003, there were 933 instances of violent crime (an increase of 1.3 percent) and 2,611 instances of property crime (an increase of 4.9 percent), both per 100,000 population.

Counterfeiting incidents tripled in Newfoundland and Labrador in 2003 over what they had been in 2002. In addition, there were double-digit increases in motor vehicle theft.

MOVING TO NEWFOUNDLAND AND LABRADOR: ONE COUPLE'S EXPERIENCE

Arnold Bennett was fifty-six and Nancy Bennett fifty-two in July 1996 when they moved from Bethesda, Maryland, to a house in Conception Bay South, just outside St. John's, Newfoundland.

They moved, in Arnold's words, with the expectation that they

Continued on next page

would "lead a life similar to the one we were leading, but in a community that is friendlier, more caring, and more socially responsible— and without the shouting matches that characterize life in the United States."

They settled in Newfoundland, he said, "because we fell in love with the people, the culture, the beauty of the place, the magical light, and the invigorating air."

Because of their ages and medical history, they felt that it was wise to use an immigration attorney. After much research and interviews with several lawyers, they settled on "a top-notch lawyer, Howard Greenberg (Toronto, 416-943-0288)," Arnold said. "It cost a few thousand dollars."

Arnold had a small research grant at the time of the move and Nancy, who is in the public relations business, brought clients with her and began to work with them at a distance. Since then, Arnold has made a couple of films with funding from Canadian broadcasters while Nancy has continued to do public relations work for clients in the United States and Canada. In addition, after the move, she worked for four years as the public relations director for a Canadian advertising agency.

That job with a Canadian company qualified her for a work visa, which made both Arnold and Nancy eligible for full Canadian health care coverage. After they became permanent residents, the health care coverage became permanent. Their experience with Canadian health care has, in Arnold's words, been "extremely positive."

On January 21, 2004, Arnold and Nancy became Canadian citizens. Would they make the move again? "Yes," said Nancy. "Yes," said Arnold. "My only regret is that we didn't do it decades sooner."

SNAPSHOT: Yukon Territory

"The Yukon to me embodies what I loved about Canada in the first place," says Chicago-born Linda Bates, who immigrated to Canada in the early 1970s and now lives in Vancouver. "It's full of people who can do everything. They can read poetry in the morning and go and shoot a moose and butcher it in the afternoon and fix their car the next day. They're real generalists."

Bates also mentions that the Yukon is cold—too cold for her to contemplate living there, as it might be for a lot of people. But not everyone. The Yukon's population is growing at a far faster rate than that of Canada as a whole.

The Yukon had its most adventurous days during the Gold Rush in the late 1890s following the discovery of gold on Bonanza Creek, in August 1896, by George Carmack and his Indian friend Skookim Jim. Bonanza Creek was a tributary of the Klondike River, which flows into the Yukon River near Dawson City. When news of the discovery of gold reached the world, thousands of prospectors came to the region.

Many of the prospectors were rough men and the North-West Mounted Police were dispatched in 1897 to keep law and order. By 1898 some 35,000 people were living in the Yukon and it became a territory with Dawson City as the capital. Between 1898 and 1904, more than $100 million in gold was mined in the region. In several years, after much of the surface ore was gone, many of the prospectors moved on. The population of the territory had declined to 4,157 by 1921.

It began to grow again during World War II when the Alaska Highway was constructed, with part of it spanning the Yukon. In the 1950s, Distant Early Warning Line radar stations brought new people to the territory. Renewed interest in mining brought still more people in the 1960s.

Rail service made the town of Whitehorse a distribution point for the territory. It eventually grew larger than Dawson City and was made the territorial capital in 1950.

In 1979, the federal government gave the territory more authority over such things as education and taxes. In the mid-1990s, the federal government granted self-government to some Yukon Indians and settled their land claims. As with other parts of Canada's vast Northwest Territories, First Nations peoples have lived in the area for thousands of years.

In 1999 the Yukon government signed an agreement with the Vuntut Gwitchin people, recognizing a First Nations tribe as a legitimate government for the first time in the territory's history.

Larger than the state of California, the Yukon's population of 30,469 people is far outnumbered by its population of caribou (185,000) and its 50,000 moose.

LOCATION (See map on pages xviii–xix.) Skagway, Alaska, is the nearest U.S. city, about 335 miles from Dawson City.

GEOGRAPHY Area, 186,661 square miles. More than 80 percent of the Yukon is wilderness. Dawson City, the first capital of the Yukon Territory, is near the border with Alaska. The present capital of the Yukon, Whitehorse, is much farther south and to the east, closer to the British Columbia border.

CLIMATE The Yukon Territory, like the other Canadian territories, has cold winters and cool summers. Average January temperature, −2°F at Whitehorse and −16°F at Dawson; average summer temperatures, 50°F in the north and 60°F in the south. Rainfall averages 4 to 10 inches a year. Annual snowfall ranges from 28 inches in the north to 79 inches in the south. Almost eight months of winter.

TERRITORIAL CAPITAL Whitehorse (population, 22,673 [2004])
 Latitude: 60° 43' N; Longitude: 135° 4' W

POPULATION 30,469 (2004); 31,227 (est., January 2005)
 Visible Minorities: Visible minorities constitute 3.6 percent of the population (2001 census).
 Population Density: 15 people per 100 square miles.
 Languages: Primarily English-speaking, but eight First Nations language groups.
 Religious Affiliations:

None	39 percent
Protestant	33 percent
Catholic	21 percent

HEALTH See Appendix, page 216, for details on the Yukon's health care coverage and how to apply for it.
 There are doctors in Dawson, Faro, Watson Lake, and Whitehorse. Dentists practice in Whitehorse and travel to other settlements. Dawson, Mayo, Watson Lake, and Whitehorse have hospitals. Other settlements have nursing stations.
 Average Life Expectancy (2001):
  Males, 74.1 years
  Females, 79.6 years

(These rates are lower than the Canadian national averages of 77.0 years for males and 82.0 years for females in 2001.)
 Infant Mortality Rate: 8.7 per 1,000 live births. (This is higher than anywhere else in Canada except for Nunavut.)

ECONOMY Large deposits of asbestos, coal, copper, gold, lead, nickel, silver, and zinc. Mining and forestry are major occupations, as is fishing, which mostly involves salmon on the Yukon River. Natural gas and oil exploration began to contribute to the economy in the early 1990s. Service occupations, including health care, education, and tourism, are the main source of jobs. The government also employs many people. In spite of the short growing season, there is some agriculture, including a number of commercial egg producers.

EARNINGS

Average earnings, working full year, full-time: $44,605 (2001)
Median family income (couples): $71,553
Average earnings of the population, 15 and over, for holders of a
university certificate, diploma, or degree (2001): $45,982

UNEMPLOYMENT RATE 11.6 percent

In 2001, males had an unemployment rate of 14.5 percent and females, an unemployment rate of 8.6 percent.

HOUSING

Average house price (2004): $153,490
Average gross monthly payments for rented dwellings: $672 (2001)
Average monthly payments for owner-occupied dwellings: $851
(2001)

EDUCATION Public and Roman Catholic schools in most population areas go up to grade 9. Grades 10 through 12 are available in Carmacks, Dawson, Faro, Haines Junction, Mayo, Pelly Crossing, Watson Lake, and Whitehorse.

Yukon College is in Whitehorse.

GOVERNMENT *Government Leader:* Dennis Fentie (Yukon Party). A commissioner, appointed in Ottawa, is the formal head of government of the Yukon Territory, but a premier who presides over an executive council is the actual head of the Yukon government. He or she is a member of the party that holds the most seats in the seventeen-member Legislative Assembly.

The Yukon is represented in the federal government by one representative and one senator.

TRANSPORTATION Airlines link the Yukon with Alaska, Alberta, British Columbia, and the Northwest Territories. Ferries run from Bellingham, Washington, and British Columbia. The Alaska Highway, built in 1942 by U.S. and Canadian army personnel (in response to the Japanese invasion of

the Aleutian Islands, threatening Alaska), covers about six hundred miles of the Yukon Territory, while the Dempster Highway connects the Yukon with Inuvik in the Northwest Territories. It is the only public highway in Canada that crosses the Arctic Circle. There are 2,942 miles of highways in the Yukon.

ATTITUDES TOWARD GAYS Same-sex marriage has been legal in the Yukon since July 2004. An organization called the Gay and Lesbian Alliance of Yukon is based in Whitehorse.

MEDIA The Canadian Broadcasting Corporation's radio station at Whitehorse transmits its programs to the entire territory. There are three other radio stations serving Whitehorse. CBC Television reaches nearly all communities in the territory via satellite or cable. There are two newspapers in Whitehorse and one in Dawson.

CULTURE Robert William Service, known as the bard of the Yukon, wrote his first famous works in Whitehorse. He went to Dawson in 1908, where his small log cabin on the edge of town has been preserved. Another famous Yukon writer, Jack London (who wrote *Call of the Wild* and *White Fang*), lived and wrote in Dawson City during the Gold Rush. Canadian writer and historian Pierre Berton was born in the Yukon.

The Macbride Museum in Whitehorse has exhibits of prehistoric mammals, the Gold Rush and First Nations' relics, as well as minerals of the territory. The Yukon Arts Centre has an art gallery featuring contemporary works, and a theatre that has concerts, plays, and musicals. There is also a Yukon Transportation Museum showing various methods of transportation used in the territory over the years. The *Queen of the Yukon,* sister plane to Charles Lindbergh's *Spirit of St. Louis,* is part of the museum's collection.

Many old buildings in downtown Dawson City have been restored, and the Dawson City Museum has Gold Rush items and First Nations' artifacts. There is also an outdoor transportation exhibit. The Palace Grand Theatre presents vaudeville shows. Diamond Tooth Gertie's Gambling Hall in Dawson City features cancan dancing as well as gambling.

FESTIVALS Frostbite Music Festival in Whitehorse (February); Yukon International Storytelling Festival in Whitehorse (June); Alsek Music Festival in Haines Junction (June); Discovery Days Festival in Dawson City (August).

SPORTS Winter: downhill and cross-country skiing, snowmobiling, snow-shoeing, dogsledding. Summer: kayaking and whitewater rafting (on rapids in Kluane National Park and elsewhere), fishing, horseback riding, mountain climbing. There is a year-round swimming pool at Takhini Hot Springs off the Klondike Highway at Kilometer Post 10. The Yukon Quest International Sled Dog Race takes place each year in February, starting in Whitehorse.

Parks: Three national parks: Kluane, in the southwest of the Yukon Territory, is the site of Mount Logan, Canada's tallest mountain (19,551 feet), and the world's largest nonpolar ice fields. There is no road access into the park; it must be explored on foot or horseback or by kayak. Ivvavik National Park is at the northern tip of the Yukon, and Vuntut National Park is south of Ivvavik. There are four territorial parks.

PUBLIC SAFETY The Yukon experienced a decline in crime rate of 2.1 percent between 2002 and 2003. There were a total of 8,075 criminal code offenses in the territory in 2003 (excluding traffic violations).

SNAPSHOT: Northwest Territories

Most people who live in the Northwest Territories are there because it's their ancestral and cultural homeland or because they want to make money. "The Land of the Midnight Sun," as the Northwest Territories is sometimes called, has increased in population since gem-grade diamonds were discovered there in 1991. However, there are still only around 42,000 people living in an area twice the size of Texas.

The Northwest Territories had been home to Inuit and Indians for thousands of years before Europeans arrived. The region was called the North West Territory and Rupert's Land by the Hudson's Bay Company, which owned it until 1870. At that time, those lands were acquired by the new Dominion of Canada. Between 1870 and 1912, portions of the Northwest Territories were parceled out to Manitoba, the Yukon, Alberta, Saskatchewan, Ontario, and Quebec.

The eastern section of the N.W.T. became the territory of Nunavut in 1999 and the N.W.T. shrank from 1,322,910 square miles to 452,478 square miles.

The N.W.T. is still a frontier where what might be strange in more southerly and temperate climates is normal. In winter, roads open across frozen seas. In Yellowknife, the territorial capital (which has its share of high-rises), some people still live in Gold Rush cabins or houseboats and paddle their way to work. Above the Arctic Circle, the sun never sets during part of the summer and never rises for part of the winter.

Radium ore was discovered on the shore of Great Bear Lake in the 1930s. During World War II, the importance of the radium mine increased because of a demand for the uranium found in the same ore. In addition, Allied armies built airfields and weather stations in the territories. After the war, the Canadian government expanded educational, medical, and social welfare programs in the N.W.T., and interest in mineral and oil exploration increased. Scheduled airline flights and road-building programs soon followed.

It is possible to drive to the N.W.T. from Alberta, British Columbia, and the Yukon. In the 1960s, a railway was built from Peace River, Alberta, to Great Slave Lake to serve mining operations then at Pine Point.

While the people of the Northwest Territories know how to enjoy themselves with festivals, powwows, drumming, and dancing, the biggest show is nature's own. From October through February on dark, clear nights, the aurora borealis, or northern lights, shimmer in the sky.

LOCATION The Northwest Territories extends from the sixtieth parallel to the seventieth parallel, far above the Arctic Circle. (See map on page xix.)

GEOGRAPHY The Mackenzie River Valley east of the Yukon and south of the tree line is where most people in the N.W.T. live. The Mackenzie, Canada's longest river, flows northwest from Great Slave Lake to the Beaufort Sea. The other important geographic section of the N.W.T. is the High Arctic, which is north of the tree line and includes several islands in the Arctic Ocean.

CLIMATE Arctic and subarctic climates. Summers in the Mackenzie Valley are warmer than on the islands of the Arctic Ocean. The Mackenzie Valley area has an average temperature of −18°F in January and 56°F in July. Temperatures in Fort Smith, in the far south, average −25°F in January and 61°F in July. The High Arctic area has an average January temperature of −25°F and an average July temperature of 52°F. The average annual precipitation is 11 inches, most of it, snow.

TERRITORIAL CAPITAL Yellowknife

The capital is the only city in the N.W.T. The population of Yellowknife was 16,541 in 2001. It is now estimated to be around 18,000. It has been the territorial capital since 1967.

Latitude: 62°28' N; Longitude: 114°27' W.

POPULATION 37,360 (2001 census); 42,944 (est., January 2005)

POPULATION DENSITY 8 people per 100 square miles

ETHNIC DIVERSITY Indians, Inuit (often referred to as the Inuvialuit), and Métis make up nearly half the population. Most of the rest descend from Europeans, although there are Filipinos and Africans from Zimbabwe and Nigeria living in Yellowknife.

Visible Minorities: 4.2 percent of the population (2001)

Religious Affiliations:

Catholic	46 percent
Protestant	31 percent
None	18 percent

LANGUAGE There are ten official languages in the N.W.T. They are English, French, Dogrib, Chipewyan, South Slavey, North Slavey, Gwich'in, Innuinaktun, Inuvialuktun, and Cree.

HEALTH See Appendix, page 213–214, for details on the Northwest Territories' health care coverage and how to apply for it.

Nurses are the largest group of health care practitioners in the territory. Community health programs include daily sick clinics, public health clinics, home care, and school health programs. Physicians and specialists routinely visit communities without resident physicians. Where insured services are not available in the territory, residents can receive them from hospitals in other jurisdictions. The N.W.T. provides medical travel assistance.

Average Life Expectancy (2001):

Males, 73.7 years

Females, 78.8 years

These numbers are well below the national averages for Canada of 77.0 years for males and 82.0 years for females.

Infant Mortality Rate: 4.9 per 1,000 live births (2001)

ECONOMY Diamonds are the leading product of the N.W.T. mining industry. The first diamond mine in Canada opened in 1998, followed by another in 2003. Both are in the Lac de Gras region about 185 miles north of Yellowknife. Two more diamond mines will be opening in the next two to three years. Canada is already the world's third largest diamond producer, after Botswana and Russia. Oil comes from near Norman Wells and natural gas from the Mackenzie Delta and the Liard Valley. Gold is mined in the Yellowknife area. Fishing and forestry are centered in the Great Slave Lake region. Tourism is a growing business, even in winter, as people come to see the northern lights.

With revenues from the N.W.T. growing, the territorial government has been trying to get the federal government in Ottawa to let more of the money stay in the territory under territorial control instead of going to fund programs elsewhere in Canada.

EARNINGS

Average earnings, working full year, full-time: $51,869 (2001)

Median family income (couples): $81,553

Average earnings of the population, 15 and over, for holders of a university certificate, diploma, or degree (2001): $56,892 (This was higher than the Canadian national average of $48,648.)

UNEMPLOYMENT RATE 9.5 percent (2001). In Yellowknife, the unemployment rate was 5.0 percent in 2001.

HOUSING In 2000, there were close to 3,000 rental dwellings in Yellowknife and 3,000 that were owner-occupied. The average price for a house in the N.W.T. in 2004 was $246,716. In 2003, the average N.W.T. household was spending $1,200 a month for shelter.

With the booming diamond business, rental costs in Yellowknife increased in 2005 by 2.5 percent over what they were in 2004, and there were fewer vacancies. A press release related to housing problems issued on May 13, 2005, by the N.W.T. Legislative Assembly stated "Affordable housing continues to be a major issue today for N.W.T. residents. It has a significant impact on businesses hiring and retaining employees and on the development of healthy N.W.T. families who can make responsible choices for their futures and that of their children."

MEDIA Yellowknife has two weekly newspapers and one that appears twice a week. There are three radio stations—the CBC, one that is privately owned, and one Aboriginal station. The CBC also broadcasts in Inuvik. A telecommunications satellite provides radio, telephone, and television to all communities. There are many cable TV stations, but the service is more expensive than it is farther south in Canada.

EDUCATION Schools in Yellowknife are operated by two district education authorities—public and Roman Catholic. In the rest of the territory, regional education boards coordinate all schools. There are high schools in

Yellowknife, Hay River, Fort Smith, Inuvik, Fort Simpson, and Norman Wells. However, the dropout rate is high (though better than it used to be). In 1997–98, only 34 percent of the students enrolled in high school graduated. By 2002–03, that figure had climbed to 43 percent.

The only college in the N.W.T. is Aurora College, which has campuses at Fort Smith, Inuvik, and Yellowknife. The N.W.T. government gives grants and loans to students who wish to study at Aurora College or elsewhere.

TAXES There is no sales tax in the N.W.T. The Canadian government gives incentive pay in the form of a tax rebate for living and working in the Northwest Territories. (On the federal government personal income tax return, it's called "Northern Residency.")

GOVERNMENT *Premier*: Joe Handley. The federal government appoints a commissioner as honorary head of government. A premier heads the government with an Executive Council (or cabinet.) The premier is elected by the nineteen-member Legislative Assembly, which governs by consensus. There are no political parties.

The N.W.T. elects one member to the House of Commons in Ottawa and sends one senator. Both of the current representatives in Ottawa belong to the Liberal Party.

TRANSPORTATION Expensive because of great distances and few passengers. The cheapest and oldest form of transportation is by water, but the Mackenzie River is frozen for eight to nine months each year. A tug and barge service operates from the Hay River Terminal of the Mackenzie Northern Railway on Great Slave Lake and continues along the Mackenzie River to the Beaufort Sea. The Mackenzie Northern Railway provides freight rail service between Alberta and Hay River, running parallel to the Mackenzie Highway. Most of the N.W.T. highways are paved. Temporary ice roads serve as supply routes for some places in winter. Scheduled flights operate in the Mackenzie Valley and the High Arctic, with seaplanes taking supplies to mining and prospecting communities. Jet aircraft serve Fort Smith, Hay River, Inuvik, Norman Wells, and Yellowknife, with connections to Edmonton and Calgary in Alberta. Yellowknife and Inuvik have scheduled air service to Whitehorse in the Yukon.

CARS AND AUTO INSURANCE Auto insurance is provided by private, nongovernmental insurance companies. The maximum medical payment covered by insurance in the N.W.T. is $25,000.

ATTITUDES TOWARD GAYS The Northwest Territories did not issue marriage licenses to same-sex couples prior to the legalization of same-sex marriage by federal law.

CULTURE The Prince of Wales Northern Heritage Centre in Yellowknife has an extensive collection relating to the indigenous people and the early history of the territory.

Indigenous artwork is increasingly appreciated and prized in the N.W.T. as well as by collectors in other parts of Canada. The Great Northern Arts Festival takes place annually in Inuvik in July. Over a hundred northern artists from the Yukon, the Northwest Territories, and Nunavut gather for a ten-day festival that includes drumming, dancing, public workshops, and artist demonstrations.

FESTIVALS Sunrise Festival (January) in Inuvik; the first sunrise of the year is celebrated with a bonfire and fireworks. Yellowknife Aurora Festival (late February–early April); includes the Canadian Championship Dog Derby and the Caribou Carnival in March. Mad Trapper's Rendez-Vous (March) in Aklavik; dancing, dog races, snowmobile races, and cultural events. Muskrat Jamboree (April) in Inuvik; muskrat skinning, snowshoe, dog, and snowmobile races, harpoon throw, pancake breakfast. White Fox Jamboree (May) in Sachs Harbour; yearly spring carnival. Folk on the Rocks Music Festival (July) in Yellowknife; music, cultural displays, arts, crafts, food. Ikhalukpik Jamboree (August) in Paulatuk; barbecues, games, and dancing celebrate the return of the Arctic char to the rivers.

SPORTS Summer: Fishing, canoeing, and kayaking. Winter: Snowmobiling, ice-fishing, dogsledding, snowshoeing.

There are currently five golf courses in the N.W.T. with a sixth under construction in Inuvik. Holman has the northernmost golf course in the western hemisphere. The eighteen-hole Yellowknife Golf Course has sand fairways with patches of bedrock.

Parks: Four national parks: Aulavik, Wood Buffalo (which is partly in Alberta), Tuktut Nogait, and Nahanni. Nahanni National Park in the southwestern corner of the N.W.T. has a waterfall, Virginia Falls, that is twice as high as Niagara Falls. The park, one of the most remote in Canada, preserves sections of the Mackenzie Mountains. There is no easy way to drive to the park. Most visitors reach it by chartered seaplane. The South Nahanni River is one of the world's premier whitewater rafting sites.

PUBLIC SAFETY The Northwest Territories has one of the highest crime rates in Canada. Between 2002 and 2003, total criminal code offenses increased by 13.3 percent. There were 2,844 violent crimes and 3,023 property crimes in 2003.

SNAPSHOT: Nunavut

Canada's newest territory comprises one-fifth of Canada's landmass, much of it above the Arctic Circle. Most residents of Nunavut are Inuit, known in earlier days as Eskimos. Their ancestors have been in the northwest country for thousands of years.

Nunavut was carved out of the Northwest Territories during the 1990s, following the Nunavut Land Claim Agreement, under which the Inuit gave up any future rights to their traditional land in exchange for the power to govern a territory of their own. They were given the eastern half of the existing Northwest Territories. It's an area three times the size of the state of Texas, mostly above the tree line, with no roads and few people. Baffin Island, where Nunavut's capital, Iqaluit, is located, is a major part of the territory.

Nunavut became a separate territory on April 1, 1999. Canada now has three territories: Nunavut, the remaining Northwest Territories, and the Yukon. In terms of population, Nunavut is one of the fastest growing regions of Canada.

LOCATION Much of Nunavut is north of the Arctic Circle. (See map on pages xviii–xix.) Canada's most northerly point is in Nunavut at Cape Columbia on Ellesmere Island.

GEOGRAPHY 769,684 square miles, extending north and west of Hudson Bay. The distance between the western and eastern boundaries of the territory is 1,242 miles. It is 1,553 miles from Alert at the northern tip of Nunavut to the Manitoba border in the south.

Nunavut has three distinct regions. Kitikmeot, the westernmost region, has expansive landscapes and tundra-bordered rivers. Baffin is an island with mountain ranges, icecaps, glacial valleys, and open tundra, and Kivalliq is the rugged west shore of Hudson Bay. Glaciers cover parts of Baffin and Ellesmere Islands. Much of the earth below the surface in Nunavut is permanently frozen.

CLIMATE Average winter temperatures range from –20°F in the south to –37°F in the north. Summer temperatures range from 50°F in the south to 36°F in the north. Precipitation is generally less than twelve inches a year.

TERRITORIAL CAPITAL Iqaluit, population 6,800, is also the largest town. It was originally a small trading post called Frobisher Bay.
   Latitude: 63°45' N; Longitude: 68°33' W.

POPULATION 26,745 (2001 census); 29,683 (est., January 2005)
   The median age of the population is 22.1 years, the youngest in Canada.

POPULATION DENSITY 3 persons per 100 square miles. There are twenty-six communities, as small as 25 people (Bathurst Inlet) or as large as Iqaluit.

ETHNIC DIVERSITY 85 percent are Inuit.
   Religious Affiliations:

Protestant	67 percent
Catholic	23 percent
None	6 percent

LANGUAGE Inuktitut, Inuinnaqtun, English, and French. Inuktitut is the official language of courts and legislation.

HEALTH See Appendix, page 214, for details on Nunavut's health care coverage and how to apply for it.
   Iqaluit has a hospital. Smaller communities have health centers staffed with nurses. Each of the larger regional centers also has a doctor. Some communities have dentists. In February 2005, Nunavut completed installation of a telehealth network connecting all community health centers. It utilizes videoconferencing for medical education and pediatric and obstetric care.
   High suicide rates and drug abuse are problems in Nunavut.
   Average Life Expectancy (2001):
   Males, 67.2 years
   Females, 70.2 years
   These numbers are well below the national averages for Canada of 77.0 years for males and 82.0 years for females.
   Infant Mortality Rate: 16.9 per 1,000 live births (2001). (This is the highest infant mortality rate in Canada.)

ECONOMY Many people live off the land (hunting, trapping, gathering, and fishing). The growing market for Inuit arts and crafts (soapstone carvings, prints, and tapestries) is worth around $20 million annually and supports around 2,500 people in whole or in part.

Most jobs are working for the territorial government. A U.S. air base provides some employment, as does a small movie business.

Mining for minerals such as zinc, copper, gold, lead, and diamonds contributes to the economy, but exploration is difficult given the terrain and the climate. The first diamond mine is scheduled to be in production by 2006. There is a small fishing industry specializing in turbot, shrimp, and arctic char. After the construction of the Distant Early Warning (DEW) Line in 1954, Iqaluit became a major refueling station for military and commercial aircraft.

An effort is being made to encourage tourism to Nunavut. Around 18,000 visitors come to Nunavut annually for hunting and fishing or just to see the wildlife and enjoy hiking, kayaking and canoeing, dogsledding, and snowmobiling. Cruise ships visit four Baffin Island communities.

EARNINGS
  Territory:
    Average earnings, working full year, full-time: $48,078 (2001)
    Median family income (couples): $48,085
  Iqaluit:
    Average earnings, working full year, full-time: $55,698 (2001)
    Median family income (couples): $86,144
  Average earnings of the population, 15 and over, for holders of a university certificate, diploma, or degree (2001): $58,992 (This was higher than the Canadian national average of $48,648.)
  Because everything has to be brought into Nunavut by air or sea, it has the highest cost of living in Canada.

UNEMPLOYMENT RATE Sixty percent of Nunavut's adult Inuit population is in the labor force, although 28 percent of that group is unemployed. Ninety-one percent of Nunavut's small non-Aboriginal population is in the labor force, with a 4 percent unemployment rate.

HOUSING Shelter costs are high in Nunavut, in part because of the high cost of utilities. A three-bedroom unit can cost more than $1,600 a month to operate. The private rental market is limited, but there are over 14,000 tenants in public housing. Almost half are on income support with rents geared to income on a sliding scale.

In 2001, there were 1,735 owner-occupied dwellings in Nunavut and 5,440 rented dwellings. The average monthly payment for owners was $1,053. For renters it was $470.

EDUCATION Education through grade 12 is available in all Nunavut communities. Often the teaching is in Inukitut in the early years and English later. While the territory's literacy rate is lower than the national rate, more and more students are attending and completing high school. Arctic College provides more advanced education at five campuses in Nunavut and has Community Learning Centers in every community.

TAXES No territorial sales tax.

GOVERNMENT *Premier:* Paul Okalik. Within the territory, a premier is elected by the Legislative Assembly. The premier heads the government with the support of an Executive Council, or cabinet. Nunavut's Legislative Assembly has nineteen members who are elected for up to five years and who govern by consent, or general agreement. There are no political parties. Smaller communities are governed by Hamlet Councils.

Nunavut elects one member to the House of Commons in Ottawa and one senator.

TRANSPORTATION With no roads, all access to Nunavut is by air or sea. Nunavut's capital can be reached by air from Yellowknife, Montreal, Winnipeg, Churchill, Edmonton, and Ottawa. Within Nunavut, there are regional airlines, serving the major communities, and charter airline services.

ATTITUDES TOWARD GAYS Nunavut did not issue marriage licenses to same-sex couples prior to the federal government making same-sex marriage legal throughout Canada.

MEDIA In Iqaluit, television: CFFB CBC, CH4161 APTN, cable from Eastern Arctic TV, private satellite. Radio: CFFB CBC, CFRT, CIQA, local radio, radio from Vancouver, Yellowknife, and Edmonton.

CULTURE Iqaluit has numerous galleries focusing on Inuit art. More than 27 percent of Nunavut's population is involved in art production. The Nunatta Suakkutaangit Museum in Iqaluit contains an excellent collection of historical artifacts relating to Inuit culture. The museum is housed in a former Hudson's Bay trading post.

FESTIVALS Toonik Tyme in Iqaluit (April); weeklong festival with games, entertainment, dogsled and snowmobile races. Top of the World Kite Festival, with kites up to sixty feet long, held during Toonik Tyme. Pakallak Time in the hamlet of Rankin Inlet (May); square dances, games, dogteam and snowmobile races. Omingmak Frolics in Cambridge Bay (May); snowmobile races, ice sculpting, arctic games, bike racing, parade, contests. Kitikmeot Northern Games in various locations (August); traditional and modern games, arctic feasts. Northwest Passage Celebrations in the hamlet of Gjoa Haven; games and contests celebrate the first ship that made it through the Northwest Passage (the *Gjoa,* in the years 1903–1906).

SPORTS Hunting, fishing, kayaking, canoeing, snowmobiling, dogsledding.
   Parks: Three national parks—Auyuittuq, Quittinirpaaq, and Sirmilik—are among the most remote in the world. There are also several territorial parks.

PUBLIC SAFETY Between 2002 and 2003, Nunavut experienced the highest increase in crime rate of any province or territory—17.9 percent. In 2003, there were 7,943 instances of violent crime and 7,222 instances of property crime, per 100,000 population. There were 34,774 criminal code offenses per 100,000 population.

APPENDIX

HEALTH CARE, PROVINCE BY PROVINCE

"There really is no Canadian medical system," says University of Winnipeg history professor, Dan Stone. "There's an interlocking system of ten provincial systems and three territories. There are some things tying it together at the top to make it reciprocal, so conditions can vary from one to another, especially in some of the details."

Alberta

To register for health care, call Alberta Health and Wellness at 780-427-1432.

No waiting period for newly arrived permanent residents. Albertans pay premiums for health care if they are under age 65. Premiums are $44 a month for an individual and $88 a month for a family, whatever the family size. Private insurance is available for prescription drugs and some services not covered by the government plan. Workers may have additional insurance through their jobs. Seniors, 65 and over, no longer have to pay premiums and have extended benefits, such as coverage for 70 percent of the cost of their prescription drugs. Alberta Blue Cross administers the plan and also has a dental and vision care plan for those with low income. Go to www.seniors.gov.ab.ca for more detailed information. For general health care information: www.health.gov.ab.ca

British Columbia

To register for health care, call Health Insurance B.C. (HIBC) at 800-663-7100; from Vancouver, 604-683-7151; from Victoria, 250-382-8400.

There is a waiting period for new permanent residents of the remainder of the month in which they arrive plus two months. British Columbia residents above a certain minimum income pay a premium for health care coverage: $54 a month for an individual, $96 for a couple, and $108 for a family of three or more. There is some premium assistance for low-income people, and partial payments for additional services may be authorized. Single people with net incomes of $20,000 or less pay no premiums, while those earning up to $28,000 net pay lower premiums. Senior couples and families of four with net incomes of $29,000 pay no premiums, and those with net incomes of up to $37,000 pay lower premiums. Private insurance is available for some services not covered by the government plan. Workers may have additional insurance through their jobs. Seniors continue to have physician and hospital coverage for medically necessary services, and to pay premiums if their income warrants. Residents 19 and under and 65 and over are eligible for free eye exams, but not glasses. Dental care is normally not covered. What seniors pay for nursing homes is based on income. All residents of British Columbia are covered by the Fair PharmaCare Program, deductibles for which are determined by family income. (Calendar year 2005 deductibles were based on 2003 income tax returns.) The program pays 70 percent of some drug costs until a family's ceiling is reached. The co-pay is 75 percent for those born in 1939 and before. Some prescription drugs are covered. The list is limited to approved drugs; the province has been slow in adding new drugs to the list. If both a generic and a brand-name drug are available, only the cost of the generic is covered. Also, in some cases, if more than one drug is available to treat a condition, provincial health care will pay no more than the cost of the lowest-priced drug. For further information go to www.hibc.gov.bc.ca.

Manitoba

To register for health care, call Manitoba Health Insured Benefits at 800-392-1207 or 204-786-7101.

No waiting period for newly arrived permanent residents. No premiums or surcharges on taxes for health care in Manitoba. Eligible prescription drugs are provided through Manitoba's PharmaCare program, which helps pay drug costs, though there are deductibles based on income. Private insurance is available for some prescription drugs and services not included in the government plan. Workers may have additional insurance through their jobs. Seniors are reimbursed for part of their eyeglass purchases, and Manitoba offers Personal Care Homes and Home Care Programs for seniors through its health system, provided through local and regional health authorities. For further information go to www.gov.mb.ca/health/guide/2/how_to.html.

New Brunswick

To apply for health insurance with the Health and Wellness Department's New Brunswick Medicare, call 888-762-8600 or from the U.S.: 506-684-7901.

It can take up to three months to process the application. No premiums or surcharges on taxes for health care in New Brunswick. Private insurance is available for prescription drugs and some services not covered by New Brunswick Medicare. Workers may have additional insurance through their jobs. Seniors, 65 and over, can qualify by income for prescription drug coverage through Blue Cross. For additional information go to www.GNB.ca/0051/0394/index-e.asp.

Newfoundland and Labrador

To register for health care benefits, call Health Community Service's Medical Care Plan (MCP) at 800-563-1557 or 709-292-4000.

No waiting period for newly arrived permanent residents. No premiums or surcharges on taxes for health care. Private insurance is available for prescription drugs and some services not covered by MCP. Workers may have additional insurance through their jobs. Seniors benefit from a drug program administered by the Department of Human Resources and Employment. For further information go to www.gov.nf.ca/health/.

Northwest Territories

To register for health care coverage with the Northwest Territories Health Plan call 867-777-7400 or use the Web site www.gov.NT.ca. The toll-free number, 800-661-0830, is only available from within Canada.

No waiting period for newly arrived permanent residents. No premiums or tax surcharges for health care in the N.W.T. In general, prescription drugs are not covered, but private insurance is available, or workers may have additional insurance through their jobs. A Seniors Benefit Program provides extended health benefits to Métis and non-Native residents 60 years of age and older. An application for these benefits must be made to the Department of Health and Social Services. Alberta Blue Cross administers prescription drug and dental benefits for seniors on behalf of the N.W.T. government. Seniors with private or employer plans must access those. Alberta Blue Cross can be called at 800-661-6995.

For further information go to www.gov.NT.ca; www.seniors.gov.AB.ca.

Nova Scotia

To register for Nova Scotia's Medical Services Insurance (MSI) or for more information, call 902-468-9700.

No waiting period for newly arrived permanent residents. No premiums or tax surcharges for health care in Nova Scotia. Private insurance is available for prescription drugs and other services. Workers may have additional insurance through their jobs. Seniors' benefits include a dental program, but eyeglasses are not covered. For further information, go to www.gov.ns.ca/health/msi.htm.

Nunavut

To register for health care in Nunavut, call 867-645-8002.

No waiting period for newly arrived permanent residents. No premiums or surcharges on taxes for health care. Private insurance is available for services not covered by the territory's health plan. Seniors' benefits include an extended health program for those 60 and over covering some vision and dental care (with a cap) and all eligible prescription drugs.

There are no long-term care facilities in Nunavut. Seniors needing this care go to Ontario, Manitoba, Alberta, or the Northwest Territories.

Ontario

To register for Ontario's Health Insurance Plan (OHIP), call the Ministry of Health and Long-Term Care at 800-268-1154 or 416-314-5518.

There is a waiting period for newly arrived permanent residents of three months from the date of arrival. Ontario has a health care tax surcharge for those earning more than $20,000 a year. That amounts to $300 a year for those earning from $20,000 to $36,000; $450 a year for those earning $36,000 to $48,000; $600 a year for those earning $48,000 to $72,000; $750 a year for those earning from $72,000 to $200,000, and a maximum of $900 a year for those earning more than $200,000. These charges are handled by the Ministry of Finance at income tax time. Private insurance is available for prescription drugs and some services not covered by OHIP. Workers may have additional insurance through their jobs. There is a TRILLIUM Drug Program for those under 65, based on income, which involves a deductible and then a $2 charge per covered prescription. Seniors continue to be covered by OHIP, and after they become 65, most of their prescription drugs are covered, although pharmacies may charge a nominal fee for servicing the prescriptions. Eyeglasses and dental work are not covered, but ambulances are subsidized so that the patient pays only $45. When necessary, Community Care Access Centres help a person find a nursing home or home care workers. Such care can be subsidized by the government if the senior is low-income. For more information, go to www.health.gov.on.ca.

Prince Edward Island

To apply for health insurance, call P.E.I.'s Department of Health and Social Services, Medicare Division, at 902-838-0900.

No waiting period for newly arrived permanent residents. No premiums or surcharges on taxes for health care in P.E.I.

Private insurance is available for prescription drugs and some services not covered by P.E.I.'s Medicare. Workers may have additional insurance through their jobs. Seniors are covered, as they are in other provinces, for medically necessary physician and hospital care, but not for nursing home care. All seniors are eligible for prescription drugs in the Canada Formulary and pay only a dispensing fee to the pharmacy of $11. For more information go to www.gov.PE.ca.

Quebec

To apply for health insurance in Quebec, call Régis de l'Assurance Maladie du Québec at 514-864-3411 in Montreal or 418-646-4636 in Quebec City. The toll-free number, 800-561-9749, is only available from within Canada.

Permanent residents are eligible for coverage in Quebec's health plan on the first day of the third month they are resident in Quebec. There is a health care surcharge on some provincial taxes, but it is only paid by employers or the self-employed. Private insurance is available to cover some services not covered by the Quebec health care program. All residents of Quebec are required to have prescription drug coverage, and generally get it through the workplace. Seniors, after age 65, have some prescription drug coverage based on income. Those without access to Canada's Old Age Pension pay 28.5 percent of the cost of prescription drugs, to a maximum (in 2005) of $71.42 a month. For further information go to www.ramq.gov.qc.ca.

Saskatchewan

To register for the Medical Services Plan, call Saskatchewan Health Registration and Vital Statistics at 306-787-3251. The toll-free number, 800-667-7551, is only available from within Canada.

Permanent residents of Saskatchewan are generally covered under the health plan on the first day of the third month following the date of arrival in the province. No premiums or surcharges on taxes to pay for health care in Saskatchewan. Private insurance can be purchased to cover prescription drugs and some services not covered under Saskatchewan Health. Workers may get additional coverage through their jobs. Foreign university students, with valid study permits, are covered by Saskatchewan Health as long as they are full-time students. For seniors, Saskatchewan Health provides funding to district health boards to cover a major portion of long-term care costs in nursing homes, health centers, and hospitals. There is also a program for those with long-term disabilities or illnesses with a range of services under Saskatchewan Aids to Independent Living (SAIL.) For more information go to www.health.gov.sk.ca.

Yukon

To register for the Yukon's Health and Social Services' Insured Health Services, call 867-667-5209.

There is a waiting period of up to three months from time of arrival in the Yukon before permanent residents can be enrolled in the Insured Health Services. No premiums or surcharges on taxes to pay for health care. Private insurance is available for prescription drugs and some services not covered by Insured Health Services. Workers may have additional insurance through their jobs.

Seniors continue to be covered by Insured Health Services for basic care but also have a PharmaCare Plan, administered by Insured Health Services, that, with no deductibles but some limits, covers dental, eye care, and glasses, as well as generic prescription drugs listed in the Yukon Pharma-Care Formulary. For more information go to www.gov.yk.ca (Programs and Services).

SOURCES

Books

AAA TourBook, Atlantic Provinces and Quebec. Heathrow, Florida: AAA Publishing, 2005.

AAA TourBook, Ontario. Heathrow, Florida: AAA Publishing, 2005

AAA TourBook, Western Canada & Alaska. Heathrow, Florida: AAA Publishing, 2002.

Brown, Craig, ed. *Illustrated History of Canada*. Toronto: Lester & Orpen Dennys Publishers, 1987.

Canada One Hundred, 1867–1967, prepared by the Canada Year Book, Handbook and Library Division, Dominion Bureau of Statistics, Ottawa, 1967.

Chronicle of Canada. Montreal: Chronicle Publications, 1990.

Colombo, John Robert. 999 Questions About Canada. Toronto: Doubleday Canada, 1989.

Defede, Jim. *The Day the World Came to Town: 9/11 in Gander, Newfoundland*. New York: Regan Books, Harper Collins Publishers, 2002.

Fodor's Canada, 27th ed. New York: Fodor's Travel Publications, 2004.

Fodor's See It Canada. New York: Fodor's Travel Publications, N.Y., Toronto, London, Sydney, Auckland, copyright: Automobile Association Developments, Ltd., 2004.

The Green Guide: Canada. France: Michelin Travel Publications, 2001.

The Green Guide: Pacific Northwest. France: Michelin Travel Publications, 2001.

The Green Guide: Quebec. France: Michelin Travel Publications, 2001.

Hurtig, Mel. *The Betrayal of Canada.* Toronto: Stoddart Publishing, 1991.

Maclean's Guide to Canadian Universities, February 2005. Toronto: Rogers Publishing, 2005.

Newman, Peter C. *Canada–1892: Portrait of a Promised Land.* Toronto: McClelland & Stewart, Inc., 1992.

The Victoria Newcomers' Guide, 5th edition, Victoria, B.C.: Campbell Communications, 2003.

Walz, Jay, and Audrey Walz. *Portrait of Canada.* New York: Times Books, 1970.

World Book Encyclopedia. Chicago: World Book, 2004.

Articles

Storer, Tina. "O Canada! The True North Strong and Free!" *Washington Times,* March 15, 2005.

Web Sites

A Look at Canada: www.cic.gc/ca/english/citizen/look/look-OOe.html.

Citizenship and Immigration Canada: www.cic.gc.ca.

Statistics Canada: www.statcan.ca.

The World Fact Book: www.cia.gov/cia/publications/factbook/geos/ca.html.

INDEX